INDIA IN THE NINETEENTH CENTURY

INDIA IN THE NINETEENTH CENTURY

By

Demetrius C. Boulger

GYAN

Published by

GYAN

Gyan Publishing House
5, Ansari Road
Daryaganj, New Delhi-110002
Phone: 011-47034999, 9811692060
E-mail: books@gyanbooks.com

Distribution Network
gyanbooks.com
India, USA, Canada, UK, Australia, France

ISBN : 978-81-212-6755-7 (PB)
First Published, 1901

2nd Impression 2022

Printed at: Gyan Press, Delhi.

INDIA IN THE NINETEENTH CENTURY
Author: DEMETRIUS C. BOULGER

INDIA IN THE XIXTH CENTURY

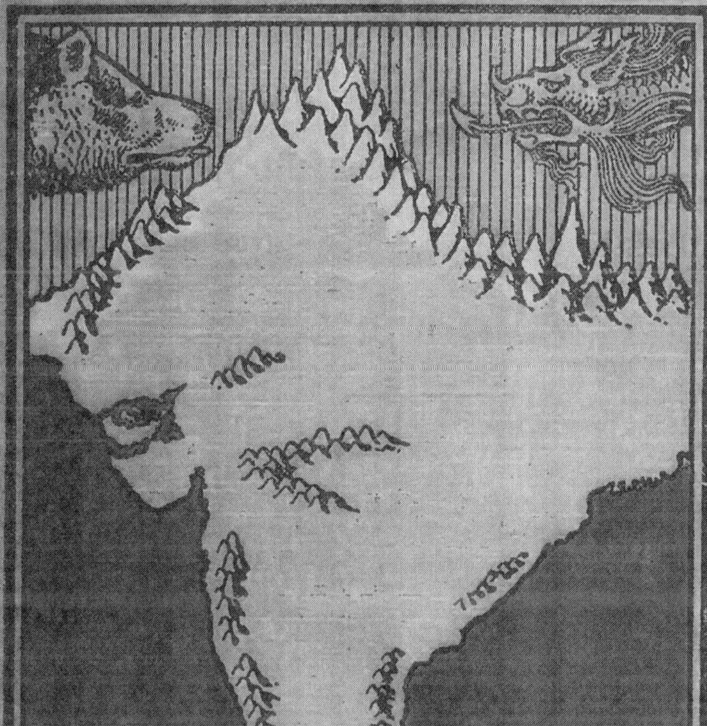

D. C. BOULGER

Photo by] [*J. Russell & Sons.*

HER MAJESTY QUEEN VICTORIA,
EMPRESS OF INDIA.

Frontispiece.]

INDIA IN THE NINETEENTH CENTURY

By Demetrius C. Boulger

AUTHOR OF "THE STORY OF INDIA" "LORD WILLIAM BENTINCK" ETC

1901

I DEDICATE THESE PAGES

TO

LIEUT.-GENERAL SIR ANDREW CLARKE G.C.M.G., ETC

ONE OF OUR GREAT PRO-CONSULS, WHO FIRST APPLIED

THE TITLES OF EMPRESS OF INDIA AND

KAISAR-I-HIND TO

HER MAJESTY QUEEN VICTORIA

Contents

Chapter I

THE QUEST OF INDIA

THE discovery of a sea route to India was the uppermost ambition of every maritime state in Europe during the second half of the fifteenth century. The old assumptions of Seneca and Pliny that there were other worlds than that known to Rome breathed again in the poetical predictions of Dante and Luigi Pulci. The belief in "another hemisphere," and that there were countries at "our antipodes," was held before Diaz discovered the Cape of Good Hope or Columbus traversed the Atlantic. The Wars of the Roses had retarded the growth of England's naval power, which in the fourteenth century had been supreme in Northern Europe; but with the Tudors came a revival of maritime spirit and adventure, although Henry VII.'s first emissaries were the Italian Cabots, in default of English mariners of sufficient experience. When Columbus sailed westward it was in the full expectation of reaching India or Cathay, conclusive evidence of the fact being furnished in his bearing a letter from the King of Spain to the Great Khan of Tartary, just as if Asia had not changed since the days of Carpini, Rubruquis, and Marco Polo. Nor was the wish to reach and tap the fabled wealth of the Orient less keen in London than in the ports of the Mediterranean; and if Columbus knew, as alleged, from the Icelanders of the old stories to the effect that Scandinavian voyagers[1] had reached land in the tenth century on the extreme verge of the Western Ocean, the probability is still greater that those reports had circulated in England. The initial fact that should remain clear in the reader's mind is that Columbus was seeking India, and confidently expected to find it, when he crossed the Atlantic to make his grand discovery of the New World.

Henry VII.'s patent to John Cabot and his three sons in 1496 was to discover the north-west passage to India. They could not discover that, but they did discover Newfoundland and much of the American mainland. The same idea dominated English maritime enterprise for a century, and during that period Spanish and Portuguese power laid a firm grip on the Americas and all the marts of Asia from Ormus

[1] Bjarni Herjulfson, A.D. 986, and Leif Erikson, A.D. 994, are credited with having reached America, near Boston, in the years named. Carpini visited the Great Khan of the Mongols, Kuyuk, at Karakoram in 1247; Rubruquis, his successor, Mangu, in 1255; and Marco Polo's residence (1272–86) in China in the reign of Kublai is historic.

to Japan. While Englishmen were breaking their strength and their hearts against an impossibility, their rivals had closed their hands on the most favoured spots of the globe, and, supported by the Church, advanced claims to clerical and commercial monopolies. Still hoping for success in the search for the north-west passage, over which no doubt, if found, they would have asserted as exclusive a control as the Spaniards and Portuguese claimed, and for a time made good, over the southern routes, the English long refrained from demanding those equal rights for all which would have been the wiser and nobler policy. Henry VIII. was less energetic than his father, but even he seems to have listened to the proposals of Robert Thorne, a sea-mate of the elder Cabot, for "the discovery north-westward of a passage to the Indies." Sebastian Cabot was sent by Edward VI., and Queen Mary, on her brother's death, renewed the sanction, to make a fresh attempt where his father had failed. Sir Hugh Willoughby had a few years before that sailed north-eastwards, to perish on the shores of Lapland, and to leave his more fortunate comrade, Richard Chancellor, to discover Russia. Then came Martin Frobisher, acting for the English "Company of Cathay"—a quarter of a century older than the East India Company—who thrice attempted in 1576-8 to find a way round Lapland to "the gorgeous East." John Davis continued the efforts made in this quarter between the years 1585 and 1587, and even after the formation of the East India Company the north-west passage lured the most daring and skilful of our national mariners along a false track. Hudson and Baffin, in seven voyages between 1607 and 1616, added immensely to the knowledge we possessed of the bays, gulfs, and straits of the country since called Canada, and they have left their names on the map, as is well known to every schoolboy, although the coast which barred their imaginary route to India and Cathay has lost the expressive name given it by Hudson of "Hopes Checked." Then at last the north-west passage was consigned to the limbo of impossibilities, and the enterprise of our ancestors concentrated itself on the task of wresting from rivals, who had in a sense forestalled them, a free passage for their ships and a free mart for their merchandise.

The influence of the successful circumnavigations of the globe by the two Elizabethan sea-captains, Sir Francis Drake in 1577–8 and Thomas Cavendish in 1586–7, is not perhaps as fully appreciated as it deserves to be. The former brought back spices, and a treaty with the King of Ternate for their supply; the latter captured a Portuguese ship homeward bound from the East Indies, and the papers found on board revealed the extraordinary richness and profit of trade in the Indies and further East, thus whetting the desire of the London merchants to share in it. The Spaniards protested against the intrusion of the English mariners in the Eastern seas, declaring that they had a divine right to navigation across them. Elizabeth disposed of this pretension in the memorable phrase that "since the sea and air are common to all men, it was lawful for an Englishman to do whatever a Spaniard might." Then followed the Armada, and with its overthrow passed away the naval ascendancy which Spain had possessed since Columbus, and which was supported by the wealth procured from the mines of Mexico and Peru. Flushed with their success, English merchants equipped several small expeditions to capture the trade of the Indies, but none of these met with any success, and the three ships that sailed in 1596 under Sir Robert Dudley's flag were never afterwards heard of. On 31st December, 1600, Queen Elizabeth signed the royal charter incorporating "the Company of Merchants of London trading to the East Indies." With that charter began the existence of the great Company which only disappeared during the throes of the Mutiny in 1858.

The command of the first expedition equipped by the Company was entrusted to James Lancaster, who had taken part in one of the abortive voyages. Five ships were fitted out for the journey, and, despite the opposition of the Portuguese, Lancaster was fairly successful, visiting Sumatra, Java, and the Moluccas, and founding the first English factory in the Far East at Bantam. Elizabeth did not live long enough to receive Lancaster on his return, and it was King James who conferred on him the knighthood he had well deserved.[1] So successful was the first voyage that a second was decided on in the year (1604) following Lancaster's return. It consisted of four ships, placed under the command of Henry Middleton. Equal success crowned its efforts. The factory at Bantam was strengthened, new factories were founded at Banda and Amboyna. Twelve "voyages," as the successive expeditions were termed, in all left the shores of this country between the years 1600 and 1612; and by these efforts not only was a vast amount of Eastern produce and merchandise imported into England at considerable profit, but a number of factories (or "houses," as they were more modestly termed) were dotted over Asia, from Anjengo and Masulipatam on the coast of India to Firando in Japan. In 1613 Captain John Saris was sent on a special mission to found a factory at Firando by the aid of William Adams, an Englishman who had gone out to the Far East in 1600 as pilot on a Dutch fleet, and who had subsequently risen to a position of power and influence among the Japanese. A diplomatic success was scored in 1608 by Captain Hawkins, one of the

[1] A few Englishmen who reached India by land before the expedition sailed deserve mention. Thomas Stevens, of New College, Oxford, was rector of the Jesuits' College in Salsette in 1579. Ralph Fitch, Newberry, and Leedes, all merchants, reached India overland in 1583.

commanders of the third "voyage," who was received by the Emperor Jehangir at Agra in the character of envoy from James I. and also from the East India Company, and who was permitted to reside there for three years. In 1613 a more imposing mission was sent, with Sir Thomas Roe as envoy, and he was given a very cordial reception at Ajmere, where, by the aid of the celebrated Noor Mahal, Jehangir's wife, whose virtues and fame are commemorated in the beautiful Taj at Agra, he obtained the right to establish an English factory at Surat, then the home of the Parsees and the principal mart of Western India.

The appearance of the English in the Eastern seas was greeted with a storm of opposition on the part of the Dutch as well as the Portuguese. The Dutch, forgetting that they owed the chance of keeping the high seas to the destruction of the Spanish Armada by the English, began to set up as close a system in Asia as ever owed its origin to the bigotry of Papists. They preceded the English by only a few years. The successful journey of Van Houtman in 1596–7 led to frequent voyages, and in 1602 to the formation of the Dutch East India Company. One of its first achievements was to prevent an English ship trading at Banda and to drive it off. The Portuguese carried their opposition to still greater lengths. When he heard of the concession at Surat, the Viceroy of Goa sent a squadron to oppose and capture the English ships. Before the factory was granted there had been several engagements between English and Portuguese vessels. But the decisive fight was fought by Captain Nicholas Downton in January, 1615, when the Portuguese were defeated with heavy loss. The following extracts from the East India Company's letters[1] will give a good idea of the fight in Swally Bay, outside Surat:—

"I wrote you of the Viceroy's coming to the bar, where he rid quietly till yesterday, and then sent three ships to Swally, with thirty-five or thirty-six frigates, whereupon one of our smallest ships went out and fought with them, and in the end forcèd the frigates to fly and took the three ships, which after an hour's possession our General (Downton) set on fire. God grant us the like success with the rest, and make us thankful for this. . . . The *Hope* being the first that began the fight, being at once laid aboard per the three Portingal ships and as many Portingal frigates as could lie about her, having entered their men into her and twice got to her forecastle, but they very lustily shipped them off again till such time as the other ships came and rescued her, else they would have put her in great danger. The Portingals came running aboard with great resolution, not so much as shooting a shot, but their courages were soon quailed. There were in their three ships many cavaliers, the most part whereof

[1] *Letters Received by the East India Company from its Servants in the East*, vol. ii., 1613–15. Edited by William Foster.

were most miserably burned and drowned. So is the report, they lost in all between four and five hundred men."

This signal victory established the reputation of the English, and facilitated the progress of Sir Thomas Roe's diplomacy at the court. The gallant Downton after achieving this victory continued his cruise—called "the first joint-stock voyage," in which more than a million and a half was invested—to Java, where he died suddenly of a fever at Bantam. His epitaph declared that he was "lamented, admired, unequalled. He was the true hero, piety and valour being seasoned by gravity and modesty." Yet such is the irony of fate that Downton was not only absolutely forgotten, but his laurels were transferred to his predecessor Best, who was very far from being a hero. Downton's fight practically ended the struggle, although there was a further naval battle in 1620, with the Portuguese; but that with the Dutch was destined to prove long and obstinate. Their policy, briefly put, was that of a monopoly, and they contended that where they stood no one else had a right to come. There was at this time an alliance between England and the Provinces known as the Treaty of Defence, but notwithstanding the Dutch began systematic proceedings for the expulsion of the English from all the islands of the Archipelago. In 1621 they expelled us from Java, and two years later they perpetrated the infamous massacre at Amboyna. As the consequence of these steps the English abandoned all their stations in the Archipelago, as well as those further east, including Firando in Japan. Reparation for the Amboyna massacre was not obtained until thirty years after its occurrence by Cromwell, but in 1629 the Bantam factory was re-established in subordination to that of Surat.

The effect of Dutch policy culminating in the Amboyna massacre was not altogether unfortunate. It may even have been a blessing in disguise, for it turned the attention of our ancestors to the peninsula of India, where a larger field and higher destiny awaited their efforts. In 1632 Masulipatam was occupied under the firman of the King of Golconda, soon to be superseded by the Nizam as lieutenant of the Great Mogul. Piplay in Orissa was assigned by the Emperor himself as the port of trade for Bengal, and the concession was made the sweeter by the expulsion of the Portuguese which accompanied it. This step was due no doubt to the marked decline in the reputation of the Portuguese, who were driven out of Ormus by an Anglo-Persian expedition, and who were obliged to sign a treaty of peace with us in 1635 framed on our terms. As early as 1625 a minor factory had been established at Armagon, on the Coromandel coast north of Madras, but this place was found unsuitable, and in 1639 it was transferred to Fort St. George (Madras). Fort St. George remained subordinate to Bantam until the year 1683–4, when it was raised to the rank of a Presidency. The privileges acquired in Bengal were largely increased because Dr. Gabriel Broughton in 1645–6 rendered considerable services in his medical capacity to Shah Jehan and also to the Governor of the Provinces. Bombay was ceded by Portugal as the dowry of Catherine of Braganza to Charles II., who in turn gave it to the Company, but it did not come into its possession until the year 1668. During this period Surat was captured and pillaged by the Maratha chief Sivaji, but the factory was stoutly and successfully held by Sir George Oxenden, to the admiration of the Mogul and the enhancement of English credit. A less known but equally heroic feat was the defence of Anjengo by the gunner Ince and a few invalids. In 1687 the head factory for the west coast was transferred from Surat to Bombay, and in the following year the head factory for Bengal was removed from Hughli to Chuttanuttee, the modern Calcutta. Fort William was built in 1689, and named after the new king. Thus, more than two hundred years ago, the formal territorial divisions still subsisting were established at a time when the Company did not possess the sovereignty of a yard of Indian territory excepting Bombay.

The experience acquired during the founding and development of these strictly commercial centres had led to the conclusion that if the Company was to continue to prosper and to retain what it had acquired it must develop the political side of its operations. The stage when it accepted gladly enough the favours and patronage of the Mogul Government was now left behind, and in the new phase the Company resolved to right itself by force for any tyrannical proceedings on the part of the Emperor's lieutenants. Sir John Child was appointed in 1689 Governor-General—a title used then for the first time, and not revived till the nomination of Warren Hastings. It was then also that the Company modified its instructions to its servants, who had previously been cautioned to confine their efforts to matters of trade and commerce. A letter written by the Court in the year 1689 enjoined them to turn their attention to political matters, and to cultivate the revenue of the many places in their occupation. It contained these words: "The increase of *our* revenue is the subject of our care as much as our trade; 'tis *that* must maintain our forces when twenty accidents may interrupt our trade; 'tis that must make us a nation in India. Without that we are but a great number of interlopers united by His Majesty's royal charter, fit only to trade where nobody of power thinks it their interest to prevent us; and upon this account it is that the wise Dutch, in all their general advices that we have seen, write ten paragraphs concerning their Government, their civil and military policy, warfare, and the increase of their revenue, for one paragraph they write concerning trade." These

SIVAJI, THE MARATHA CHIEF.

[*To face page 12.*

memorable words were written nearly seventy years before Plassey.

The exactions of the Mogul Government, the breaches of faith committed by the Bengal Governor, and a general increase of hostile sentiment among all "the native powers" towards Europeans explained the apprehension of the Court. The tension generally noticeable was especially acute at Calcutta, where the English were described by the nabobs as "a company of base quarrelling people and foul dealers," and perhaps this insult was the cause of the Company giving its servants permission to wage war on the Mogul. This permission was conveyed in the following passage from the instructions of the Secret Committee which directed the policy of the Company during two hundred years: "You must always understand that, though we prepare for and resolve to enter into a warr with the Mogulls (being necessitated thereto), our ultimate end is peace; for, as we have never done it, so our natures are most adverse to bloodshed and rapine, which usually attend the most just warre. But we have no remedy left but either to desert our trade, or we must draw the sord His Majesty hath entrusted us with to vindicate the rights and honour of the English nation in India."[1]

The campaign, if it may be so called, in Bengal was short, sharp, and decisive. It was waged on the Hughli River and on some of the islands forming the Gangetic

[1] The old spelling with its inconsistencies is retained.

delta. Several Mogul vessels were seized, and a fortified position on Hidgley Island was captured. The English, twice repulsed in an attack on a battery mounting eleven guns, were led to victory at the third attempt by a Captain Arbuthnot, who captured and spiked the guns. The Moguls left sixty killed on the ground, while the English loss in this first battle was only two killed and two wounded. After this success peace followed, and the English were left undisturbed in their new possession of Chuttanuttee or Calcutta for more than sixty years—in fact, down to the episode of the Black Hole. The energy with which the Company had upheld its rights was consequently well repaid by the results in Bengal, which was described in a letter of the period as "the best flower in the Company's garden." In other parts of India disputes and fighting continued, but before summarising them some important passages in the internal life and constitution of the East India Company must be made clear.

While the East India Company had had to struggle with foreign rivals during the whole of the seventeenth century, it had also troubles nearer home. The Company of which we have been speaking represented the parent stem of the greatest private association known in history, but it did not enjoy an unbroken monopoly. Incorporated by Queen Elizabeth's charter of 31st December, 1600, its full title was "The Governor and Company of Merchants of London trading to the East

Indies," and when rivals appeared on the scene this title was curtailed into the London Company. The first of these competitors was known as Courten's Association, and received a charter from Charles I. in 1635. This Association traded not only with India, but with Madagascar, Sumatra, and China, and its proceedings generally were marked by vigour, not to say violence. In the first year of its existence it seized some Mogul ships at Diu and Surat, and a little later (1637) Captain Weddell, one of its commanders, bombarded Canton because the Chinese authorities showed themselves obstructive. There is, however, no authority for the statement made by a recent writer (Mr. Alexis Krausse) that Captain Weddell first brought tea to England. Tea was not introduced into England until after the establishment of the factory at Amoy, and the first reference to it (as yet discovered) is in Pepys' diary for 25th September, 1660,[1] where he says, "I did send for a cup of tee (a China drink), of which I had never drank before." Courten's Association was bought up by and absorbed in the London Company in 1650. Cromwell gave the Merchant Adventurers' Association a charter in

[1] Sir George Birdwood is the authority for this statement, contained in his exceedingly interesting report on some of the records of the India Office in 1878. There are, however, frequent references in the E.I.C. letter-book as early as 1615-6 to "chawe," the Japanese for tea being "cha." It seems to have first come into use at the factory of Firando in Japan.

1654, but in two or three years it also was merged in the London Company.

During forty years no further competitors appeared upon the scene, but shortly after the accession of William and Mary rumours became current that a rival was in the field, and that it enjoyed the powerful support of William Bentinck, Earl of Portland, among others. The London Company spent great sums of money in the endeavour to prevent the grant of a charter to the new society, and in 1693 alone £90,000 was expended in bribing the Privy Council. But these efforts proved fruitless, for in 1698 a charter was granted to the General Society or English Company trading with the East Indies. Evelyn said in his diary that "the old East India Company lost their business against the new Company by ten votes in Parliament, so many of their friends being absent, going to see a tiger baited by dogs." The London and English Companies were keen rivals for ten years, and then they very wisely decided to amalgamate. In 1708–9 the two Companies combined as the United Company, and from that time to its extinction the East India Company encountered no more opponents or rivals of its own nation.

At the same time there were a good many merchant adventurers who ignored the Company and sailed under their own flag. "These men were called Interlopers, and the Company pursued them in the East with sword and imprisonment, in London with fines and other legal penalties, as only the powerful can oppress the weak.[1] They were denounced as rats and treated as vermin, yet the national character was as well vindicated by their reckless bravery as by the systematic, but more selfish, proceedings of the Company's servants. We can only refer to the greatest of all the Interlopers, Thomas Pitt, the founder of the family which gave England two of her proudest names. For twenty years of his life he was the terror of the East India Company. He was a 'desperate fellow,' the leader of the Interlopers, a man to be hunted down wherever found. Fined in London, imprisoned in India, he still sailed his ship under the nose of the Company's squadrons and sold his goods on the London market in despite of the Honourable Court, for he was 'cool in action, saw what to do and did it.' At length admiration or helplessness suggested another course. Thomas Pitt, having expended some part of his Indian profits in gaining a seat in Parliament, was taken into the Company's service and sent out as President of Fort St. George, at Madras. For more than ten years he governed that important possession to the profit of the Company and the enhancement of his own credit, being known as 'The Great President,' or 'The Great Pits.'"

President Pitt was famous not only as the grand-

[1] I reproduce the description of the Interlopers given in my *Story of India*.

father of the Earl of Chatham, but as the purchaser of the Pitt diamond, which he brought to England. It was originally a stone of 410 carats, but on its being recut and reduced to 137 carats it was valued at twelve times its cost price. For some time Pitt wore it in his hat, and had his portrait thus taken. In 1717 the Regent Orleans purchased it for £135,000. The transaction is buried in some mystery, and doubt has been cast on the fact of the payment having ever been made. But the records in the India Office show that two boxes of gems were lodged as security by the French, and there is little or no doubt that they sufficed to meet the price. In France the diamond was renamed the Regent, and at the time of the Revolution its value was estimated at half a million sterling.

Before concluding this chapter, reference may be made to the Company's foreign rivals, who shared with it the efforts and the reward of the quest of India. The Portuguese, who were the first in the field by more than a century, exercised their rights under what might be termed a national guarantee; that is to say, the king never delegated his sovereignty to any chartered company, and left the trade open to all his subjects without restriction. We have seen how Spain, when Portugal was united to it, advanced the pretension to exclude English and other heretic mariners from the Eastern seas, and how that pretension fared at the hands of Elizabeth and her sea-captains. Dispelled on the

Atlantic, the pretension was revived in the Indian Ocean, to be again consigned to the limbo of human vanities or baseless hopes. Downton in Swally Bay, Shirley at Ormus Island, destroyed it as effectually as had been done in the Channel and at Cadiz.

To the Portuguese succeeded a sterner competitor, the Dutch, allied with us in religion and politics, but not allowing those ties to interfere with or restrain the working of a commercial procedure based on the rigid exclusion of every one else, to which Philip II. could not have lent an additional touch of colour or severity. As navigators the Dutch preceded the English by about five years in the seas of the East, but their Company was not founded until 1602, when James Lancaster was on his way back from his first voyage. Their success was rapid and extraordinary, and far in excess of that achieved by the English. The scene of their activity and exploits extended from Mocha and the Mauritius to Japan and Corea. Java, Ceylon, and Sumatra were the special centres of their activity, and to them belongs the credit of the discovery of Australia, which they fondly believed was destined to be a new Holland, just as firmly as they thought that New York would go down in history as New Amsterdam. The tyrannical exclusiveness of the Dutch laid the seed of a national enmity and resentment that would never have arisen but for the massacre of Amboyna, the cruel proceedings in Japan, and the expulsion, wherever possible of the English from the Archipelago, a course of procedure not confined to the seventeenth century, but almost as marked in the nineteenth, and especially pronounced at the time of our acquisition of Singapore. Dutch pretensions were at their height when Pepys entered in his *Diary*, February, 1664, the following passage: "Great talk of the Dutch proclaiming themselves in India lords of the Southern seas, and denying traffick there to all ships but their own upon pain of confiscation." Before the century closed these preposterous pretensions were ended, and the two rival races were beginning to devote their attention to two distinct spheres. The Dutch hold on Java, Sumatra, Borneo and the minor islands was not to be easily shaken. But the English had obtained compensation in India. Fifty-eight factories, great and small, encircled the peninsula, and the English alone had bearded the Mogul. The massacre of Amboyna had results its guilty perpetrators never contemplated. But for it English ambition might never have soared above the spice trade. Commerce with, or even the conquest of, a group of islands would never have bred the consciousness of power, the sense of imperial responsibility, which have been stimulated by the charge of the destinies of India.

Chapter II

THE CONQUEST OF INDIA

THE discovery of India and the establishment round its coasts of a number of trading factories need not have entailed its conquest. The real cause of that event must be held to have been the internal divisions of the Indian princes and peoples and the weakness of the central Mogul Government. If India had been united, if she had even possessed in the eighteenth century what she did in the sixteenth, a wise and resolute ruler in the person of Akbar, it is not to be conceived that one of the principal passages in the historic rivalry of England and France would have been enacted on the plains and off the shores of India. The clash of Briton and Gaul in mortal fray shook the fragile edifice of Mogul authority to its base. The proof of the superiority of European troops over native levies conveyed a lesson too obvious and too easily learnt not to be applied to the events of the day, and the fact that the Emperor was held in thrall by warlike races inimical to trade, settled government and the foreigner was at once a provocation and an excuse for the English, who found it necessary to enforce the tranquillity essential for the prosecution of the commercial enterprise, that was after all their first object, at the sword's point. Rivalry with France supplied the match that exploded the magazine of India's internal weakness, disunion and strife, but the contents of that magazine were bound to have exploded under the blows of invaders from Persia and Afghanistan some day or other, and to have wrecked the Mogul Government. It did not deserve to live. Its system was rotten, the good of the people never entered into its thoughts, and the sword which Baber the Lion had wielded with such effect had become brittle, and was held by a nerveless arm.

These facts, sufficiently clear when scanned in the light of history, were not generally appreciated at the time of their occurrence. There is no evidence that any Englishman was able to apply the lesson taught by the successes of the two Shahs Abbas, or of the Afghan founders of the Candahar and Khorassan kingdoms, or of the plunderings of Lahore and Delhi by Nadir Shah, although they were clearly the writing on the wall. To Dupleix belongs the credit of perspicacity in seeing that the Mogul regime was doomed, and that it would not be difficult to put an European one in its place.

Obstructions to its trade, diminishing the totals in its ledgers or the rate of interest to its subscribers, touched the East India Company in its tenderest part, for it was conducted on strictly business principles. The sword was only to be drawn to right the wrongs inflicted on the English trade by corrupt and false-dealing governors of the Mogul ruler. The policy of a corporation guided by these principles would long have been controlled by timid scruples and reluctance to enter upon the political arena. The competition of the French not merely removed these restraints, but soon made it a question of a life and death struggle for existence. Richelieu founded the first French East India Company in the year 1642, and the minister Colbert did much to encourage its operations. It is worthy of notice that, during the long wars between England and France in the reigns of William III. and Queen Anne, there were no hostilities in India. There both nations were embarked on commercial undertakings, and they remained content with the pacific competition of their calling. Chandernagore, in the Gangetic delta, and Pondicherry, on the coast of Coromandel, were the two principal French stations, but they attempted no attack on their English neighbours at Calcutta and Madras during the long and bitter struggle which concluded with the Treaty of Utrecht. It was different when the two countries were next engaged in hostilities during the first Silesian war, partly because possessions beyond the sea had begun to be prized in Europe, and partly because France was at themo ment represented in the East by a man of great ambition and considerable ability in the person of Dupleix.

At the moment of his appearance the French stations in India were in a flourishing condition, and those who only looked on the surface might have hesitated to predict whether the English or the French Company would most prosper. Pondicherry had flourished under three intelligent governors — Caron, Martin, and Lenoir. Chandernagore was raised to a considerable degree of prosperity by Dupleix himself, who had held the post of its intendant for eleven years when in 1741 he was summoned to assume at Pondicherry the supreme direction of French affairs in the peninsula. The French had two advantages over their English rivals. They had made themselves more agreeable to the native princes and rulers than the English, and they had ingratiated themselves with them by taking an interest in their political affairs and by affecting to look down upon commerce. They were in the first place representatives of *la grande nation*, and only in the second merchants interested in the exchange of goods and money. This kind of relationship was far more agreeable than the strictly business transactions carried on in the English factories and counting-houses. It was more pleasant, but it was not profitable, and it could not prove permanent. The French had to draw the resources for their operations in India from France; the English were able to provide them on the spot. If the first advantage possessed by the French was qualified by the consideration to which attention has just been drawn, the second advantage was one that was incontestable, and that goes far to explain French successes in the earlier stages of the struggle, as well as the narrowness by which the English triumph was eventually attained. The French possessed a considerable European-trained army of native sepoys, which at the moment of Dupleix's arrival at Pondicherry did not number less than 5,000 men.

The French thus possessed the military power. On the other hand, the English possessed the bulk of the trade, a very considerable revenue, and ten times the number of commercial stations round the coast. The opponents were not unequally matched. The struggle could not fail to present some interesting features, and its final solution would necessarily follow the fortunes of the Power that secured the command of the sea.[1]

Dupleix saw very clearly the advantages possessed by the English, and with admirable candour he declared that Madras overshadowed Pondicherry. Notwithstanding his trained sepoys and the cordiality of his relations

[1] Captain Mahan has made a great reputation by exploiting a very old idea, and even the phrase "command of the sea" was employed long before we, or any single Power, possessed it. In a curious pamphlet, *The Letters of an Officer of the Irish Brigade to his Friend, a French Officer*, 1756, I find the Irish officer laying down the law that if France was to beat England she must keep "the command of the sea," and assist the Irish in their rebellions.

with the native powers, Dupleix was under no delusions as to the severity of any struggle with the English on the Coromandel coast. The greatness of his ambition even led him to wish to defer any action until he felt certain of success, for which he saw that a concentration of French power east of the Cape was necessary. His first measures were consequently of an amicable character, when tidings reached India, in 1742, that England and France had taken opposite sides in the first war between Austria and Prussia. He wrote to Governor Morse, of Madras, proposing that there should be an abstention from all hostilities between the two peoples in India. The reply made by Governor Morse was of a non-committal description, and intended to leave his hands free. It is possible that there was some reason to distrust the sincerity of the French governor, but, on the other hand, Governor Morse may have derived such confidence from the presence of a considerable English squadron under Commodore Peyton that he did not feel inclined to deprive his country of the advantages it might obtain by dealing France a forcible blow in the East. Governor Morse had no intention of attacking the French, nor had he the means of doing so, but he would not go out of his way to make an arrangement that would prevent the king's captains from bombarding Pondicherry or Mahé if they chose.

Dupleix wanted time for maturing his plans. If he could not get it by direct negotiation with the English representative, he must seek it in another direction. He accordingly appealed to Anwar-ud-Din, the Governor of the Carnatic, for whom the French had done a good many commissions, including the annual production of his coinage at a very considerable profit, and he asked him to forbid the English to make war on the French on Indian territory. This was a very clever move on his part. It screened his own plans, and it seemed to put the English in the wrong. The Governor of the Carnatic complied without any hesitation, and sent a peremptory order to Governor Morse forbidding him to undertake any military operations on Indian territory, and supporting this order with a display of military force. Governor Morse had no option save to obey. There is no proof, indeed, that he ever entertained any idea of undertaking any offensive measures against his neighbours. None the less he was subjected to this public affront, which enhanced the prestige of the French as the allies of the Emperor's governor.

Dupleix's move had been made with the idea of gaining time. He wished to bring his project for establishing French supremacy in India to the knowledge of his king, and to make sure of the assistance of the French fleet anchored off the isle of Bourbon. The French governor of the island which we know to-day as Mauritius was La Bourdonnais, who had served with distinction in India, and who might not be averse to co-operate in schemes for the humbling and perhaps the expulsion of the English. Dupleix found in the captor of Mahé a ready listener, but time was needed in those days for the arrangement of any plan that entailed the movement of any considerable armed force across the ocean. Before La Bourdonnais could do anything to support his colleague in India, he had to make the position in his own governorship secure, and to provide for its defence against any descent on the part of an English squadron. He had also to organize out of rather unpromising materials an efficient land and sea force to give his expedition any reasonable prospect of success. The year 1746 had arrived before he was ready to sail. Even then his squadron was weaker in armament, if not in numbers, than the English squadron, under Commodore Peyton, which watched the sea approaches round the island of Ceylon. He admitted that his chief hope of reaching Pondicherry ay in slipping by the English frigates. Disappointment attended this expectation as the English watch was good, but in the encounter that followed the English commander did not distinguish himself. After some cannonading the English seemed to have victory in their grasp, when, finding a few of his ships damaged, Commodore Peyton, instead of pressing home his attack, drew off his squadron, and retired ignominiously to Achin, the northern part of Sumatra, with the intention of refitting. The French ships were left a clear course to Pondicherry, and Madras, so recently lulled in a sense of absolute security became exposed to the gravest peril. Dupleix had received the reinforcement essential for the execution of his bold project, which the lapse of years had not rendered less attractive.

The French governor had used his friend Anwar-ud-Din to keep the English in an enforced state of inaction while they possessed a superior naval force to his own, but now that the position was reversed the promise to abstain from hostilities on Indian soil was thrown aside like an old glove. At that time the defences of Fort St. George, Madras, were quite inadequate to resist an attack by artillery, and La Bourdonnais, finding that the English squadron had really departed, proceeded to attack it by land and sea. The English were wholly unprepared to make any resistance, and when Governor Morse heard of the approach of the French he sent off a messenger to Anwar-ud-Din asking him to order them to retire. This, for some unknown reason, the Governor of the Carnatic refused to do, and it was supposed that his connivance had been secured by the promise of a share in the spoil of the rich English factory. Be that as it may, he did not interfere with the French bombardment, and after a few days Governor Morse made a surrender on honourable terms. Negotiations were then entered into between Morse and La Bourdonnais for the ransom of the town, and, notwithstanding the opposition of Dupleix, they were concluded with that object. There can be no reasonable doubt that La Bourdonnais was induced to make this arrangement by the receipt of a large bribe, but the English were disappointed in their expectations, because they could not compel the French commander to remain and carry out his own undertaking. La Bourdonnais was most anxious to leave the coast before the bursting of the monsoon, and when a terrible storm shattered several of his vessels, and cost him the lives of 1,200 of his soldiers, he at once went on board his ship and sailed away, declaring that he wished he had never come to India.

The departure of La Bourdonnais, with whom the Governor of Pondicherry's relations had become those of open feud, left Dupleix master of the situation. He refused to recognize the convention signed by La Bourdonnais, and he retained possession of Madras. At this moment Anwar-ud-Din became alarmed at the magnitude of the French success, and he sent Dupleix an order to restore Madras to the English. Dupleix haughtily refused, and when the Mogul governor sent an army to enforce his command, Dupleix despatched all the troops he could collect to oppose it. Dupleix was no soldier, and he entrusted the command to a Swiss soldier of fortune named Paradis, and the result justified his choice. The two forces met at St. Thomé, a name to be remembered as forming the turning-point in modern Indian history, for there was revealed for the first time the hollowness of the military power of the Moguls. An immense force of thousands of men, with a cumbrous artillery carried on elephants, was put to the rout by a small body of native troops trained and led by Europeans. The victory may have been gained by the small corps of Frenchmen present rather than by Dupleix's own sepoys, but none the less the latter established a marked superiority over the untrained thousands of the Moguls. The victory of St. Thomé filled Dupleix with hope and presumption. For the success of his schemes it only remained to sweep away the English. He proclaimed the annexation of Madras to France, carried off the chief English residents to parade them in triumph before the inhabitants of Pondicherry, and gave orders that Fort St. David, where the English had collected, was to be attacked. A few of the stouter-hearted among the English made their escape from Madras, and among them was Robert Clive, a young writer in the Company's service, who in this stormy period was about to find his true vocation. In May, 1747, Clive obtained his commission as ensign in the Company's service, because he was "of a martial disposition and had distinguished himself as a volunteer in some recent engagements." Among those engagements was the successful defence of Fort St. David against two French attacks, one led by Paradis, the victor of St. Thomé, in person. The arrival of Admiral Griffin with a small squadron turned the scale in favour of the English, and Major Stringer Lawrence, an experienced soldier, arrived to take command of the

Company's troops. He obtained a considerable success over the French at Cuddalore in January, 1748, where Clive especially distinguished himself, but a little time later Lawrence[1] had the misfortune to be taken prisoner while besieging Ariakuram. The English force was soon afterwards increased by the arrival of another squadron under Admiral Boscawen, and it was decided to effect the recovery of Madras by attacking the French at Pondicherry. Dupleix, aided by Paradis until he was killed in a sortie, made an able and determined defence, and after six weeks Boscawen was obliged to retire with the loss of one thousand men. What would then have happened is doubtful, but news arrived of the Treaty of Aix la Chapelle, and the struggle closed with the restoration of Madras and a general reversion to the *status quo ante.*

The first act in Dupleix's programme thus ended with little definite result, but it was clear that the harmony previously existing between the English and French merchants could not be restored, and that the ambition of both had been excited by the evidence furnished of the weakness of the native governors and the inferiority of their armies. The second act began with intrigues in which the chiefs of the province filled

[1] In a letter, dated 24th April, 1748, to the Court, thanking it for making him a Member of Council, Major Lawrence specially praised the Company's European troops, saying, "I should not blush to show them before any king's troops."

a prominent *rôle*, and with movements in which the Europeans played a more or less concealed part, for England and France were then at peace, and there could be no open and official war. In one of Major Lawrence's letters at this period occurs the following characteristic passage: "The whole country round us is at war, and the French governor, M. Dupleix, is trying all the villainous low methods to involve us in it." Dupleix had indeed decided to turn the rivalries and disputes of the native chiefs to advantage on his own account, and the course of events was certainly in his favour. The French had acquired some claim on the family of the Nabob of the Carnatic, and Dupleix greatly increased it by paying the Marathas the ransom they demanded for the surrender of Chunda Sahib. Chunda Sahib on being released captured Arcot, with the assistance of some French troops under Bussy, and assumed the style of ruler of the Carnatic. At the same time Dupleix took up the cause of Muzaffir Jung in his efforts to become Subahdar of the Deccan, or, in other words, the principal Mogul viceroy south of the Nerbudda. At first both of these plans met with remarkable success, and within a year of the close of Admiral Boscawen's siege of Pondicherry the French could boast that the two principal rulers of Southern India were their allies and even their dependants. Without any recourse to arms, Dupleix by clever political moves made French influence for the moment supreme in Southern India, and the year 1750 beheld the high-water mark of French power.

The English had taken no part in these affairs, and it seemed to Dupleix as if they had gone back contentedly to their ledgers and bales, leaving him alone to play the game of high politics. If he could have played it without coming into collision with the English all might have gone well with him, but this was really impossible, and the sudden death of his principal ally, Muzaffir Jung, in a skirmish was the first of a long series of reverses and disappointments. The English said that "the French will not be restraint by any laws," and they saw that there would not be room for the two nations on the Coromandel coast. The scheme of Dupleix in setting up potentates at Hyderabad and Arcot aimed at the expulsion of the English. In 1751 the tension proved too much for the most pacific, and the seizure of the English factory at Masulipatam, for the purpose of making it a French hospital, was followed by a declaration of war between the Companies.

The real dispute arose over the succession to Muzaffir Jung. The French recognized Salabat Jung, an ardent admirer of themselves; the English, moved at last to action, declared for Mahomed Ali, whose title certainly seemed the better, but whose only possession was Trichinopoli, whither a small English garrison was despatched. War openly began in 1751, and it began with the defeat of an English force at Volconda. The garrison at Trichinopoli was in consequence reduced to the lowest straits, and if Clive, who was present at Volconda, had not hastened back to Madras with the view of representing that the situation could only be saved by making a diversion in the rear of the besieging force, its fate would have been sealed. Clive drew up a plan of campaign, the main object of which was to capture Arcot, which would have the probable effect of drawing off Chunda Sahib from Trichinopoli. When we remember that the bold proposer of this scheme was a young man of twenty-four without military training, the principal matter of surprise is that those in authority sanctioned his undertaking. But Mr. Saunders, the Governor of Fort St. George, was a man of broad views and free from prejudice. He saw the advantage of the plan, and he placed at Clive's disposal a small force of 200 English and 300 native troops. Clive captured Arcot without difficulty, but the French officers before Trichinopoli saw through his plan, and if their advice had been followed Clive's object would have been baffled. At first Chunda Sahib listened to their counsel and refused to yield to the impulse to rescue his own capital. But Trichinopoli held out, and at last Chunda Sahib set out at the head of the bulk of his army and a small French contingent.

By this time Clive's force had been greatly reduced in numbers by sickness and disease, but he had made skilful preparations for a defence which will live for ever in the memory of the English race in perhaps the most brilliant of the many brilliant descriptions left us by Macaulay. If the seven weeks' defence of Arcot established the reputation of Clive, the manner in which he followed up this success showed that he possessed the highest qualities of military genius. Mr. Saunders supported his youthful lieutenant with all his vigour. He sent him a fresh force of 200 Europeans and 700 natives. The Maratha chief Morari Rao, struck with admiration for the English, whom he thought "could not fight"—he must have been ignorant of Sivaji's repulse by Sir George Oxenden—agreed to fulfil his convention with Mahomed Ali, for which he had been paid, and placed at the orders of the English leader a force of several thousand irregular cavalry. With this mixed army Clive advanced to attack Chunda Sahib's force on the banks of the river Arni. It had been increased by a further French contingent, and on this occasion for the first time there were as many Frenchmen on the ground as Englishmen. Clive's tactics proved as successful as his defence of Arcot. He turned a more numerous enemy out of a strong position, and he had the supreme satisfaction of seeing the better part of Dupleix's own force flee before him. He did not rest upon his laurels. He gained several further successes, and destroyed the city and monument of Dupleix Fattehabad—city of the victory of Dupleix—which the

French governor had erected to celebrate his triumph two years before. Thus in a few months the genius of Clive raised the fallen fortunes of his countrymen, and snatched from the grasp of Dupleix the triumph that seemed almost assured.

Clive's health broke down under the strain of a campaign conducted in the tropics without any of the comforts which are now considered essential to life in India, and when Major Stringer Lawrence returned from Europe Clive resolved to visit England for his health, but before his departure in 1752 he captured the forts of Covelong and Chingleput, as a final offering to his employers. The cordiality of the relations between Lawrence and Clive deserves notice, on account of its rarity between professional soldiers and outsiders. Lawrence called Clive "a man of undaunted resolution, of a cool temper, and of a presence of mind which never left him in the greatest danger—born a soldier"; and Clive, mindful of the consideration this soldier by profession had shown him, refused the jewelled sword offered him by the Company on his arrival in London, unless a similar one were given to his chief and friend, Major Stringer Lawrence.

The departure of Clive left Dupleix baffled but still hopeful of recovering what he had lost. Lawrence gained a considerable success over the French at Bahur, and Chunda Sahib was taken prisoner and executed in the summary manner which, if it takes little note of the individual's rights, conduces to the settlement of great questions. In 1753 Dupleix made a supreme effort to capture Trichinopoli, and thus restore the fortunes of himself and France. While he laid siege to it, Lawrence covered the place with his small force and obtained the advantage in several skirmishes. At last Dupleix ordered a desperate assault to be made, and when this was repulsed he called off his forces. It was his last act of authority, for shortly afterwards he was recalled by his own Government. The war between the English and the French in the Carnatic from 1751 to 1753 had been an unofficial and indeed an unauthorised war, because there was peace between the two countries. If Dupleix had been victorious Versailles might have consented to keep its eyes closed, but a defeated lieutenant must always pay the penalty of disobedience. We will not deny to Dupleix the credit of having been animated by patriotic motives, but his countrymen put him on his trial and persecuted him till the day of his death in penury and grief.

The outbreak of the Seven Years' War in 1756 induced the French Government to make a fresh effort to recover their lost ground in India. An expedition,[1] composed of two veteran and distinguished regiments, those of Lally and Lorraine, was fitted out in 1757 and placed under the command of Lally Tollendal,

[1] I reproduce the description given of the Lally expedition in my *Story of India*, 1897.

a gallant and experienced soldier, whose desperate courage and quick decision at the head of part of the Irish Brigade had turned Fontenoy from a defeat into the most brilliant victory the French ever gained over an English army. As the son of an Irish chieftain who had left his native country after the surrender of Limerick, he was animated by a special hostility to the English, and he threw himself with extraordinary energy and zeal into the task of overthrowing his hereditary enemies. He was joined soon after his arrival by Bussy, the military director of the Subahdar of the Deccan—or the Nizam, as he soon after this began to be generally called—but Bussy, although experienced in Indian warfare, had not the same professional skill or honesty as Lally. Bussy was envious of the greater fame of his colleague; and, on the other hand, Lally formed the lowest opinion of Bussy, and indeed of every one connected with India. Lally's operations were conducted in a vigorous and daring manner that had not been seen in India except when Clive was present; and now Clive was heavily engaged in Bengal, realizing the fruits of Plassey. Lally sat down before Fort David and captured it. He laid siege to Madras, and the English emporium seemed on the eve of a second surrender. Troops arrived from Bengal, under the command of Eyre Coote, just in time to save it, and a fleet hastily assembled under Admiral Pocock brought the French covering squadron under D'Ache to an action, and defeated it on 10th September, 1759.

But the decisive engagement had to be fought on land and not on sea. Sir Eyre Coote had a force of nearly 2,000 Europeans and over 3,000 natives. The French commander had 1,500 Europeans and 4,000 natives. Lally and Bussy, although not in close accord, were both brave and capable officers, and when the rival armies faced each other on the field of Wandiwash on 21st January, 1760, no one could have confidently predicted the result. Although both armies contained a larger number of natives than Europeans, the former took little or no part in the action. They seemed to be the spectators while the fate of India was being decided between the European combatants. Lally's position was a strong one, with his left resting on a hill crowned by a battery manned by sailors, and on his right he placed his European cavalry, 150 in number. He decided to commence the action with a cavalry charge, in the hope of turning the English left and thus assisting his main infantry attack from the centre. Placing himself at the head of the cavalry he sounded the charge, but the men refused to follow him. It was only at the third attempt that they could be induced to charge, and then in a faint-hearted manner. In the meantime the battle became general, and an accidental shot caused the explosion of a powder magazine on the hill, killing eighty sailors and destroying the battery. Notwithstanding this misfortune and the capture of Bussy, Lally made a strenuous resistance, and at one moment it seemed as if he might have inflicted on the English in India almost as severe a defeat as he had been the chief cause of bringing about in Europe. This was not to be, and all hopes of a French triumph in India were practically swept away in the battle-clouds of Wandiwash.

After the battle Lally defended Pondicherry against the English for a whole year, and on 7th January, 1761, he made a surrender on honourable terms, which permitted him to return to Europe with the remnants of the two regiments he had brought out four years earlier. Lally was thrown into the Bastille; and in 1766, despite the petition of the Duke de Soubise, in the name of the French army, that his life should be spared, the hero of Fontenoy was executed. Dupleix and Lally represent in their names French failure in India, and in their persons they experienced French ingratitude.

We did not, however, conquer India from the French; it would be correct to say that we prevented the French conquering it. The story of the conquest centres in Clive, whom we left on his way to England in 1752. Three years sufficed to restore his health, exhaust his savings, and make him ready to resume active service. In 1755 he sailed for India in the capacity of Governor of Fort St. David, and with the military rank of Lieutenant-Colonel, conferred upon him by George II. On his way he destroyed, with the co-operation of Admiral Watson, the piratical stronghold of Gheriah, the residence of the Maratha chief Angria, who had successfully defied the Bombay authorities, and whose raids extended to the Persian Gulf and Red Sea. A few weeks after Clive's arrival at Fort St. David, news came from Bengal of the terrible tragedy of the Black Hole.

The great province of Bengal[1] had been quite unaffected by the events in the southern and senior Presidency. The French held Chandernagore, but there was no contest between that place and Calcutta in imitation of the struggle between Madras and Pondicherry. Still the tendency to regard Bengal as "the fairest flower in the Company's garden," noted in an earlier epoch, had been strengthened by the increase of the trade in the Gangetic delta, and by its exceptionally profitable character. But, on the other hand, the Mogul Viceroy of Bengal was supposed to wield a far superior military power to that possessed by any of the southern satraps. Behind his deputy at Moorshedabad stood the great Emperor himself on the throne of Delhi, and, diminished as was the respect paid in Madras to the mere numbers of the native armies, it was still otherwise in Bengal. Moreover, it is only fair to note that the establishment at Calcutta

[1] Here again I can merely reproduce the description of the Black Hole and Plassey given in my *Story of India.*

was a civil and commercial one, whereas that at Madras had assumed an essentially military character, with its European regiments and thousands of trained sepoys. Surprise should not be felt, therefore, at the attitude of the Calcutta authorities being more respectful and even servile towards the native rulers than that of their colleagues in Madras, where easily won victories had taught a correct appreciation of the superiority of discipline over numbers. The events that led to the establishment of British power on the Ganges can in no wise be attributed to the arrogance or self-assertion of the East India Company's representatives there. Their policy was peace, and they would submit to any exactions short of absolute repression and extortion. There is absolutely no evidence to warrant the charge that Mr. Holwell and his colleagues had any political designs, and they must be wholly acquitted of having contributed in any way to the hostile and tyrannical proceedings of the Bengal viceroy, Surajah Dowlah.

That youthful potentate succeeded his grandfather at the age of twenty, almost at the moment of Clive's return to India. It is said that he hated the English from his childhood, and that he gave himself up to debauchery. It is certain that if there had never been a Black Hole tragedy his name would long ere this have passed into oblivion. Taking offence at some trifles which he considered a reflection on his dignity, Surajah Dowlah marched with a large army upon

Calcutta. It must be admitted that the English at Calcutta showed great pusillanimity, and acted after a very different fashion from stout Job Charnock and Captain Arbuthnot, who stormed the Mogul battery seventy years earlier. The governor fled to the ships, and the ships sailed down the Hughli, leaving Fort William to surrender at discretion. Surajah Dowlah entered the British factory, and summoned the English prisoners into his presence—20th June, 1756. They were 146 in number, and Mr. Holwell, member of Council, was the chief of them. The viceroy abused them in language made more forcible by disappointment at having found so little treasure, but he promised them their lives; and he probably meant it, for they were valuable for ransom. But, unfortunately for himself as well as his ill-fated prisoners, he retired from the room without giving any orders for their disposal, and some cruel and careless subordinate forced these 146 Europeans into the room, twenty feet square, which had been used for the few prisoners of the factory, and which was familiarly designated the Black Hole. The officials who perpetrated this act of cruelty refused to repair it by asking the Nabob for fresh orders, on the ground that he was asleep. In the morning Surajah Dowlah ordered their release, but 123 of the captives were dead, and several of the surviving twenty-three died later or never recovered their reason.

The tragedy of the Black Hole created great commotion at Madras, where steps were immediately taken for the despatch of a punitive expedition under Clive. It was not, however, until December, 1756, that the expedition, under the joint command of Clive and Admiral Watson, arrived in the Hughli. The interval had given Surajah Dowlah confidence, but it had also caused him to realize that by suppressing the English factory he had lost a productive source of revenue. He had no fear of retribution at the hands of the English, but he was disposed to restore Calcutta, still in the hands of his garrison, and to grant fresh trade facilities. Such were his feelings at the moment when news reached him that Clive had entered the river, recovered Fort William, and destroyed his garrison at Hughli. He was still anxious for an amicable settlement, and proposed to compensate the members of the Calcutta factory for their losses and sufferings. These Englishmen themselves were quite willing to meet him half way. They had run away from Calcutta in the first place, excepting the few survivors of the Black Hole, and thought nothing of glory or political expansion. They wanted their money-bags replenished out of the Mogul treasury, and to resume their ordinary pursuits. But Clive took a very different view of the situation, and although hampered by the Calcutta Board and also by the Madras Council—who wanted him back to fight the French—he succeeded in carrying out his own policy.

The conduct of Surajah Dowlah himself no doubt largely contributed to Clive's success. That prince took military steps which were incompatible with his pacific protestations, and his agent Omichund played a double part. Clive saw all the possible perils of the situation when Surajah Dowlah began to intrigue with the French, and he determined on a bold counter-stroke. War had not then been declared between England and France, but it was known to be imminent, and Clive came to the resolution to nip in the bud all danger in Bengal from French hostility by conquering their settlement at Chandernagore. The expedition was secretly fitted out and admirably led. The French were too surprised and taken too completely at a disadvantage to offer much resistance, and the 500 French soldiers who might have turned Plassey into a Mogul victory were disarmed and made prisoners of war. At this juncture several of Surajah Dowlah's principal relatives and officers, disgusted by his treatment or disappointed by his want of success, began to plot for his overthrow. Into these intrigues Clive threw himself with energy, for he quickly saw that they provided him with the means of thwarting the pusillanimous counsels of Bengal, and at the same time of turning a deaf ear to the messages of recall from Madras. Mir Jaffir, the commander of Surajah's troops, was the leader of the plot, and on its success he was promised the succession to Surajah Dowlah.

At the moment when the plot was ripe for fulfilment Omichund turned traitor, or, rather, he demanded the enormous sum of £300,000 as the price of his keeping faith. Clive, brought face to face with a peril that threatened the success of the whole design, resorted to villainy to catch a villain. He expressed his readiness to comply with the Hindu's request. An agreement was drawn up, but Clive had two copies prepared—one on red paper, the other on white. The former contained the promise to Omichund, but was fictitious, and bore the forged signature of Admiral Watson, which Clive did not scruple to append himself. The white treaty was the genuine one, and was only produced when the Hindu asked to be paid and discovered that he was to get nothing. It is unnecessary here to go into the moral side of this unpleasant matter. Clive vindicated himself some time afterwards by declaring, in a letter still in existence at the India Office, that "delay and chicanery is allowable against those who take advantage of the times, our distresses, and situations."

Having completed these preliminaries, Clive gave the signal by assuming the offensive and marching towards Moorshedabad at the head of 3,000 men who, as he said, had never turned their backs. Surajah Dowlah collected all his forces to repel the English, and Mir Jaffir, his courage failing him at the last moment, held back and did not join Clive with his followers as had been arranged. In this grave position when the two armies were only separated by the plain of Plassey, Clive called a council of war, and, although Eyre Coote was in favour of attack, the majority decided for retreat. Clive seemed to yield to the majority, and for an hour the fate of the English in Bengal hung in the balance. Clive then came to the momentous decision to resume his advance and attack the Nabob's army of nearly 60,000 men with the 1,000[1] British and 2,000 native troops under his orders. The battle, which was fought on 23rd June, 1757, was short, sharp, and decisive. The Bengal army was put to the rout one hour after the first cannon shot, and, although it lost only 500 killed, its camp guns and baggage formed the prize of the victors. Mir Jaffir came into Clive's camp to congratulate him, not without doubt as to his reception, but his fears vanished when Clive greeted him as ruler of Bengal and its dependent provinces. Some days later the English commander installed him in the seat of Surajah Dowlah at the provincial capital of Moorshedabad. The new ruler's position was assured by his capture and murder of Surajah Dowlah.

The territorial reward to the East India Company for the victory of Plassey was not much. For the chief part of its possessions south of Calcutta it paid

[1] Among these was the old 39th regiment, which bears on its colours *Primus in Indis.*

a rent to Mir Jaffir. The pecuniary reward was a sum of £800,000 out of the Bengal treasury, but the most important result was the establishment in the north of the same military power and reputation which the English had acquired in the south. Having made this striking commencement, Clive hastened to ensure and extend the authority and influence of his country. He despatched one expedition, under the command of Major Forde, into the region which is termed the Northern Circars, and when Shah Alum, the son of the Great Mogul, advanced against Mir Jaffir at the head of a large force, boasting that he would re-conquer Bengal, Clive went himself to encounter the new danger. At that moment Shah Alum was closely besieging Patna, which seemed on the point of falling, but such was the terror of Clive that on hearing of his rapid approach the Mogul army broke up its camp and fled in all directions. In his gratitude for this rescue Mir Jaffir assigned to Clive the rent paid him by the Company for the district mentioned—namely, the Twenty-four Pergunnahs. Clive in return made this grant over to the Company as the nucleus of the Bengal Pension Fund.

At this juncture Clive was called upon to face a new and unexpected peril, which threatened to destroy all that had been done. The appearance of Lally had compelled him to send Eyre Coote and the larger portion of his European troops to Madras, and, as the French power in Bengal had been destroyed, there seemed no special risk in this step. But Mir Jaffir, fearful lest the power that had set him up might destroy him, had been intriguing with the Dutch at Chinsura, and the Dutch were induced to believe that by a bold stroke they might obtain on the Ganges the monopoly they had acquired in the Eastern Archipelago. They wrote to Batavia a full account of the position in Bengal, and the Dutch Governor of the Indies sent a powerful squadron and a land force of 1,500 good troops to snatch the prize which Providence seemed to have placed within his reach. He reckoned without Clive, and he presumed too much on the nominal peace between Holland and England deterring the English from attacking even an armed expedition directed against themselves. Such considerations had not prevented the Dutch murdering Englishmen at Amboyna ; they did not weigh a feather with Clive when he saw that he had to preserve the British possessions in Bengal. To reach Chinsura the Dutch had to sail up the Hughli past Calcutta. Clive, at the head of a very inferior naval and military force, met them on the way, attacked and defeated them, destroyed several of their largest ships, and imposed on the Dutch of Chinsura the onerous condition that they were never to interfere in politics again as the price of their being allowed to retain their factory. The surprise of the French at Chandernagore had paved the way for Plassey; the discomfiture of the Dutch of Chinsura made its fruits assured.

After Clive's second return to England Mir Jaffir was deposed for his double dealing, but his successor, Mir Casim, proved a worse selection, for he massacred 200 English prisoners at Patna and then fled into Oude. The Nawab Wazir of that state and Shah Alum, who had succeeded to the imperial throne, took up the cause of Mir Casim, and the federated princes placed in the field the most formidable native army that had ever been gathered in Northern India. On 23rd October, 1764, it met and was signally defeated by the Anglo-Indian army under Major Munro at Buxar. That battle was in its way as decisive and striking as Plassey. The Mogul emperor visited the English camp as a suppliant. Bengal, Behar, and Orissa were ceded to the English in perpetual sovereignty. To these were added, in the following year, the Northern Circars surrendered by the Nizam, and thus England became for the first time a territorial power in Bengal. In the seven years from Plassey to Buxar the military position in Bengal was placed on so indisputable a basis that it passed without challenge in that vast province from the day of Munro's victory to the Mutiny.

Not long after Clive's final departure from Calcutta in January, 1767—his third stay in India was marked by administrative reforms and army reorganization and not by military triumphs — a crisis arose in Southern India which threatened to prove more difficult to deal with than the rivalry of French governors and adventurers. In the productive and interesting kingdom of Mysore the native Hindu dynasty, which had maintained its independence long after the Mogul advance south of the Nerbudda, had been lately set aside by a Mahomedan soldier of fortune named Hyder Ali. Before Dupleix fell or Clive established his military reputation Hyder Ali had begun the career which made him the most striking Indian figure of the eighteenth century and our most formidable adversary. When Munro won Buxar he had become the sovereign of Mysore and a potentate with whom his neighbours must reckon. It was not till the end of the year 1767 that he crossed the path of the English, and then only because the Nizam of the Deccan, regretting the loss of the Circars, resolved for the first and last time to array his forces against them. Bussy took a considerable part in organizing the campaign, but treachery was the main weapon relied on. The Nizam's army was defeated at Vellore, and the worst peril from the confederacy seemed past, when Hyder Ali, descending from his mountain kingdom at the head of 30,000 men, plundered the Carnatic, and compelled the English authorities at Madras to purchase an ignominious peace by concluding an alliance with him on his own terms. For ten years after this incident Hyder Ali's power seemed greater than that of the English in Madras.

During that period the affairs of the Company were guided in India by little men, but in the year 1774 Warren Hastings, appointed the first Governor-General of Bengal, resumed the execution of the task begun by Clive. The military exploits of Clive might never have borne the fruit they did if at so short an interval the statesmanship and administrative skill of Warren Hastings had not supervened for their consolidation. Warren Hastings reformed the European administration, but his chief achievements were the repudiation of the Mogul's authority by refusing to pay any longer the tribute of 300,000 rupees a year, the seizure of Allahabad, and the increase of the Company's revenue by these and similar high-handed measures. From the moral point of view there may be nothing to be said for them. They were the acts of a conqueror, and made the more remarkable because effected without the least employment of force. In this manner Hastings added a quarter of a million to the Company's revenue and obtained a capital sum of half a million, which was doubled by the subjugation of the Rohillas for the benefit of the ruler of Oude. These funds provided Hastings with the means of carrying on the important and serious wars that marked the later years of his administration. Without them he could never have brought those military operations to a triumphant issue.

The first opponents with whom Hastings felt it necessary to deal were the Marathas, who had founded the three great military states of Baroda, Gwalior, and Indore, governed respectively by chiefs known as the Gaikwar, Scindiah, and Holkar, while the Peishwa, representing a nominal headship ruled at Poona. It was said that the French, baffled in the south, had sent emissaries to these courts to stir them up against the English, and the authorities of Bombay were filled with alarm as to whether they could hold their own. Hastings at once realized the gravity of the situation. He raised ten new native regiments, and he sent two expeditions across India to Bombay. One attacked Scindiah, and Captain Popham captured by assault his reputedly impregnable fort of Gwalior. The other, under Colonel Goddard, overthrew the Gaikwar of Baroda. Peace with the Marathas was concluded on favourable terms.

In the meantime the long-pending conflict with Hyder Ali had commenced, and Bussy, the French officer who had fought at Wandiwash, acted as the European adviser of the Mysorean ruler. Fortunately, before a shot was fired, Warren Hastings had by diplomatic means succeeded in detaching the Nizam from the side of Hyder Ali. In 1780 Hyder Ali invaded Madras, and carried all before him. One force, under Colonel Baillie, was destroyed; the main body, under Sir Hector Munro, the victor of Buxar, was compelled to retreat; and, for the first time in history, the English turned their backs on a native foe. A French fleet, under the skilful Suffren, the ablest sailor that country ever produced, had been sent from Europe to co-operate with Hyder Ali; and, for a time, it met with no inconsiderable success. The situation, from every point of view, was extremely critical; but Warren Hastings, with characteristic promptitude, and by an assertion of authority in excess of the written letter of his warrant, superseded the incompetent Governor of Madras by sending his most experienced and capable officer to conduct the war with Hyder Ali. He induced Sir Eyre Coote, the victor of Wandiwash twenty years before, to take the command, although the force placed at his disposal was very meagre, and scarcely exceeded that with which he had defeated Lally. Eyre Coote arrived just in time. When he reached Madras, in November, 1780, he found the French fleet in possession of the roadstead, the town of Wandiwash on the eve of surrender to Hyder Ali, and a state of panic prevailing at Fort St. George. The most pressing step was to draw Hyder Ali away from Madras and to relieve Wandiwash. With this object Coote executed a difficult march to the south of Pondicherry; but, although he succeeded in his main object, he found that he had placed himself in a disadvantageous and dangerous position in face of Hyder Ali's numerous army, with which the French squadron was able to co-operate. When he reached Cuddalore, a short distance south of Pondicherry, he endeavoured to recover the ground he had lost by assuming the offensive, but in an attack on the pagoda of Chelambakam, he met with a repulse, which might have had grave consequences. It was then that he retired a few miles further south, and took up a strong position at Porto Novo. The spirit of this gallant general, untamed by years or by his recent reverse, would not brook a defensive battle. He again assumed the offensive, and inflicted on Hyder Ali as crushing a defeat as any recorded in Anglo-Indian history. He followed up his victory with remarkable energy, and without leaving the enemy time to breathe. When he halted his small army in February, 1782, he had, in little more than twelve months, rescued the whole of the Madras Presidency from a confident and daring assailant, and inflicted a succession of defeats on the ablest native soldier and ruler Southern India had ever known. The struggle proved fatal to its author, Before peace was signed Hyder Ali, broken in spirit, died of baffled rage and spleen at his discomfiture, and his power and ambition passed to his son, Tippoo Sahib.

The close of the struggle with the usurping Mahomedan power in Mysore was not reached for many years after the departure of Warren Hastings, and only as the result of two severe campaigns. The Marquis Cornwallis was forced, by Tippoo Sahib's invasion of Travancore, to draw the sword at the end of the year 1789, and it was not until the year 1791 that he succeeded in driving "the tiger of Seringapatam" into his capital and compelling him to sue for peace. Tippoo surrendered half his territory, and paid us an indemnity of three millions sterling; but his spirit was not broken, and French encouragement was not lacking to bid him prepare and hope for revenge. The struggle reached its most critical stage in 1798, when the Marquis Wellesley arrived in India, specially charged with the mission of establishing British predominance throughout the peninsula. At that moment Bonaparte was in Egypt, and every vestige of French power in India became of magnified importance. The Nizam's army had been trained by Bussy and other French officers, Scindiah's army was becoming really formidable in the hands of De Boigne, and Tippoo's sympathies were strongly with Bonaparte, who had promised his co-operation. Wellesley set himself to his task at once. He cajoled or frightened the Nizam into dismissing his French officers, disbanding their regiments, and signing a treaty promising to employ no Europeans except Englishmen. Having made himself secure at Hyderabad,

Wellesley declared war on Tippoo, invaded his state with two armies, and captured his capital by assault. Tippoo himself was slain in the breach of Seringapatam on 4th May, 1799, and from that day to the present the peace of Southern India has been practically undisturbed.

A more serious task awaited Lord Wellesley than the overthrow of the power of Tippoo, much diminished by the previous war with Lord Cornwallis. He endeavoured to make the Maratha chiefs accept an arrangement similar to that which he had imposed on the Nizam; and when he exacted from the Peishwa the Treaty of Bassein, embodying such an arrangement, it seemed as if his end might be attained by peaceful means. But the militant Maratha chiefs repudiated the action of the Peishwa, who had been expelled from his capital by Holkar, and Scindiah and the Rajah of Nagpore formed a defensive and offensive alliance to resist the pretensions of the English. It was in this grave emergency that Wellesley showed the highest gifts of statesmanship, and he was fortunate in finding in his younger brother, Sir Arthur Wellesley, the future Duke of Wellington, and in General Lake, two extremely able commanders to lead his armies and realize his plans. The campaigns which followed were among the most brilliant and successful in the whole of our Eastern experiences. Sir Arthur Wellesley won the battles of Assaye and

THE EARL OF MINTO.

[To face page 58.

Argaum, and captured the strong fortress of Ahmednugger. Lake gained still more striking victories at Aligarh and Laswari, and concluded a most remarkable march at Delhi with the rescue of the Mogul emperor from his Maratha gaolers. These battles were fiercely contested, and gained with difficulty and at considerable loss. Want of funds prevented the prosecution of the war with Holkar to its bitter end and a hollow peace prevailed until, in the time of the Marquis of Hastings, the second war with the Marathas brought to a conclusion the struggle with that vigorous race.

An interval of peace ensued, marked only in the time of Lord Minto by the expeditions undertaken to expel the French from the islands of Mauritius and Java. Both these expeditions were crowned with success; and while Mauritius, as a French possession, was permanently annexed, Java, after six years' beneficent administration by Sir Stamford Raffles, was restored to the Dutch. The war in 1814–6 with the Goorkhas of Nepaul, who offered a stubborn resistance and only succumbed to the military skill of Sir David Ochterlony, formed a prelude to the campaigns that established the question of supremacy in Central India. The year 1817 began with a war against the Pindari bands which held the whole of Central India. With these the greater Maratha chiefs were either in sympathy or in open alliance. Holkar and the Rajah of Nagpore openly supported them, and the Peishwa lent the allies all the influence of his name. At the battle of Mehidpore Holkar's army was routed (21st December, 1817), and that chief compelled to sue for peace. In the following spring the Pindari bands were overthrown and dispersed, and the Peishwa surrendered and resigned his power and authority. The fall of the Peishwa signified the collapse of the Maratha confederacy. It had never presented an absolutely united front, but after the fall of the descendant and representative of Sivaji the rivalry and jealousy between the militant ruling chiefs became still more pronounced. Each had been willing to yield precedence to that titular leader when none would cede a point or a pretension to the other.

The conquest of India may be considered to have ended with the second Maratha war in 1817–8. It is quite true that large portions of territory were subsequently added to the dominion of the Company even within the limits of Hindostan, but they were appropriated not from the mere love of conquest, but from absolute necessity in completing or consolidating what had been conquered. In sixty years, dating from Plassey, the East India Company had extended its dominion from the few factories and trading ports stationed around the coast over the whole of the peninsula outside the Punjab. The viceroys of the Mogul in Bengal, the Deccan, and Oude had been either superseded or reduced to a position of subordination. The most formidable military races—the Mahomedans of Mysore, the Marathas of every principality from Delhi to the Nerbudda, and the Rohilla Afghans of Northern India—had in turn been compelled to yield to the steady discipline and unsurpassable courage of the British. Kings held their states at the pleasure of that trading Company, whose origin had been humble, whose fortunes had long been checkered by reverses, and whose greatness had been thrust upon it. The Great Mogul, whose imperial power seemed so irresistible at the beginning of the seventeenth century, had become in the early years of the nineteenth the puppet of the English, thankful to find that their protection was less irksome and less costly than that of the Marathas.[1]

[1] *The Story of India.*

Chapter III

THE FIRST EPOCH OF REFORM

THE general interest of the British public in the affairs of India may be said to date from the throwing open of trade with that country at the time of the renewal of the Company's charter in the year 1813. The abolition of the trade monopoly which the East India Company had enjoyed for the century following the amalgamation of the Companies was the signal for a great development of trade and also of interest in India, but so long as the Company retained the monopoly of trade with China its commercial character could not be considered inferior to its political. The consequences of these changes and warnings of change could not but be far-reaching. There was not only an increased sense of responsibility, but an increased appreciation of the necessity of defence against possible attack. It was well known that the China monopoly had only been renewed in 1813 for twenty years as a last sop to the Company, and when its term approached the fear was even prevalent that the demand for reform so general after the accession of William IV. might extend to the very existence of the Company. It would scarcely be going too far to say that, after the close of the long governor-generalship of Lord Hastings in 1823, the directors of the Company laboured under a feeling that to some extent the institution which they represented was on its trial.

Under this combination of circumstances it was not surprising that the idea of reform based on financial retrenchment and legislative amelioration should be in the air. India could no longer be regarded merely as the milch cow from which might be drawn an endless succession of dividends. Its conquest had entailed the responsibility of governing a vast population with a due regard for its rights, and also for the moral obligations of a higher civilization. It was perfectly clear to everybody that we should stand self-condemned if we failed to give India something better than the Mogul Government. When a successor had to be appointed to Lord Hastings, Lord William Bentinck, who had had some Indian experience as Governor of Madras, and who had played a considerable part in Sicily and Italy during the Napoleonic struggle, was one of the candidates, but the Court chose the Earl of Amherst, who had conducted the second English embassy to China in 1816. What the Company expected from its representative above everything else was economy and retrenchment, and it so happened that events forced Lord Amherst to undertake the costly campaign in Burma which not only swallowed up all his available resources, but produced a greater deficit than ever. In great alarm the Court determined that its next governor-general should at all events be a champion of economy and a capable financier, and, remembering that Lord William Bentinck had been one of its most thrifty representatives, it chose him as Lord Amherst's successor in July, 1827.[1]

Lord William Cavendish Bentinck was the second son of the third Duke of Portland and Lady Dorothy Cavendish, only daughter of the fourth Duke of Devonshire. In 1803, when he was not twenty-nine years of age, after some military service in various parts of Europe, he arrived at Madras as governor in succession to the second Lord Clive. Although he took no direct part in the campaign with Holkar, he assisted Sir Arthur Wellesley in the Assaye campaign by sending him supplies, and he was thanked for his co-operation by the general, and also by his brother, the Marquis Wellesley, then Governor-General. In a communication written at this time Lord William Bentinck speaks of "British greatness being founded upon Indian happiness"—a memorable phrase written more than twenty years before the idea of reform had been seriously

[1] He did not arrive in India till July, 1828.

entertained in Anglo-Indian circles. The details of his governorship in Madras do not concern our subject, except the remarkable incident which brought it to an end—namely, the mutiny at Vellore.

Vellore, a town west of Madras and not far distant from Arcot, was an important cantonment of the Madras army. Several sons of the famous Tippoo Sahib lived there, surrounded by some of their family retainers, on the bounty of the Company. It was rather a turbulent little community, and it was believed that intrigues were often set in motion for the recovery of Mysore. About this time too various innovations had been introduced into the Madras army, with the idea of smartening up the sepoys' appearance on parade. In 1805 a new turban was introduced; in 1806 the sepoys were forbidden to wear their caste marks and earrings on parade. Sir John Cradock, afterwards Lord Howden, the Madras commander-in-chief, was a severe martinet of the old pipe-clay school. These injudicious steps were not long in producing the consequences that might have been foreseen.

The first mutiny occurred in April, 1806, at Vellore, when the 2nd battalion of the 4th Native Infantry, one of the most distinguished regiments in the service, refused to wear the turban. An English cavalry regiment, the 19th Dragoons, was sent to Vellore, twenty-one sepoys who had acted as ringleaders were arrested, and after a court-martial two were sentenced to severe corporal punishment and dismissal from the army, while the other nineteen were pardoned. This partial measure did not much improve the situation. The agitation continued, and Sir John Cradock, alarmed at the attitude of the soldiers, talked of giving way, and at last asked the governor what should be done to abate the excitement. Lord William replied that, "whatever might be the objection to the measures, yielding in the face of force was to be avoided," and thus made himself responsible for the maintenance of the original order.

On 10th July the native troops at Vellore rose, attacked their officers, murdered several of them, and besieged the small European force which was cut off from the arsenal. A message was sent summoning the 19th Dragoons to come to the rescue, and fortunately this regiment arrived in time. The native troops were promptly attacked, routed, and dispersed. Many hundreds were cut down by the cavalry, and the captured ringleaders were blown from the guns. For a moment there was some apprehension lest the spirit of insubordination might spread to Secunderabad, but the well-timed measures of Colonel Montresor checked the spread of the movement. The famous Vellore mutiny, the warning and model of 1857, was promptly suppressed, and it might have passed into oblivion but for the ndignation of the Court with its representatives at Madras. In April, 1807, it recalled or rather removed Lord William Bentinck in a summary and discourteous fashion, although it recognized "the uprightness of his intentions and regard for its service." On his return to England he endeavoured, by petitioning the Court and publishing a defence, to obtain reparation, because he had been "condemned as an accomplice in measures with which I had no further concern than to obviate their ill consequences." The Court would not on this occasion withdraw or modify its censure, but in 1827 it rendered him the fullest satisfaction by his nomination to the post of Governor-General. Lord William Bentinck accepted the appointment with special satisfaction, because he interpreted it as the justification of his conduct in 1806.

The administrative measures and political reforms to which Lord William Bentinck devoted himself during the seven years he was in India might be divided under three main heads—financial reorganization; the suppression of crime and cruel practices which disqualified the Hindus from being regarded as civilized, and reflected on the Government responsible for their actions; and the dissemination of education based on the English language, with its necessary corollaries of political liberty and a share in the government.

The most pressing of all the questions with which the new Governor-General had to deal was the state of the finances. The revenue showed a deficit of more than one million sterling, and, as Sir Charles Metcalfe said, "the Government which allows this to go on in time of peace deserves any punishment." His own instructions from the Court enjoined on Lord William Bentinck above everything else to effect retrenchment and economies, but they only indicated one direction in which this could be done, and that was by the abolition of batta. The word "batta" means "extra pay," and long usage had accustomed the officers to regard at least the half batta allowed them even in their cantonments during peace as part of their regular pay. Lord William Bentinck was strictly ordered to reduce all full batta to half batta. This step gave rise to much clamour and to considerable agitation in military circles. Petitions were addressed to the Governor-General and sent home to England. The Calcutta press found two years' amusement in abusing Lord William Bentinck personally, to which he philosophically replied by saying that "he knew of no subject which the press might not freely discuss." But finally the orders of the Court on the subject of batta were made law in September, 1830. From the noise and volume of the agitation one might fancy that the stake at issue was exceedingly large. As a matter of fact, the change effected an economy of twenty thousand pounds a year, which went but a small way towards restoring an equilibrium.

Further economies of trifling amounts were effected by the abolition of the Provincial Courts of Appeal and Circuit, and by a reduction of the civil establishment. But the real reform was attained by the substitution of native clerks and functionaries in all subordinate offices for Englishmen, and when this step had been effectually carried out the burden on the exchequer was lightened to the extent of half a million a year. At the same time army expenditure was reduced in a summary fashion, and the establishment was diminished to a sufficient extent to lessen the vote by a million a year. By these radical steps an equilibrium was soon brought within sight, if not actually attained.

While controlling the expenditure Lord William Bentinck did not neglect the sources of revenue. The land revenue of Bengal had been fixed by the permanent tenure of Lord Cornwallis. During the whole period of his stay in India Lord William was occupied with the settlement of the land revenue in the North-West Provinces. When carried into effect in 1833, it materially added to the revenue of the Government of India. Another considerable addition was made by the successful carrying out of an arrangement with the Maratha chiefs of Central India for licensing the direct conveyance of opium from Malwa to Bombay. The necessity for this arrangement was proved by the fact that Malwa opium not only escaped all contribution to the Government of India, but, being exported from the Portuguese ports of Diu and Daman under the Portuguese flag, entered into competition in China with Patna opium and undersold it. The joint result of the economies noted and of the new sources of revenue provided was that before Lord William Bentinck left India the deficit of one million, which he had found on his arrival, had been converted into a surplus of two millions.

Lord William Bentinck's financial and other reforms were of the greatest assistance to the Company in obtaining the renewal of its charter in 1833. The Select Committee appointed to consider the facts began its labours in 1829, with very hostile intentions towards the Company. But its energies were exhausted long before the final scene in the House, when the charter was renewed with the benches deserted and all interest in the question evaporated. The renewal of the charter was not, however, done in its entirety. The monopoly of the trade with China was cancelled, and trade with that country was thrown open, just as that with India itself had been in 1813. The loss of the China trade, which earned the shareholders their dividend, as was said in somewhat far-fetched language, was declared to signify ruin, but a very brief experience sufficed to show that this fear was baseless. During the whole of the discussion the East India Company was more or less on its trial, and it was undoubtedly due to Lord William Bentinck, whose reforms quickened the life of India and advanced the clock of progress by half a century, that the verdict was one tantamount to an honourable acquittal.

At the beginning of his administration Lord William Bentinck was compelled to adopt strong measures for the suppression of the gangs of professional robbers called "thugs" or "thags."[1] The word "thag" in Hindustani means "cheat," but it does not give a very true idea of the thug's mode of operations. Their other name of phansi-gar (noose-throwers) is more explicit, as they strangled their victims with a scarf or rope. They seem to have long been a pest of India, as the French traveller Tavernier mentions "the stranglers of the highway" as one of the chief perils of the unwary or unguarded traveller in the seventeenth century. These secret murderers formed a guild of their own, into which admission was difficult, and rarely granted except to members of families that had been long enrolled among the initiated. Religious ceremonies were introduced to glorify and exalt the base profession of a highwayman operating by the perpetration of murder. The secrecy of the method, the long impunity of the criminals, and the helplessness of a fatalistically disposed people enhanced the reputation of the thugs and the timidity of the incapable and corrupt native Governments. The impunity enjoyed by the thugs was only disturbed when Lord William

[1] "Thag" is the so-called scientific spelling, but the pronunciation is "thug."

Bentinck took up the question of their suppression by the appointment of a Thug Commission, and by deputing special officers, of whom Colonel Sleeman deserves special mention, to hunt them down.

The following description of their methods is summarised from my own *Life of Lord William Bentinck*. Having performed certain propitiatory rites of a quasi-religious character, and obtained some favourable prognostications as to the result of their enterprise, they set out along one of the main roads frequented by merchants and travellers. To all appearance they were a party of unarmed and harmless men, either pursuing their business as traders or returning to their villages from a pilgrimage. In days of open robbery travellers were only too glad to meet with companions, and the thugs never experienced any difficulty in picking up one or more than one unsuspecting wayfarer *en route*. There was nothing in their demeanour or conduct to excite suspicion. At the well or caravanserai they seemed like inoffensive travellers, and the only ground for suspicion was that which least arouses it—an excessive affability and a too conciliatory attitude towards strangers. Having once selected their victim, their patience in waiting for the most favourable moment to strike the blow was remarkable, and constituted the main secret of their power and protracted impunity. In nearly all cases the deed was done at a moment when the victim would be least prepared and most off his guard—engaged in either his prayers or his ablutions—and the noose was always used with such deadly precision that the murdered person never had a chance of raising an alarm. The larger proportion of victims were single individuals, but if the gang was sufficiently numerous—and sometimes the thugs travelled in bands of sixty or seventy—they would not be afraid to entice a considerable body of travellers, and to murder as many as a dozen at a single massacre. In all cases they resorted to every precaution to prevent surprise from interruption, and with such success that no instance of failure is recorded. The younger members of the family or band served their apprenticeship as scouts, and it was only after many years' employment in this innocent capacity that they were even allowed to witness the perpetration of a crime, while the act of throwing the scarf was always entrusted to the most expert and experienced member of the band. Their skill in effecting the murder was matched by that with which they concealed the body and removed all traces of the crime.

At the time of which we are speaking Central India had become the chief scene of their operations, and the chiefs of Malwa and Rajputana were too weak to crush them. Their officials are even believed to have connived at their proceedings for bribes or a share of the plunder. In the year 1829 the suppression of thuggee was taken seriously in hand, and the task continued during six years. Two thousand thugs were arrested during that period, and of that number fifteen hundred were punished either with death or long terms of imprisonment. The native Governments, stimulated by British example, took an active part in hunting down the bandits, but the native Courts of Justice showed great reluctance to pronounce a death sentence in any case. To meet this difficulty plenary judicial powers were conferred on the agent in Central India, to whom was entrusted the chief direction of the pursuit and prosecution. The chief culprits were captured and punished, the more formidable bands were broken up, and the family ties and secrets of initiation were destroyed or forgotten. In this way the suppression of the thugs was effected, not merely for the immediate period, but permanently for all time, and it is exceedingly improbable that they will ever be revived.

A still more memorable achievement, and one which will be always associated with the name of Lord William Bentinck, was the abolition of sati, suttee, or widow-burning.[1] This practice was sanctioned by religion and custom; the unfortunate women who performed the sacrifice were extolled as model wives and paragons of virtue. It was specially in vogue in

[1] Suttee, or sati, means simply "a pure and virtuous woman"; the act of immolation was saha-gamana, "accompanying a husband's corpse," but suttee has been adopted by common usage as the phrase for the act.

Bengal, and the holy river Ganges had witnessed countless acts of self-immolation during the progress of centuries. The custom, shocking as it would have been under any circumstances to the European mind, was rendered more horrible by the knowledge that these immolations were often not voluntary, that sometimes they were only rendered possible by drugging the victim, and that a suttee was consequently often only an euphemism for murder. At the same time it was impossible for the English to take up the position adopted by the native reformers Dwarakanath Tagore and Rammohun Roy, viz., that suttee was an innovation not sanctioned by or in real accordance with the true teaching of Hinduism. It was no part of our duty or mission to attempt to draw a dividing line between the true and the false in the religious beliefs of the people. It was the sheet anchor of our policy in India to leave all those burning questions alone, and neither to define nor to challenge the Code of Manu. But the same indifference that was shown to a religious custom or conviction could not be extended to a crime, and the more closely the question was examined the clearer did it appear that suttee was a crime perpetrated at the expense of the weak, the unoffending, and the helpless.

It must be conceded to the English rulers of Bengal that, from their first appearance in that province, they did not conceal their disapprobation of the practice, and various measures were proposed by some of the earlier governor-generals for putting an end to it. For fear of seeming to interfere with the religion of the people and for other reasons no steps were taken, and a hope was even encouraged by some of the native magistrates that the practice would die a natural death. Far from this proving the case, it showed a tendency to increase, and especially among the races from which the Bengal army was recruited. Lord Minto passed the only practical measure dealing with it before the time of which we are now speaking, by making the sanction of the English authorities essential for the ceremony to be performed. In this way it was hoped to put an end to involuntary sacrifices; but this well-intentioned regulation was rendered quite inoperative by native ingenuity, the fanaticism of the devotees, and the terrorism exercised over the women. To give an idea of the number of suttees, it may be stated that in the Lower Provinces of Bengal the average for the ten years ending in 1828 was six hundred per annum. The Marquis of Hastings, whose courage at least no one could think of disputing, did not think it safe to interfere with "the horrid superstition," because it was the practice of the high-caste Bengal army. The hesitation shown in suppressing suttee was not due to any doubt as to the evil or the abuses of the practice, but to apprehension lest its suppression might disturb the discipline and allegiance of the Bengal native army.

Such was the position of the question when Lord

William Bentinck assumed the government of India. The weight of experience was against stirring up unnecessary agitation and danger by grappling with it. The instructions of the Court of Directors, if they did not fetter his action, at least inculcated the need of caution. The personal experience of Lord William Bentinck was certainly calculated to make him opposed to any hazardous legislation. There was no incumbent duty on him to deal with the question at all. He might have passed it on to his successor in the same manner as his predecessors had passed it on to him. He might have accepted the dictum of the Marquis of Hastings that it required great personal influence with and a certain ascendency over the native troops to carry out such a measure successfully, and he could have truthfully declared that he did not possess the influence of the conqueror of the Marathas. Or he might have based his refusal to act in the matter on Lord Amherst's not unreasonable "apprehension of evils infinitely greater than those arising from the existence of the practice." But he at once, and without hesitation, came to the conclusion that he could not remain indifferent to this crime, and abstain from action against it, without himself being guilty of "the crime of multiplied murder."

As a prudent preliminary to any action, an inquiry was instituted as to the feelings of the sepoys of the Bengal army in the matter. A number of questions was put to forty-nine officers of special experience and knowledge of the native troops. Twenty-four advocated the total and immediate suppression of the practice, and only five reported against any interference. The remaining twenty were in favour of suppression by indirect measures. An overwhelming majority agreed that the sepoy was far less interested in the subject than was supposed. This conclusion removed the great deterrent in the path of reform, and immediate measures were decided upon. Judicial authority supported the military, and in 1829 the Nizamat Adalat, or High Court composed of native judges, reported unanimously in favour of the permanent and immediate abolition of suttee. The conclusion to which Lord William came on this and other evidence—nine-tenths of the public functionaries of the province were declared to be in favour of abolition—was that it was perfectly safe as well as expedient to order its immediate suppression.

Suttee was formally suppressed by Regulation No. 17 of 4th December, 1829, and pronounced to be a crime of culpable homicide, punishable with imprisonment or fine, or with both. The Courts of Justice were also left the option in extreme cases of passing a capital sentence. This regulation applied at first only to Bengal, but in 1830 it was extended to the rest of India. I am tempted to repeat the deliberate conclusions expressed on a former occasion[1] on the subject

[1] *Lord William Bentinck.* Rulers of India Series.

of Lord William's great reform in, to use his own words, "washing out a foul stain upon British rule."

These words of Lord William Bentinck suggest some remarks, in conclusion, on the principles underlying our policy in India, which have as much force to-day as they had sixty years ago, when Indian reform was first taken seriously in hand by the abolition of suttee. Non-interference with any native practice was the first article of faith with the East India Company, which, while admitting in their fullest extent the services it rendered to the State, was after all a commercial body in its essence. It may be admitted that the determination to show all possible respect and consideration to the practices and prejudices of the Indian population was and still is sound policy. But after all there is another side to the question. It may be difficult to fix on paper the limits of toleration, and to declare beforehand the points at which active intervention should commence. But practical men could never experience any difficulty in deciding when a Hindu practice must be considered a foul stain on British rule. It is unjustifiable from every point of view except religious bigotry, and impolitic in the extreme, to take steps to coerce the Hindus and other Indian creeds to adopt Christianity. Their religion should be as sacred in the eyes of those who govern them as it is in their own. When we refuse to recognize this truth and act in contravention of it, we shall have taken the first step towards the loss of our Indian Empire. But respect and protection for the religion of the Hindus cannot allow us to be blind to acts which are opposed to the clearly established rights of humanity. No religion can justify the sacrifice of innocent persons. A civilized Government is bound to protect them, or to lose its own reputation.

It was for this reason that, even if the Hindus had made the abolition of suttee an excuse for revolt, we were bound, sooner or later, to intervene for the protection of women who could not help themselves, and who were the victims of a senseless and brutal tyranny and bondage. The enlightened and educated Hindu must realize that the legislation directed against special acts of what can only be considered human cruelty, arising from ignorance sanctioned by long usage, does not injure his religion in the least. With the doctrine and religious ceremonies of Hinduism the Government of India has no more inclination or intention of meddling than it has with the creeds of the Mahomedans and the Parsis. But a solemn and imperative duty rests upon us to put an end to cruel and brutalising acts wherever committed under our jurisdiction, and for these we cannot allow either religion or long usage to be an excuse or a safeguard. The suppression of suttee was and still remains the most striking instance of the fulfilment of this obligation.

Having dealt with the great social reform and financial improvements, the subject of the general

THE MAHARAJA OF MYSORE.

[To face page 80.

administration naturally suggests itself in the next place for consideration. One great reform in the civil service of the country was the prohibition of the acceptance of gifts or presents by its members from any native. Before this regulation was passed the practice had been general, and it was rightly considered to open the door to a number of abuses.

Although Lord William Bentinck's rule was the most peaceful before the Mutiny, he had to sanction two important annexations, both caused by the excesses of the princes and incapacity or worse of the ministers of the states in question. Mysore and Coorg were incorporated in British India, the former to be restored in 1881 to the descendant of the Maharaja deposed fifty years earlier. The internal condition of the kingdom of Oude was also extremely bad, and it was undoubtedly aggravated by the manner in which the Governor-General's hands were tied by the East India Company, whose orders were peremptory in forbidding him to interfere with the native states. They did not prevent the two annexations referred to, but they saved Oude from annexation for a further quarter of a century. It may be noted, however, that the despatches of Lord William Bentinck in 1831 and 1832, advocating annexation, furnish the justification for the step when it was taken twenty-five years later by Lord Dalhousie. In two trifling matters the relations with the native states were not without interest. The Maharaja of Patiala, who also deserves mention for having lent the Government, in a moment of difficulty, twenty lakhs without interest, sold us the greater part of the hill on which stands Simla, and the site of Darjeeling was also purchased from the Rajah of Sikkim. Lord William Bentinck will thus be remembered for having established the two most important sanitaria and hill stations in Northern India.

All these measures may be said to have had their objective and their consummation in the education and public employment of the natives, for which education was essential. The adoption of English as the official language of the civil and judicial administration was regarded by some of the older school with a very lively sense of apprehension. The measure that was above all others to unify a British India was pronounced on high authority to be certain to provoke trouble and entail disaster. The majority were of this view, but a few enlightened men, like Sir Charles Metcalfe, Sir Charles Trevelyan, and Mr. Russell Colvin, held the contrary opinion, and in 1833 they received a powerful ally in Mr. Macaulay, who came out as legal member of Council. It does not appear to be any exaggeration to say that the genius and assiduity of Macaulay turned the scale against the Orientalists who championed Arabic and Sanscrit. In a minute of remarkable lucidity and power, Macaulay turned the arguments of his opponents against themselves, and proved to the dullest mind that no other language was practically possible or desirable except English. The force of Macaulay's brilliant periods was not diminished by the plain words of an Anglo-Indian administrator when Sir Charles Metcalfe added : "The English language seems to me to be the channel through which we are most likely to convey improvement to the natives of India."

But the most convincing argument of all in favour of the adoption of the English language was that it was essential to the admission of the natives to a proper share in the government of the country. If the Orientalists had triumphed, they would have injured their own clients, because we could never have trusted men trained by a standard of Eastern antiquity to carry out or conform with the teaching of civilized government. In all empires there must be some connecting link, and in India it could only be that of language. The adoption of English as the official tongue, in 1835, was accompanied by Lord William Bentinck's strong recommendation in favour of throwing open the higher posts of the civil service to natives. As Sir Charles Trevelyan said in his evidence before the committee in 1853: "To Lord William Bentinck belongs the great praise of having placed our dominion in India on its proper foundation, in the recognition of the great principle that India is to be governed for the benefit of the Indians, and that the advantages which we derive from it should only be such as are incidental to and inferential from that course of proceeding." It should also be recorded that Lord William was the first Governor-General to admit native gentlemen into his intimacy. He did not exclude the leaders of native thought and intelligence from his splendid hospitality, and for the first time in Anglo-Indian intercourse the social barrier between the several races was removed. This practice disappeared with him, and was not revived for another thirty years. It contributed not a little to the exceptional reputation Lord William Bentinck enjoys to this very hour among the natives of India.

Lord William Bentinck's governor-generalship was also remarkable for the revival of the old fears as to the possibility of an invasion of India from the side of Afghanistan. Russia's activity in Persia and Central Asia was one cause of this apprehension, and the internal division of Afghanistan was another. The reigning family of the Sudozais had been deposed from the throne of Cabul, and in its place ruled Dost Mahomed, of the rival Barukzai family, which is represented to-day by the Amir Abdur Rahman. The representative of the Sudozais at this time was Shuja ul Mulk, an exile in British India. Although more than a quarter of a century had elapsed since his reception of Mountstuart Elphinstone at Peshawur, and despite several intermediate failures, Shuja still retained the hope of recovering his own again. In 1833–4, equipped with funds supplied by the generosity of Runjeet Singh, the

Sikh ruler of the Punjab, Shuja made a determined effort to reconquer his kingdom, and as his army was far superior to that of Dost Mahomed, and included two good regiments of old Hindustani soldiers, led by an Englishman named Campbell, his chances of success might well have been pronounced favourable. He was however completely defeated by Dost Mahomed in 1834, and escaped once more to India, where he remained as our pensioner until his cause was taken up by Lord Auckland, as will be described in the next chapter. It is very remarkable, when we remember the errors about to be committed, to find Lord William Bentinck writing in his minute of March, 1835, about "the wretched army that Shah Shuja had under *his feeble guidance*," and predicting that the supremacy of Dost Mahomed might give greater strength and consolidation to the Afghan confederacy, and tend to create a stable state as "an intermediate barrier between India and Persia."

Lord William Bentinck contributed something more than words to the settlement of our difficulties on the north-west frontier, then defined in general terms by the Sutlej. He secured from the Amirs of Scinde the opening of the Indus to navigation and commerce. By his interview with Runjeet Singh at Rupar, he undoubtedly made that suspicious and vigilant ruler more cordially our ally than he had ever been before, and this improvement bore fruit in the famous tripartite alliance of 1838.

This was the more remarkable as Lord William was under no misconceptions as to the solidity of his power or of the friendship of his people after his death. In the minute from which I have quoted he wrote: "Runjeet Singh is old and infirm, and there is no apparent probability that the wisdom of his rule will be inherited by his successor. Troubles upon his decease will certainly arise, and it is impossible to foresee the result as relates to the line of conduct which we may be called upon to pursue." But the most remarkable portion of the minute was that dealing with the possible co-operation of a Russian army in a movement on India. It is possible that Lord William Bentinck was largely influenced by Napoleon's views on the same subject. As a soldier and a statesman he declared the line of operation of a Russo-Persian army to advance on Herat—"the key of Cabul," as he calls it—was short and easy, yet at that time the distance was nearly 1,200 miles, while the further march to the Indus, *via* Candahar, Cabul, and the Khyber, was another 1,100 miles. These enormous distances have in the last sixty-five years been greatly reduced, and there are now English and Russian outposts within 100 miles of each other. Lord William's invasion minute contains some pregnant passages about the native army and our own position in India, which are still deserving of consideration, although the circumstances and the composition of our Indian army have completely changed.

To give further point to Lord William Bentinck's observations, it is only necessary to quote a few extracts from Sir Charles Metcalfe's comments on them. Sir Charles Metcalfe was, it may be observed, the true originator of the policy of "masterly inactivity," which is generally associated with the name of Lord Lawrence. He wrote:—

"Some say that our empire in India rests on opinion, others on main force. It, in fact, depends on both. We could not keep the country by opinion if we had not a considerable force, and no force that we could pay would be sufficient if it were not aided by the opinion of our invincibility. Our force does not operate so much by its actual strength as by the impression which it produces, and that impression is the opinion by which we hold India. . . . He (Bentinck) admits that we have no hold on the affections of our subjects; that our native army is taken from a disaffected population; that our European soldiery are too few to be of much avail against any extensive plan of insurrection. This is quite enough, and more than I have hitherto alluded to, for it is possible to contemplate the possibility of disaffection in our army without seeing at once the full force of our danger. As long as our native army is faithful, and we can pay enough for it, we can keep India in order by its instrumentality, but if the instrument should turn against us, where would be the British power? Echo answers, where? It is impossible to support a sufficient army of

Europeans to take the place of our native army. The late Governor-General appears also to adopt, in some measure, the just remark of Sir John Malcolm, that 'in an empire like that of India we are always in danger, and it is impossible to conjecture the form in which it may approach.' This sentiment expresses the reality of the case in perhaps the truest manner."

On another occasion Metcalfe, who succeeded Lord William Bentinck as acting Governor-General, and who was soon afterwards created a peer, said "we were sitting on a barrel of gunpowder in India, which might explode at any moment"—a forecast of the Mutiny which should take a high place among successful prophecies.

It is, however, as a reformer, and not as a military expert, that Lord William Bentinck will be remembered in history. His name will certainly be always identified with the first epoch of reform in British India. The work he did has been described at sufficient length, but undoubtedly his chief achievement was to attract the sympathy and stimulate the hopes of the natives in receiving a share in the government of their own country. He first put in practice the loftier ideal of Indian government which had insensibly grown up as one of the consequences of the Warren Hastings trial. He convinced the natives of India that one at least of the dominant considerations in our policy was a disinterested desire for their welfare and elevation in the scale of civilization.

During the twelve months following the departure of Lord William Bentinck in March, 1835, the governor-generalship was held officially by Sir Charles Metcalfe, and during that term he gave the final imprimatur to several of Lord William Bentinck's reforms, among others to his press law. The long interval between the departure of Lord William and the arrival of his regular successor was due to an extraordinary occurrence in official life. Sir Robert Peel had appointed Lord Heytesbury to be the next Governor-General, but Lord Melbourne, on coming into office a few weeks later, had resorted to the extraordinary step of revoking that appointment and nominating Lord Auckland in his place. The second nomination was made in September, 1835 but it was not until March, 1836, that he landed in India. Lord Auckland is so generally associated with our first Afghan wars, and with nothing else, that in closing this chapter it is only necessary to state that in the year 1837–8 he had to deal with the first famine on a formidable scale that afflicted India after our assumption of the government. This famine devastated Oude and the North-West Provinces in particular. Lord Auckland directed the relief works in person, and to him is due the credit of having promoted a permanent remedy, or at least mitigation, of the evil in the construction of the Ganges Canal. This little matter is, however, quite overshadowed in the great drama of the Afghan wars.

Chapter IV

OUR FIRST AFGHAN WARS

THE immediate and direct cause of our intervention in Afghanistan, and of our taking part in the long struggle between the rival families of Afghanistan at the moment when the triumph of one of them through the genius of Dost Mahomed seemed assured, was the success and progress of Russian arms and policy in Persia. The treaties of Gulistan in 1813 and Turkomanchai in 1827, concluding victorious campaigns, had given the Czar an ascendency at Teheran greater than which he does not possess to-day. The effect of Russian victory was enhanced by what was considered the English betrayal of its obligations to Persia, and it is not surprising that the Russian diplomatists, like Simonich, should have found at Teheran every disposition to acquiesce in schemes that promised Persia some compensation for loss on the Aras by conquest on the Heri Rud. The unconcealed *rapprochement* between Russia and Persia aroused in India no inconsiderable apprehension, and revived the old and never-to-be-removed idea that India is always exposed to invasion from the north-west. Lord William Bentinck, in the weighty minute[1] already referred to, showed that there was nothing improbable in a force of 20,000 Russians, supported by a Persian corps, to which the adventurers of Afghanistan and Central Asia, attracted by the prospect of loot in India, would speedily attach themselves, reaching the Indus. If such was the opinion of a man not disposed to take an alarmist view of any military question, and writing with a full sense of his responsibility as governor-general and commander-in-chief, it can readily be understood how much farther went the general opinion in Anglo-Indian circles. That opinion was largely based on the reports of travellers like Burnes and Conolly, Masson and Pottinger, who traversed the region between the Caspian and the Indus, and who possessed the only trustworthy information as to the position of affairs in Afghanistan. The least imaginative observer saw that changes were at hand in this region, and that the Persian designs on Herat rendered it more than ever desirable that there should be a united Afghanistan.

When Burnes returned from Cabul after his first visit in 1832 he brought back a very favourable account of Dost Mahomed, and he even went so far as to make

[1] In this minute it is noteworthy that Lord William speaks of Herat as the key of Cabul. It is only in more recent times that it came to be called the key of India.

a comparison in his favour between the ruler of Cabul and the Sudozai prince Shuja, who was then preparing to make his last single-handed effort to recover his crown. The graphic and interesting narrative of Burnes aroused considerable interest in the personality of Dost Mahomed, if it failed to direct our policy into the natural channel of an alliance with that prince. Before we committed ourselves to the foolish course of championing the discredited and unlucky Shah Shuja, however, Burnes was sent on what, by an euphemism then in fashion, was called a commercial mission to Cabul, but it was never clearly ascertained with what object. Dost Mahomed had himself opened the way to this diplomatic relationship by a letter congratulating the new Governor-General, Lord Auckland, on his assumption of office, in which he asked for advice as to the best way to come to an amicable arrangement with the Sikhs, and declared that "he and his country were ours." The flowers of Oriental rhetoric are not to be interpreted literally, and Lord Auckland replied very properly by expressing our wish that "the Afghans should be a flourishing and united nation," a phrase that has been repeated through all the succeeding stages of our political relations with Afghanistan.

Burnes, with his admiration and sympathy for Dost Mahomed fully aroused, had conceived the idea that our best policy would consist in a close alliance with that chief, and he also believed that he had been granted by

Providence the privilege of bringing this to pass. When he reached Cabul in September, 1837, he was fully persuaded that our best policy was to conclude a hearty alliance with the Dost. He set about his task with sanguine expectations as to success, and these were naturally increased when he found that Dost Mahomed was entirely of his own way of thinking and most anxious for the English alliance. But these hopes were speedily damped and dashed to the ground, first by the absence of instructions, and then by his being officially reprimanded for having exceeded them. While he was negotiating at Cabul for the settlement of all the difficulties pending between the Afghans and the Sikhs, including the delicate question of the possession of Peshawur, as well as for the establishment of English influence on a firm basis at the Afghan capital, the views of the authorities in India had become more definitely in favour of Shah Shuja. In a despatch received by Burnes in February, 1838, Lord Auckland stated positively that Peshawur must remain with the Sikhs, and that the utmost we would do in return for the Amir holding no relations with either Persia or Russia would be to restrain the Sikhs from attacking him. We asked a great deal at the hands of Dost Mahomed, and in return we offered him nothing, for the Afghans did not fear the Sikhs and frankly admitted that they were always the aggressors. Under any circumstances this declaration would have put an end to all the chances of success of Burnes' mission, but as it happened that a Russian officer named Vickovitch was at Cabul, and had for several months been making lavish promises, with or without authority, in the name of the Czar, it was only natural that Dost Mahomed should at once abandon the hope of an agreement with the English and turn to the quarter whence he received encouragement. In April, 1838, Burnes left Cabul for India precipitately and with threats of assassination freely uttered among the turbulent Cabulis; and in the same month Vickovitch was carried in triumph through the streets of the capital, where he had raised hopes in the bosoms of the Afghans that could not be fulfilled. Vickovitch [1] departed soon after Burnes, to arrange, if he could, for the fulfilment of the pledges he had made; but events at Herat destroyed the visionary expectation of Russian aid, and dissolved before they could be ratified the treaties he had concluded with Dost Mahomed and his brothers at Candahar.

[1] The end of the unfortunate Vickovitch may here be briefly described. Notwithstanding his energy and ability he was repudiated by his Government. On calling upon Count Nesselrode at St. Petersburg he was refused an interview, and informed that that minister "knew no such person except an adventurer who had been lately engaged in some unauthorised intrigues at Cabul and Candahar." Vickovitch returned to his hotel and blew out his brains. It was said he destroyed all his papers, but recently a statement was circulated in Russia to the effect that his correspondence would be published.

While Burnes and Vickovitch were carrying on their diplomatic duel at Cabul for the favour of the Amir Dost Mahomed, events of a dramatic character were occurring at Herat which controlled those in every other part of Afghanistan, and, by putting an end to the pretensions of both Russia and Persia, encouraged the English Government to undertake the task of setting up an Afghan sovereignty which would owe its existence to British protection and support. The province of Herat was still ruled by an independent Sudozai prince. Kamran, the nephew of Shah Shuja, and whose cruelty had most contributed to discredit his own family—the worst of a bad race, as Kaye calls him—was *de facto* King of Herat, and ruled over the larger part of the districts between Candahar and the Persian frontier. But his resources were not great, and his authority outside the gates of Herat was little more than nominal. Although maintaining an Afghan administration on the western frontier, he was cut off from the support of his countrymen by the success of the Barukzai brotherhood, and it was known how anxious the sirdars at Candahar were to dispossess him of Herat. The weakness of his position tempted the Persian ruler, Mahomed Shah by name, to assert his pretensions to that city, and he was undoubtedly encouraged to attempt its capture by the advice of the Russian minister at his court, and by the belief that the English would not go to war for the sake of Herat. After some hesitation the Shah marched with a considerable army, part of which had received some European training and was led by a few foreign officers, to lay siege to Herat. He arrived before that fortress on 23rd November, 1837, and the siege, which is one of the most memorable in Asiatic history, is considered to have begun on that day. As the Shah was accompanied by both the English and Russian ministers, it is not very surprising if he thought that he would not meet with any vigorous opposition from the English Government. If his arms had been crowned with immediate success it is possible that his view would not have proved incorrect.

The importance of Herat has been the theme of so many pens that it is unnecessary to give much space here to the subject. It possesses two natural advantages, of which neither the lapse of time nor the changes in its political fate have been able to deprive it. It is situated in the centre of one of the most fertile valleys of the world, which enjoyed in old days the name of the Granary of Central Asia, and which would at the present day support a large population. Here, and only here within the limits of Afghanistan, could an army of 100,000 men be fed for an indefinite period on the resources of the locality. Its second advantage is that it lies on the only good road practicable for artillery between Persia on the one side and Candahar, Cabul and India on the other. The fortress, which has considerable natural strength, and which sixty years ago was secure against artillery, forms the only bulwark of Afghanistan on the west. Every invader of India has made its possession the first step in the execution of his design, and hence it has been called the gate or the key of India. Its importance to-day is not less than it was when Mahomed Shah sat down before it in 1837, although the increased range of artillery has probably placed it at the mercy of an assailant provided with the necessary siege guns. The Amir Abdur Rahman, in his lately published autobiography, declares that he has provided against this danger by fortifying the surrounding heights. As even science cannot destroy the effect and influence of individual heroism in war, we may retain the hope that when Herat is next besieged there will again be an Eldred Pottinger among its defenders.

The officer named, then a young subaltern in the Bombay artillery, entered Herat in August, 1837, after an adventurous journey through the Hazara and Aimak country from Cabul. Kamran and his minister Yar Mahomed [1] were absent on a fruitless expedition to Seistan at the date of his arrival, but they were recalled a few weeks later by the rumours of the approaching Persian army. Almost immediately after their return Pottinger was received in audience by both the king

[1] This remarkable man, a member of the powerful Alikozai tribe, was the real ruler of Herat, and after Kamran's death he established his own authority. He is entitled to much of the honour for the successful defence of Herat in 1837–8.

and his vizier, but it was not until the siege had lasted for six or seven weeks that his counsel and military knowledge were specially invoked for the defence. Before his aid was thus formally solicited he had taken, however, no inconsiderable part in the defence, and his presence and example had inspired the garrison with renewed fortitude, based no doubt on the belief that their fate was not altogether a matter of indifference to the English. After he was called in Eldred Pottinger became the chief member of the council of war, the encourager of Yar Mahomed in his moments of doubt and fear—in short, the soul of the defence. He took part in all the sorties, and was ever foremost in repelling the assaults of the Persians, having several hair-breadth escapes, the record of which must be sought for in his modest journal. But for him the town would undoubtedly have been captured by assault on 24th June, when the Persians made a furious attack which almost succeeded, and when even Yar Mahomed showed every sign of giving in. The crisis of the siege was reached and passed on that day, for although no relieving force was sent to Herat the Persian army was obliged to retreat less than three months later, without repeating the attempt to storm the place, because the English Government made an effective demonstration [1] in the Persian Gulf. But the imperishable credit of having

[1] Space will not admit of the details of that expedition being given. But the following dates may be recorded: In June, 1838, Sir John

defended Herat, when its walls were in a state of decay and its garrison miserably inefficient and ill-armed, during a siege of ten months, rests with the young English officer whom chance quite as much as a spirit of adventure had brought to that city at so opportune a juncture.

At the same time that the Government of India sent an expedition to the Persian Gulf to bring the Shah to reason, it came to the momentous decision to support the Sudozai pretender and exile, Shah Shuja. All the arguments and efforts of Burnes, the declaration of Dost Mahomed himself that he "would not abandon the English alliance while the chance of obtaining it remained," were futile to prevent Lord Auckland from taking this step, which seemed warranted by neither justice nor expediency. In May, 1838, Lord Auckland wrote an important minute, laying down that the scheme most worthy of attention for settling the affairs of Afghanistan was that of "granting our aid or countenance in concert with Runjeet Singh to enable Shah Shuja ul Mulk to re-establish his sovereignty in

McNeill, having learnt that an expedition had been sent to the Persian Gulf, quitted the Persian camp before Herat. On the 17th of that month the British expedition occupied the island of Karrack. In the middle of August the Shah declared that he would not go to war with England, and that if he had known his coming against Herat would have risked the loss of his friendship with us he would not have come at all. On 9th September the Persian army retreated from before Herat.

the eastern division of Afghanistan, under engagements which shall conciliate the feelings of the Sikh ruler and bind the restored monarch to the support of our interests." It does not appear that Lord Auckland contemplated originally the despatch of an English army into Afghanistan. It was thought that a liberal subsidy and a small number of officers would be quite sufficient to enable the Afghan prince by the aid of a Sikh army to regain his throne, but the Sikh ruler was not disposed to pluck the chestnuts out of the fire for us. The Sikhs had a real dread of passing through the Khyber, and nothing could make a war in Afghanistan popular with the Khalsa army. After his last failure it was evident that Shah Shuja would require some fighting force superior to the army of Dost Mahomed, and, as the Sikhs became more reluctant to supply the army of invasion, the Government of India was gradually drawn on to take their place, and provide the necessary force as the only means of averting the failure of the policy that had been adopted.

The whole of the summer of 1838 was passed in negotiations between our Government on the one side, and the Afghan prince at Loodiana and Runjeet Singh at Lahore on the other. These brought out two facts in the situation. One was that the brunt of the work would have to be borne by the English, and the other that the difficulties of the enterprise became the greater the more nearly the subject was approached. No doubt it was thought that the Afghan claimant would be so delighted at the prospect of English military support, which would make the success of his cause morally certain, that he would not dream of raising any objections or of criticizing our proposals. But it was made clear in the early stages of the question that even for success Shah Shuja would not sacrifice his dignity, and also that he knew a great deal more about the Afghan temperament than any of the other parties engaged in the adventure. The two conditions he made showed that he was most anxious to sustain his importance as a sovereign prince, and to prevent the Afghans thinking that he was a mere puppet of the English Government. They were first that no interference was to be made with his authority over his tribe and household, and secondly, that he should be allowed to raise an army of his own. In all his statements he laid special stress on the latter point, as it would prevent his being deemed the tool of the English. It was unfortunate that Shah Shuja's nondescript army of Afghan and other adventurers was not of the calibre to support his dignity and realize the object of his policy. Let it be stated now that the worse Shah Shuja's fortunes became the more did he cling to his dignity, and the more hollow his power was found to be the less consideration was paid to his susceptibilities by his English allies.[1]

[1] Notwithstanding his misfortunes, Ferrier seems right in saying that Shah Shuja was both an able and a courageous man.

In August, after many councils[1] and after the opinion of every man entitled to express one on the subject had been taken, the weak and hesitating Lord Auckland, who was, by the agreement of every one competent to judge, a most peace-loving man, gave his assent to the project of supporting Shah Shuja with English bayonets. He was driven to this decision by the convincing proof furnished that the Sikhs would not invade Afghanistan, and that Shah Shuja's success, even if aided with our money and some officers, was highly doubtful. If the enterprise was to be carried out at all, it was clear that it would have to be performed by the Government of India. The only alternative was to risk a discreditable reverse, and such a contingency was calculated to lend firmness to the most irresolute governor-general. The decision was therefore taken to collect a large army and to invade Afghanistan with an overwhelming force, which should impress the whole of Central Asia with a sense of the power and resources of the English Government. The expedition originally formed was far larger than that actually employed. The commander-in-chief, Sir Henry Fane, took personal charge of the arrangements, and two brigades of artillery, two English

[1] Burnes was in favour of supporting a united Afghanistan. Sir Claude Wade, whose influence was very great, wished Afghanistan to be split up into several states, so that we might be supreme. There is no doubt that Burnes was right, and the unity of Afghanistan has become the sheet anchor of our policy.

cavalry regiments, five English regiments of infantry, and thirteen regiments of native foot, or about 20,000 fighting men in all, were to form the army of invasion. In addition to this there were Shah Shuja's own army and the Sikh contingent with its English representative, Sir Claude Wade, the latter of which was to operate through the Khyber. The military arrangements being practically completed, it only remained to launch the enterprise on the world in an effective and formal manner, and this was done in the official proclamation which is known as the Simla manifesto.

The careful student of the subject will peruse the exact text[1] of this document, but to keep up the current of the story it will be sufficient to state here that it refers to the still doubtful result of the siege of Herat, that it represents Shah Shuja as making the main attempt for the recovery of his own crown, and that it declares the intention of the Government of India to withdraw its troops as soon as its protégé was placed in power. The policy of Lord Auckland was not at the time of its declaration a popular one. The Anglo-Indian public had no opinion of Shah Shuja, and, if Burnes had failed in his more serious political projects, he had at least aroused interest in the individuality of Dost Mahomed. An expedition which seemed to consign the British army to a secondary place, and to leave the honour to an Afghan adventurer who had never

[1] To be found in the Parliamentary Papers and Kaye's *History*.

been successful, could not exite much enthusiasm in military circles, and, although hopes had been entertained that the advance into Afghanistan might lead to a far bigger game in Central Asia, these were dispelled by the progress of events. By some strange irony of fate, the more resolute Lord Auckland and his advisers became in their determination to do something vigorous and to commit themselves beyond the Indus, the more clearly and irrefutably did facts show that there was no necessity for such action, that the Russian danger was then a myth, and that we had serious matters to attend to within our borders without seeking for shadowy perils beyond it. For within a few days of the publication of the Simla manifesto—before, metaphorically speaking, the ink was dry on the paper—the news came that the siege of Herat was at an end, that the Persian army was in full retreat, and that any designs Russian statesmen might have entertained had collapsed. A wise governor-general in face of that very altered situation would have revised the policy of which the Simla manifesto was the formal expression, and would have left Shah Shuja to take his chance of regaining his own country by the aid of a liberal subsidy alone. But *dis aliter visum!* It was decreed that we should be precipitate in Afghanistan, with the penalty that afterwards we were to be timid and vacillating, and that the very name of that country should become in English ears hateful and unpopular.

The only result of the deliverance of Herat was that the grand army which Sir Henry Fane was to have led into Afghanistan was reduced to one half its intended size, and its command transferred in consequence to the Bombay commander-in-chief, Sir John Keane. The orders went forth that the selected troops were to assemble at Ferozepore, then the extreme north-west station of British territory, and at that place accordingly an admirably equipped army of 9,500 fighting men, with, however, the preposterously large non-combatant body of 38,000 camp followers, was assembled by the beginning of November. An interview between Lord Auckland and Runjeet Singh, a great review of the British and Sikh armies so soon to be pitted against each other in hostile fray, marked the end of the preliminaries to the first invasion of Afghanistan. The *fêtes* at Ferozepore ended on 10th November, and one month later the army of the Indus began its march towards Scinde and the Bolan.

The undertaking was marked at its very beginning by an unpleasant and discreditable episode. In order to reach Afghanistan it was necessary to traverse either the Punjab or Scinde. No choice was left in the matter, because Runjeet Singh withheld his consent to the English army passing through his territory. Scinde was at that time ruled by its Amirs, who had been the tributaries of the Sudozai family until its fall. They had shaken off the Afghan yoke more than twenty years before this date, and ruled over the valley of the Lower

Indus from the Punjab border to the sea. It was at first agreed that the Amirs should purchase their independence by paying a sum of twenty lakhs, which should be divided between Runjeet Singh and Shah Shuja. This agreement was changed to one of a more arbitrary nature, providing that Runjeet Singh should receive fifteen lakhs and that Shah Shuja should get as much more as he could squeeze from the Scinde rulers. When this demand was made upon the Amirs they not merely declined to pay, but they produced two solemn releases sworn on the Koran by Shah Shuja of all future claims upon them. The English agent, Colonel Henry Pottinger, saw the justice of their contention that they had already purchased their own liberty, and endeavoured to obtain for them more lenient treatment. But in vain. He was instructed to tell them that, unless they co-operated in a hearty manner with the Afghan prince and his English allies, the power of the Government of India would be employed to annihilate them. They yielded to force, but with a bad grace. They gave up the fort at Bukkur, the possession of which was necessary to a secure passage of the Indus, and when a column of troops was on the march to Hyderabad, their capital, they gave way on the question of the subsidy and agreed to pay twenty-five lakhs. But the whole incident served as an unpleasant opening to our operations in Afghanistan. It showed that we were committed to champion Shah Shuja's claims even when he had surrendered them, and to support the lack of justice with the display of superior force. Our treatment of the Amirs of Scinde in 1838, and again in 1843 when we annihilated their power, is one of the least creditable pages in our Indian history, over which prudence bids us draw a veil.

It took the army of the Indus three months to march from Ferozepore to the mouth of the Bolan. The Khojak was not reached until April, by which time there had been a great loss of baggage animals, and the soldiers had experienced a considerable scarcity in supplies. The approach of the great Anglo-Indian army sufficed to overawe any attempt on the part of the Afghan chief to oppose it. Dost Mahomed's brothers, the so-called Sirdars of Candahar, fled on its approach, and Shah Shuja entered the ancient capital of his family without firing a shot on 25th April, 1839. He had been joined by some chiefs, but on the whole his reception was chilly and discouraging. Curiosity, not loyalty, seemed to be the predominant feeling among the Afghan population, and it soon became evident that the Sudozai prince commanded no strong section among those whom he called his subjects.

A further delay of three months ensued at Candahar, where the army had to halt for the collection of supplies, and it was not until the 27th June that it set out on its northern march to Cabul, with a view to bringing the question with Dost Mahomed to an issue. That chief, with his usual prudence, had done nothing to commit himself against us in Southern Afghanistan. When he had only to deal with Shah Shuja in 1833, he had hastened to his brothers' aid and had won a signal victory. But now he confined his attention to the defence of Ghuzni and Cabul. Of the two Ghuzni, the strongest natural fortress in the country and secure against any but siege guns, was the more important, and any hopes Dost Mahomed may have entertained of successful resistance must have centred in the English army being delayed before Ghuzni. The army pressed on rapidly, considering the extent of its impedimenta and the heat of the season, and reached Ghuzni on 21st July, but the siege guns had been left at Candahar. Mistaken views seem to have been held as to the strength of this place, but Sir John Keane at once appreciated that it was of "great strength both by nature and by art," and if he had not learned from an Afghan deserter—a nephew of Dost Mahomed—that the Cabul gate was not bricked up like the rest, he might have despaired of carrying the place by assault and adopted Shah Shuja's advice to ignore it and advance on Cabul. With this knowledge the English general resolved to blow in the Cabul gate and carry the place by assault.

The incidents of this assault, the only heroic episode of the first campaign in Afghanistan, have been carefully preserved and frequently recorded in history The Cabul gate was successfully blown in by the engineering party under Captain Thomson, and consisting, besides himself, of Lieutenants Durand and Macleod and Captain Peat. How narrowly the explosion succeeded may be inferred from the fact that Durand had to scrape the hose with his finger nails, and that the portfire did not at once ignite. The storming party was also within an ace of being left without its support, owing to a belief that the entrance into the fortress was blocked. Fortunately the troops pressed on, and, although the Afghans offered a desperate and gallant resistance, carried everything before them. Within a brief space of time the whole fortress was in our possession. Five hundred of the Afghans were killed within the walls, 1,600 remained prisoners, and of those who got out of the doomed fortress most fell by the swords of the pursuing cavalry. The spoil included a large supply of grain and provisions, besides arms, horses, and some treasure. The British loss—and all the fighting was done by English troops—amounted to seventeen killed and the large number of 165 wounded, of whom eighteen were officers. The British success did not end with the capture of Ghuzni. An Afghan army, under Afzul Khan, father of the Amir Abdur Rahman, fled, leaving his camp in our hands, on seeing the English flag floating from the citadel of Ghuzni.

With the dispersion of this force and the capture of the reputedly impregnable fortress of Ghuzni all Dost Mahomed's schemes for delaying the advance of the English army fell through. It is true that he collected the whole of his fighting force, that he selected the position for a last stand, and that he marched from Cabul to Urgundeh. But his troops would go no farther and refused to fight. They even reviled and plundered the chief whose salt, as he said, they had eaten for thirteen years, and in despair Dost Mahomed, accompanied by the few members of his household who remained faithful, fled for the Bamian Pass and Turkestan. He was closely pursued by a small party of English officers and Afghan cavalry under the command of Captain Outram, and there appears to be no doubt that, but for the delays of the Afghan traitor, Hadji Khan Kakar, he would have been captured. This would have rendered complete the effect of the fall of Ghuzni and the rapid advance on and unopposed occupation of Cabul. On the 6th August, four days after the last Afghan army turned on Dost Mahomed at Urgundeh, the invaders were before Cabul, and on the following day Shah Shuja entered the city and rode in triumph to the palace in the Bala Hissar. A few weeks later communications were established through Jellalabad with the Sikh army operating from the Khyber, and thus the ostensible programme of the Indian Government was carried out with complete success and without a hitch before the summer had ended in the valleys of Afghanistan. The Barukzai Amir was a fugitive and deserted by his own army. The legitimate Sudozai sovereign had recovered his throne and was the proclaimed friend and ally of the English. There was ample time to withdraw the English army before the winter closed communication through the passes.

But the same reasons which had compelled the Indian Government to send its troops into Afghanistan induced it to leave them there. A very brief experience at Cabul sufficed to show that Shah Shuja had no hold on the country, and that his authority could only be maintained by our military occupation of it. There was no alternative between the admission that our Afghan policy had failed, which would be the immediate consequence of our evacuation, and making an endeavour to procure a successful issue by retaining our garrison for an indefinite period. The escape of Dost Mahomed added an unknown peril to the situation, for it was impossible to say what new forces he might not obtain from the Usbeg chiefs of Turkestan and Bokhara. As Sir William Macnaghten, the resident at Cabul, who held the supreme direction in Afghanistan, wrote: "The Afghans are gunpowder and the Dost is a lighted match." So long as Dost Mahomed was at large the opinion prevailed that we could not leave Shah Shuja to his fate, and no one suggested that, as it was clear that he had no chance of restoring the Sudozai sovereignty, the proper course for us was to take him back with us to India. It was, therefore, resolved to remain in Afghanistan during the winter of 1839-40, and as an additional argument in support of this policy the rumoured Russian expedition against Khiva was quoted, as evidence that the danger from Russia had not passed away with the relief of Herat and the disgrace of Vickovitch.

Although the English garrison was kept in the country its numbers were reduced. Sir John Keane[1] returned to India with a portion of the army, and Sir Willoughby Cotton was left in command of all the troops at Cabul. Shah Shuja and his English advisers passed the coldest months of the winter at Jellalabad, and nothing happened to disturb the tranquillity of the country or to suggest any reason for uneasiness at our having remained. The Bala Hissar was held by English troops, and a mixed detachment was sent to occupy the Bamian Pass. The only incident of importance was calculated to render our position more

[1] Sir John Kaye quotes a story of this general which establishes his foresight. Before his departure Keane said to an officer who was to accompany him: "I wished you to remain in Afghanistan for the good of the public service, but since circumstances have rendered that impossible I cannot but congratulate you on quitting the country, for, mark my words, it will not be long before there is here some signal catastrophe." (Kaye, vol. ii. p. 23 *n.*)

secure. In November it was found necessary to send troops against the ruler of Khelat, whose action had been suspicious, and in that month his capital was besieged and carried by assault. Mehrab Khan fell while valiantly defending it, and a new Khan was chosen and proclaimed by the British authorities, but the northern districts of this state were assigned to Shah Shuja. This was done with a view to gratifying the frequently expressed wish of Shah Shuja to rule over the original limits of the Durani monarchy, although he could not maintain unaided his hold on Cabul and Candahar. His appeals to Sir William Macnaghten so far influenced that officer that he too embraced the view that to be secure the Sudozai sovereign must rule over the whole region from Peshawur to Herat, and he expressed the wish in a semi-public manner that Lord Auckland were either a Wellesley or a Hastings, so that he might sanction an expedition to Herat on the one side and precipitate a quarrel with the Sikhs on the other. For our difficulties in Afghanistan had been largely aggravated by the half-heartedness of our Sikh allies, who after the death of Runjeet Singh, which occurred almost simultaneously with the capture of Cabul, had done nothing but thwart our plans, encourage our enemies, and play generally a treacherous part. At Herat too matters had gone from bad to worse. The minister, Yar Mahomed, resented our interference and our attempts to put down the slave trade by which he profited, while the possibility of an English expedition to Herat in the interests of Shah Shuja threatened to extinguish the Sudozai authority that had been so long maintained there by Shah Kamran. The mere discussion of an expansion of our policy served to aggravate our troubles. How much more serious they would have been rendered by an attempt to carry it out can be realized from a consideration, not of our later disasters in Afghanistan alone, but of our long and arduous tussle for power with the Sikhs some years later when our hands were free everywhere else.

The return of spring brought with it the advent of troubles in a practical form. The opinion was confidently held that Dost Mahomed would make some hostile movement upon Cabul, and the garrison in the Bamian Pass was strengthened and placed under the command of Colonel Dennie, who had led the storming party at Ghuzni. This expectation was soon realized, for Dost Mahomed had been badly treated in Bokhara, whose ruler was jealous of him and wished to reduce him to the position of a vassal. He therefore returned to Turkestan, where he found for a time a loyal friend and supporter in the Usbeg chief of Khulm. They succeeded in raising a force of six or seven thousand men, and with this they advanced to overwhelm, as they hoped, the small body of troops at Bamian. In that pass we had thrown out advanced posts. When the foe attacked them they were repulsed, but our officers thought it right to evacuate them, and in the retreat most of our baggage was abandoned. An Afghan regiment, commanded by an English officer, went over bodily to the enemy. But here the Dost's successes stopped. On 18th September, four days after Colonel Dennie had assumed the command, was fought the first battle of any significance since the capture of Ghuzni. It was not known that Dost Mahomed had entered the Bamian Pass with all his forces when Colonel Dennie marched out to expel an enemy that was signalled as advancing. Our artillery never gave the Usbegs a chance, and when they were broken the cavalry was let loose and completed their discomfiture. Dost Mahomed himself barely escaped capture, and when he reached a place of safety he found that the most serious consequence of his defeat was the desertion of his cause by the Usbeg chief of Khulm. The Dost received notice of this meditated treason. He succeeded in making his way to the Kohistan, where there was much dissatisfaction with Shah Shuja and where he could still assemble a party of his own. Ten days after the fight at Bamian Sir Robert Sale led a force against the Kohistanis and captured several of their hill forts. But Dost Mahomed succeeded in rallying them, and on the 1st of November was in a position to oppose the English force, notwithstanding its successes. On the following day he drew up his men in line of battle at the village of Purwandurrah. He did not intend to fight at that moment, but an engagement was brought on by the precipitancy of the cavalry, and Dost Mahomed, fired by a fit of enthusiasm, ordered his horsemen to charge and redeem the honour of Islam. For a moment it looked as if there would be a brilliant collision between the Afghan and Anglo-Indian cavalry, but by one of those sudden and inexplicable panics which sometimes seize the best disciplined troops the Indian cavalry turned tail and fled, leaving their English officers alone to resist the Afghan horse. Of the five English officers three were killed.

But Dost Mahomed was not carried away by his success in this cavalry engagement. He saw that it possessed no real significance, that it could not affect the issue of the struggle, and that his resources were quite unequal to prolonging it. The clearness of his vision induced him to make a heroic decision and to carry it out in a kingly manner. He resolved to surrender to the English, but, instead of yielding to the commander of the force which he had defeated at Purwandurrah, he rode off with a single companion to Cabul, and, meeting Sir William Macnaghten outside the city, surrendered to him in person. There was the more heroism in the act because the English authorities had only a few weeks earlier taken the high-handed course of placing a price upon his head.

However hostile our intentions may have been so long as Dost Mahomed was a formidable enemy at large, they were modified when he became a prisoner who had voluntarily thrown himself on our generosity. Every consideration was shown him, he was spared the humiliation of a personal interview with his public and private enemy Shah Shuja, and he was sent off to an honourable place of exile in British India, where he remained until after our withdrawal from the country.

The surrender of Dost Mahomed and his deportation to India provided us with another opportunity for evacuating Afghanistan. So long as he was at large our success might be termed partial and problematical, while the ability of Shah Shuja to maintain his position was very doubtful. But with Dost Mahomed disappeared, as far as we could see, the only opponent who could possibly dispossess Shah Shuja of his throne. We might fairly have said to the Sudozai prince: "We have placed you on the throne, and we have removed your only formidable rival to India, where we will keep him in safe custody, and now we intend to withdraw our troops." If the Sudozai monarchy had any vitality in itself or any hold on the affections of the Afghan people he should have been able to maintain his position without the presence of British troops. At all events we had done all we had engaged to do. Another reason co-operated at this moment to justify Lord Auckland in ordering the evacuation of the country. The apprehension of Russia's designs on Herat had been one of the main causes of our first advance into Afghanistan, and the rumoured attack on Khiva by the expedition under General Peroffsky in 1839-40 had been one of the arguments employed to justify our remaining in the country. The Peroffsky expedition indeed set out, but it met with nothing but misfortunes. The force was vanquished by the snow and compelled to retreat, leaving the punishment of Khiva for another generation. The news of this repulse was received at the very moment that the movements of Dost Mahomed were again beginning to attract attention. Anxiety from both causes was consequently allayed within a few weeks of each other. Both Russia and Dost Mahomed were reduced to a position of impotency to work us any mischief in the autumn of 1840. How then was it that we did not leave the country at this favourable moment? It can only be attributed to that aberration of judgment which sometimes afflicts a nation and government as much as an individual, for, as Sir Henry Durand wrote in his interesting memoir of the first Afghan war, "No more striking event could be conceived for an honourable termination to the armed occupation of Afghanistan and for the triumphant return of the Anglo-Indian army to its own frontier. By furnishing so unhoped an occurrence

Providence removed all reasonable ground of excuse for hesitation, and afforded the Indian Government the very moment which it professed to await. But man in his short-sighted elation clung to ill-gotten conquests, and, rejecting the proffered opportunity, was overtaken by a fearful and terrible retribution."

If Sir William Macnaghten was blind to the facts of the situation and passed from the extreme of confidence to despondency, writing one day that "we are in a stew here," and the next deriding Major (afterwards Sir) Henry Rawlinson's warnings that we had to reckon with an outbreak of national hostility, there was not the same obtuseness among responsible observers of the manner in which the Indian Government had become involved in Afghanistan. The Secret Committee of the East India Company drew up a very able report on the situation, and recommended the immediate selection of one of two courses. They declared that there was no course between the two alternatives, a speedy retreat or a considerable increase of the military force garrisoned in Afghanistan. Unfortunately the Governor-General did not act upon these views, but left the control of events in the hands of Macnaghten, who, lulled into a false sense of security by the tranquillity of the country in September, 1841, determined to prolong the occupation through another winter. The decision had scarcely been come to when there was a recrudescence of hostility among the

Durani tribes west of Candahar and the Ghilzais north of that city, but the ease and unvaried success with which General Nott, who commanded there, broke up both factions encouraged the belief that no gathering of the Afghan tribes would stand any chance with regular troops. It was while this feeling of complacency was at its height that events occurred at Cabul which rudely undeceived those who believed that the Afghans were neither formidable nor fanatical.

The return of Akbar Khan, the principal of the sons of Dost Mahomed, from Bokhara to Bamian was the signal for the revival of hostility in the Cabul region. Almost under the nose of the British representatives a plot was hatched for the seizure of that city and the capture of the treasury, where lived Sir Alexander Burnes with a very inadequate guard; and, although many warnings were given by those among the Afghans who were friendly, no precautions whatever were taken. On 2nd November a commotion began in the city, and it soon assumed the dimensions of an insurrection. The treasury was attacked and carried by the mob before assistance could arrive. Sir Alexander Burnes, his brother, and another English officer were massacred, and the national rising of the Afghan tribes was inaugurated by a success more complete and striking than they could have expected. It was due to the apathy and indifference of the English authorities in the first place, and secondly to the tardy and ill-directed movement of troops from the cantonments outside the city, that these English officers were murdered when "6,000 British troops were within half an hour's march of the spot." Ferrier, the able French writer on Afghan affairs during this period, calls Macnaghten's inaction at this critical moment incredible, and Shah Shuja could only exclaim that "the English had gone mad."

But if the inaction of the English officers during the outbreak of 2nd November was inexplicable and little to their credit, their proceedings after that occurrence were still more extraordinary and incredible. General Elphinstone did nothing whatever to punish the insurgents or to restore order, although it was seen at the time and admitted by every one since that "a prompt and vigorous movement on the morning of that day would have strangled the insurrection at its birth." But neither General Elphinstone nor Sir William Macnaghten appreciated the situation, and they were as indifferent to the butchery of a colleague as to their own peril. Even in the face of such unequivocal events they succeeded in persuading themselves that the Cabul outbreak was an accident and not a warning. In this opinion they were soon undeceived by the harsh proof of experience. The successful affair of 2nd November, followed by the apathy of the English, gave the Afghans immense confidence and brought thousands of fighting men to the standard of the insurgent chiefs. The English troops were compelled to retire into the cantonment, which was too large for their numbers and still more for their inadequate artillery force. In more than one encounter the Afghans obtained the advantage, and the vacillation and miserable incompetence of General Elphinstone cost us the loss of the two outlying forts, in which were stored all the grain and other necessary supplies of the army. In this conjuncture the only remedies tried were unworthy of the reputation of the English Government and illustrative of the demoralisation that had descended upon the leaders of the force. General Elphinstone, when he should have thought only of redeeming his tarnished military honour, begged Sir William to negotiate for a safe and honourable retreat, and Macnaghten had recourse to bribery and thought to find a safe issue from his troubles by appealing to the cupidity of the Afghan chiefs. Had he stopped here it would have been possible to speak only of his folly, but unfortunately for his reputation he made himself a party to, if he did not absolutely originate, schemes for the assassination of the Afghan chiefs. A reward of 10,000 rupees was offered for the head of every leader of note, and our native agent, Mohun Lal, was incited to arrange their secret murder. There is not a more discreditable passage in English history, and it can scarcely be regretted that this infamous machination recoiled on its principal originators. Some allowance for these facts, which came to the knowledge of the Afghan chiefs by the murder of two of their number, must be made before condemning the moral turpitude shown by them towards the English representative when he placed himself within their power.

Meantime the position of the small British force in the cantonment had been rendered desperate by the incompetence of the general and the divisions among his colleagues. On 9th November the Bala Hissar, which was in every respect a superior military position to the cantonment, was evacuated. A few days later a Goorkha regiment, stationed at Charikar, a place north-east of Cabul, was annihilated, mainly through its sufferings from the want of water. On 18th November Sir William Macnaghten wrote strongly in favour of holding on "in the hope that something may turn up in our favour," and if the only sane course had been pursued of abandoning the cantonment and concentrating the whole force in the Bala Hissar—which could have been done, though not without loss—the main body of the army would have been saved and a deep humiliation averted. But neither sanity nor courage was to be found among those in authority, and, as Kaye says, "the only measure which could have saved the British force from destruction and the British name from degradation was rejected in this conjuncture." How deteriorated the *morale* of the troops had become by fighting under unnecessary disadvantages, and commanded by officers in whom they had lost all confidence, was shown by the result of the action of Behmeru on 23rd November, when the British force was ignominiously defeated, and when the Afghans could have carried the cantonment if they had only pushed on their advantage. This disaster completed the moral disorganization of the force, and even a withdrawal into the Bala Hissar was pronounced too hazardous for disheartened troops. There remained no other alternative to negotiating with the Afghan leaders for the secure retreat of the army, and General Elphinstone gave many reasons in an official letter for the opinion "that it was no longer feasible to maintain our position in this country."

The negotiation was easily commenced with the Afghan chiefs, who had already expressed their desire for peace, but its beginning did not promise well, for they declared that as they were the victors they would accept nothing but the unconditional surrender of the English force. Sir William Macnaghten, whose courage at least was superior to that of many of the military officers, rejected this suggestion with scorn, stating that he preferred death to dishonour and that a higher power must decide. At this moment Akbar Khan appeared on the scene, and, setting aside the Cabul leaders, took that foremost part in the conduct of affairs which he retained to the end of the war. Sir John Kaye describes his character in the following sentences: "He was a man of an eager, impetuous nature; susceptible of good and of bad impulses, but seldom otherwise than earnest and impulsive. His education had been neglected; in his youth he had been unrestrained, and now self-control—a virtue rarely exercised by an Afghan—was wholly foreign to the character of the man. He was indeed peculiarly demonstrative and sudden in his demonstrations, passing rapidly from one mood to another—blown about by violent gusts of feeling, bitterly repenting to-day the excesses of yesterday and rushing into new excesses to-morrow. His was one of those fiery temperaments—those bold, dashing characters—which in times of popular commotion ever place their possessors in the first rank. But in seasons of repose he was one of the most joyous and light-hearted of men; no man loved a joke better; no man laughed more heartily or seemed to look more cheerfully on the sunny side of life."

Although negotiations were resumed they did not promise to produce any speedily satisfactory result. Fighting continued round the cantonment with generally doubtful results, thus further disheartening the troops, while the supply of stores was reduced to starvation point. Sir Robert Sale had been summoned to bring his brigade back from Jellalabad, and he had replied that it was impossible. A force had marched northwards from Candahar for the relief of Cabul, but had been obliged to retreat through commissariat difficulties. The really feasible course of a retirement through comparatively easy country to Ghuzni, held by an English garrison, where the English army could have held out till the spring, isolated but secure, was, so far as the records show, never suggested, and the only project mooted was a retreat to Jellalabad through some of the most difficult passes in Afghanistan. In the execution of this project, which, if carried out immediately on its being decided upon, would have been as successful as could have been expected, and which would have saved the main part of the force, there was the delay that ruined everything connected with the whole enterprise. It was on 8th December that General Elphinstone wrote his official letter stating that there was no alternative to negotiating for a safe retreat to India *viâ* Jellalabad, yet it was not until more than four weeks later that the first march was made in that direction. The approach of winter quite as much as the absence of supplies rendered every day's delay inadvisable and dangerous. It was not until 18th December that the first snow fell, so that there was a sufficient margin of time, had it only been utilised.

Sir William Macnaghten did not enter on these negotiations either very willingly or very hopefully. He would have preferred to stake everything on a military effort to formally admitting the failure of all his policy and schemes in Afghanistan. Even while negotiating he was intriguing in the hope of being able to put a new face on affairs, and by some desperate remedy removing the worst features of the deplorable fiasco which had been reached. Although he had comparatively little difficulty in concluding a treaty with Akbar Khan by which the English force was to be allowed to retire to Peshawur without molestation, he does not seem to have rested quite satisfied with this arrangement, but to have resorted to intrigues, through Mohun Lal, with Ghilzai and Kizilbash chiefs by whose aid he hoped to maintain himself in Afghanistan throughout the winter. He seems to have hoped that these intrigues would not come to the knowledge of Akbar, but of course this was impossible, and in a game of finesse and duplicity the English officer was no match for the Afghan chief. Akbar at once proposed to fall in with the envoy's scheme, and declared his willingness to join the English who should remain in the country until the spring, while he was to become vizier to Shah Shuja. It seems almost incredible that an official acquainted with Oriental character, and who had had so many opportunities of proving Afghan falseness, should have been deceived by so transparent a device. Every one else, even simple General Elphinstone, saw through it and at once declared it to be a plot, but Macnaghten, relying on his superior wisdom, derided the idea of his being deceived, and rushed blindly on his fate. On 23rd December Sir William Macnaghten, accompanied by three officers, rode out from the cantonment to hold the interview that was to conclude the new arrangement with Akbar Khan. Before the conference had proceeded very far the Afghans seized the Englishmen, and in a personal struggle between Macnaghten and Akbar the former was shot, and afterwards hacked to pieces by the Ghazis or fanatical warriors who had taken the vow imposed by their religion to prosecute the war against the infidel to the death. One of the officers accompanying him shared his fate, but the others were detained prisoners and released after the end of the war. We are not concerned here to vindicate the character of Sir William Macnaghten, whose faults were not merely fatal to the great enterprise on which he was embarked, but left a legacy of timidity and vacillation to the councils of India in all Afghan matters. But at least his courage cannot be aspersed, and it was rendered more conspicuous by the craven conduct of his military colleagues. Kaye says that, although a civilian, he was the best soldier in the camp, and Sir Henry Durand wrote that "his high courage almost atoned for his moral and political errors." But his political devices and shifty expedients aggravated a situation that was bad enough without them, by giving Afghan treachery a colour of excuse in the example of the English representative.

The low state to which the courage of the military authorities in the Cabul cantonment had sunk can be inferred from their taking no steps to avenge the murder of Macnaghten, perpetrated almost under their eyes. An attempt was made to represent his fate as doubtful, and so far as this was intended to prevent the army being discouraged it might be deemed justified. But there was never for any moment a doubt on the subject. The escort, seeing the scuffle, fled instead of attempting a rescue, and the two regiments drawn up in support did nothing. Some watchers of the scene on the wall declared that they saw the commotion and feared the worst, but it was given out that Macnaghten had only gone off to the city, and with this transparent deception a justification was found for doing nothing. When the murder became known, or rather publicly admitted, Eldred Pottinger, the hero of Herat, now a major and suffering from a severe wound received at Charikar, was appointed successor to Macnaghten, and at the same time requested to resume the negotiations for a safe retreat. As a matter of duty he undertook the task, but his courage and good judgment impelled him to make one more effort to raise the sinking courage of the military chiefs, and to point out that the best course was still to fight their way into the Bala Hissar or back to Jellalabad without negotiating at all. Such was the inspiring effect of his example and exhortation that Elphinstone himself was inclined to take his counsel, but the inclination, finding no encouragement, soon passed away.

On 1st January, 1842, the ratified copies of the treaty, bearing the seals of eighteen of the principal Afghan chiefs, were exchanged, and despite warnings from many quarters that their promises were not to be trusted and that treachery was meditated—one of Akbar's alleged boasts being that he would destroy the whole of the English army with the exception of one man, who should be allowed to carry the tale to India—all the guns but six were surrendered. An arrangement had been made that the sons of the chiefs should accompany the English force as hostages, but by a crowning act of folly the army began its retreat without this safeguard, and once it left the comparative shelter of the cantonment behind, it is not surprising that the Afghans did not see the necessity of complying with a stipulation which the impatience of the English as much as their own doubtful faith had rendered void. The retreat began on 6th January, and the dispirited force of 4,500 fighting men and 12,000 camp followers proceeded from the beginning in almost inextricable confusion along the arduous and snow-covered route that led to India. When the march began snow had been falling for nearly three weeks, and the unfortunate camp followers suffered incredibly, and were reduced to such a condition of panic that they seriously incommoded and detracted from the efficiency of the small fighting force, which without their presence might have made a better stand. The simplest precautions had been neglected, and from the first day of the retreat there was nothing but confusion and fear, so that this English army lost all the appearance of a disciplined body, and invited the overwhelming disaster from which greater fortitude would even at this eleventh hour have enabled it to escape. It is unnecessary to dwell upon the details of the catastrophe to what, as Kaye says, was "no longer a retreating army, but a rabble in chaotic flight," for they will be found admirably described in that writer's history of the Afghan war. From the very first day of the retreat the Afghans assailed the English force with increasing confidence and numbers. In the first three days of the retreat such were the losses and so remote did the prospect of escape appear that the English ladies were handed over to the dubious protection of Akbar Khan, who pretended to disapprove of the excesses to which the Afghan tribesmen had gone. As the result showed, it was the best course that could be pursued, and the incompetent commanders, Elphinstone and Shelton, were so far fortunate that they saved their lives by being detained as prisoners after a conference with Akbar Khan. No similarly kind Providence looked after the safety of the brave officers and soldiers whose military ardour had been restrained and broken by the incompetence and pusillanimity of their generals. They met their fate and were exterminated in the terrible

Khourd Cabul and Jugdulluck Passes, before Gundamuck and Futtehabad, leaving of an army of over 16,000 men only one solitary Englishman, Dr. Brydon, to escape and tell the tale at Jellalabad of the dreadful work that had been done since the force left Cabul. This campaign resembles in miniature the retreat of Napoleon's army from Moscow, but it was more discreditable to the military reputation of England than that reverse was to France. For the French were vanquished by nature, whereas our misfortunes were due to the shortcomings of English commanders and the moral degeneration of our army. Thus was expiated in the blood of our soldiers a policy which has been termed, not inaccurately, "truthless and unscrupulous," and which from a practical point of view was both precipitate and unwise.

Before reciting the measures taken to exact an exemplary revenge, two gratifying and honourable incidents, showing that there were still left in the British army in Afghanistan some officers who had not lost their heads and some soldiers who retained their national courage, may be referred to and briefly described. Some weeks before the murder of Burnes and the first outbreak at Cabul, Sir Robert Sale had been sent with a brigade to clear the passes of hostile clans along the route to Jellalabad and Peshawur. He entirely succeeded in his task, but one action that he fought should, from its stubbornness, have conveyed a warning that the hostility and confidence of the Afghans were reviving. When matters became serious at Cabul Sir William Macnaghten sent several messages to Sale to return with his brigade. But Sale, instead of retracing his steps from Gundamuck to Cabul, pushed on to and occupied Jellalabad, and so calm a writer as Sir Henry Durand terms Sale's decision to defend that place and not to return to Cabul as "inexcusable." The opinion is generally held that if Sale had returned to Cabul the whole force would have been saved; but it must be noted that Sale's own indecision of character, as evinced during the siege of Jellalabad, where he was as much in favour of capitulation as Elphinstone, would not have imparted much of the greatly needed vigour to the councils of war in the Cabul cantonment. As excuses may be found for every act, Sale could put forward many in vindication of his decision. The number of his sick and wounded, the want of baggage animals, and other similar causes rendered his return march, as he said, simply impossible. But a more difficult charge to answer is why he did not remain at Gundamuck, where he would have been nearer the beleaguered force at Cabul and able to give it a helping hand through the passes. His answer to that was that in his position there he could not command a day's provisions or even water, and that he was threatened with being hemmed in on every side by hostile tribes. By seizing Jellalabad he obtained a position which he represented he could hold until the Cabul force retired on him or until reinforcements came up from India. The strength and plausibility of this defence were only weakened by his eagerness to capitulate when the pinch came at Jellalabad, and when, but for Broadfoot and the resolute minority on the council, he would have surrendered to Akbar Khan.

But the error of judgment and the disobedience to orders being admitted, further criticism is silenced by the vigour shown in placing Jellalabad in a posture of defence, and by the courage exhibited in holding it against a numerous and confident enemy. When Jellalabad was entered it was in no state to stand a siege, but Major George Broadfoot threw himself with all his energy into the task of raising walls and excavating trenches, so that in a short time it presented a sufficiently formidable front to any assault. There were only two days' provisions in the place, but energy soon supplied the need, and throughout the whole of the winter sufficient food for the garrison was always forthcoming. Iron and wood were obtained from the neighbourhood, and the deficiencies of ammunition and shot were supplied by ingenuity and foresight. The Afghans were encountered in the open and defeated a few days after the entrance into Jellalabad, and again with greater loss on 1st December. These successes both sustained the courage of the garrison, diminished that of the Afghans, and gained time for the completion of the defences. When Afghan officers brought an order from General Elphinstone to surrender Jellalabad, compliance was refused pending a further communication as to the security for a safe march back to Peshawur. That communication never came, for within a week of the receipt of this summons Dr. Brydon, the sole survivor of the Cabul force, reached Jellalabad, when Sale and his colleagues felt no longer bound by any conventions made at Cabul, but only called upon to act as they thought best for themselves and the national interests.

After the destruction of the Cabul brigade, doubts began to be felt at Jellalabad as to whether there was any intention on the part of the Indian Government to send up a relieving force; and Sale, whose personal courage had always been praised, showed some of the moral degeneration that Elphinstone under similar circumstances had exhibited. At this juncture a letter came from Shah Shuja, calling upon the troops to evacuate Jellalabad; and for several reasons, among which the most honourable was the apprehension that refusal would endanger the lives of the English prisoners in the hands of Akbar, Sir Robert Sale and the majority of his council were disposed to assent. Fortunately, the energy and vehemence of Major Broadfoot enabled him to fight single-handed the whole of the council, and, by delaying an irretrievable step, to gain all the advantage of time. When the Afghans would not give a sufficient guarantee for a safe retreat, the hollowness of their declarations became evident, and several members of the council rallied to the views and side of Broadfoot. When it became known that troops were concentrating at Peshawur, the council became unanimous that Jellalabad should be held to the last extremity. While this uncertainty was apparent among those responsible for the defence, Major Broadfoot had thrown himself with his characteristic determination into the work of improving the defences of the place, so as to enable it to withstand the large force which Akbar had collected in the neighbourhood. Even when an earthquake undid all that he had accomplished, he repaired its ravages by extraordinary activity within a fortnight, and when the Afghans showed signs of renewing the attack, a sortie was made on 11th March, which resulted in their dispersal with heavy loss. Then Akbar endeavoured to starve out the garrison; but one month later, on its becoming known that the relieving force was entering the Khyber, Sale assumed the offensive, and attacking Akbar's army of 6,000 men, inflicted upon it a signal defeat, thus re-establishing the military superiority of English troops in the most satisfactory and convincing manner. The garrison of Jellalabad—which, by a happy inspiration, Lord Ellenborough christened "the illustrious garrison"—thus really effected its own relief, and had the honour of routing the main Afghan army, under Akbar Khan, which had vanquished the Cabul division.

Gratifying as the Jellalabad incident was, amid the gloom of surrounding discredit and disaster, it was well matched by the vigorous defence of Candahar, where General Nott and Major Rawlinson kept at bay the tribes of South and West Afghanistan. General Nott was a brave and single-minded soldier, knowing his duty well, and able to inspire his soldiers with the confidence he felt in himself. He thoroughly distrusted the Afghans; refused to be a party to any intrigues with them; and, with his "beautiful sepoy regiments," never doubted that he was a match for any number of the Afghan tribes. Rawlinson, who also possessed the *feu sacré* of the soldier, was a diplomatist and organizer of the first rank. In striking contrast with what occurred at Cabul, the authorities at Candahar, by keeping their heads cool, defied the Afghans with success, and maintained untarnished the military reputation of their country.

The details of the siege must be sought elsewhere; but it must be noted that, from the very beginning of the winter troubles, General Nott never allowed the Afghans to beleaguer the city. As soon as the enemy collected in any force in the neighbourhood, he marched out to attack them, and whenever he came up with them he completely defeated them. The most important of these earlier engagements was that fought on 13th January, 1842, when he routed, at what has been called the battle of Urgundah, an Afghan army of many thousand men. When letters were sent from Cabul ordering the evacuation of Candahar, in compliance with the convention with Akbar Khan, Nott proudly declared that he would not treat with any one for the evacuation of that city until he received explicit orders from the Government of India. Well would it have been for Elphinstone and his troops if that officer had shown equal fortitude.

No precaution was omitted to place Candahar in an efficient state of defence. The Afghan troops nominally in the service of Shah Shuja were got rid of after one regiment had mutinied, and the further very necessary step of expelling the Afghan population—then about 1,000 families—was carried out early in March. By this measure, not merely was the supply of provisions husbanded, but a source of weakness and serious embarrassment in the event of any Afghan attack was removed. It was immediately after this expulsion that General Nott resumed the offensive against the Afghan clans, who had gathered in great numbers under the Durani chiefs. Leaving a small force under Major Rawlinson to hold the city, General Nott made a sortie at the head of his main body, and after two days' marching and desultory fighting he found that the Afghans had disappeared and that he was a considerable distance from the city. Subsequent information showed that the Afghans had purposely enticed the English commander to a distance from Candahar, so that they might fall upon the weakened garrison in his absence. Major Rawlinson, from the numbers of Afghans who appeared in the old city of Candahar, came to a rapid and just conclusion as to the scheme of the Durani leaders, and at once sent off messengers in hot haste to recall General Nott to the city; but, before he could return, the blow had fallen and been warded off. On the night of 10th March the Afghans delivered their attack in force on the Herat gate, which had not been bricked up, and for a time it looked as if they must succeed. Had there been the least faltering among the small garrison, Candahar must have fallen, and its loss could not but have entailed that of Nott's force as well, as it would have been deprived of both provisions and ammunition. But, fortunately, Major Rawlinson and his supporters met the furious charge of the Ghazis with equal heroism and more skilful opposition. The Afghans destroyed and passed through the Herat gate, only to find that fresh defences had been erected, and that their swords were inadequate weapons when brought to face grapeshot. After many hours' fighting the Ghazis were driven off, with the loss of 600 of their number; and when General Nott returned, two days later he found the triumphant garrison had inflicted a more severe loss on the enemy than he had done during his week's vain endeavour to bring the Afghan army to an engagement. The credit of this successful defence belonged exclusively to Major Rawlinson; and as it was the only occasion on which the Afghans ventured to attack the city, the circumstance was the more memorable. With it the siege of Candahar may be said to have begun and successfully ended. Unfortunately, the courage and prudence shown in its successful defence were not emulated at Ghuzni, which place, notwithstanding its great natural strength, was surrendered to the Afghans only a few days before the assault just described. The surrender of Ghuzni was considered more discreditable than the capitulation at Cabul, and furnished a striking contrast to the gallant defence of Khelat-i-Ghilzai, which was held throughout this trying winter by its small garrison of forty English artillerymen and a few hundred sepoys, under the command of Captain Halkett Craigie.

Successful as were the defence of Candahar and also General Nott's steps in breaking up the Afghan forces whenever they collected in any numbers, the efforts made to reinforce the garrison and to furnish it with fresh supplies from India resulted at first in some unexpected and unnecessary humiliation. General England, at the head of a considerable force escorting treasure and ammunition marching up from Quettah, reached Hykulzye, at the southern entrance to the

Khojak Pass, on 28th March, and found that the Afghans had assembled in considerable numbers to oppose his advance. An engagement followed, with disastrous results; for after the repulse of the first attack, with the loss of nearly one hundred killed and wounded, General England determined to retreat, instead of making any fresh attempt to retrieve the day. This involved a month's delay; and when General England reached the same spot on 30th April with a larger force, he found that a portion of the Candahar garrison had deprived him of the opportunity of regaining his laurels by occupying the pass and opening the road for the relieving army. Ten days later the whole British force was concentrated at Candahar, and awaited there the decision of the Government as to whether it should return to India by way of Quettah or Cabul. A brigade was, however, despatched to rescue the garrison of Khelat-i-Ghilzai, to bring it back to Candahar, and to destroy the defences of that place. While the brigade was on the march, the Afghans made a supreme effort to capture the place; but, although the assault was delivered with great fury and considerable numbers, Captain Craigie had the satisfaction of repulsing it, with much loss to the Afghans and none to himself.

It will be most convenient to summarise here the subsequent movements of General Nott's force. After an interval of three months, during which the policy of the Indian Government remained uncertain, it was decided that General Nott with the main portion of his force should march by Ghuzni and Cabul to India, and that General England should return by Quettah with the sick, the stores, and the less efficient portion of the troops. General Nott's march was unmolested as far as Mookour, 160 miles north of Candahar, and a place which has often been selected as a battle-ground in the internal wars of Afghanistan on account of its admirable position. In the vicinity of this place several skirmishes were fought, and in one instance with an adverse result to the English ; but these doubtful engagements were amply atoned for by the decisive success at Goaine, which cleared the way to Ghuzni. The Afghans were so disheartened by this reverse that they did not attempt to defend that place, which was occupied without a shot being fired. As part of the decreed work of expiation, the fortress of Ghuzni was as far as possible destroyed, but the injuries were not such as to seriously impair its great natural or acquired strength. Then the army resumed its northern march to Cabul, bearing with it the sandal gates of the mosque attached to the tomb of the celebrated conqueror, Mahmud of Ghuzni, which he had carried off from the famous Hindu temple of Somnath, in Guzerat. This act was intended to signify the triumph of Hindu India over the representatives of its old Mahomedan conquerors, and although the authenticity of the gates was problematical, it would seem from the local excitement that the blow was not as empty as has been alleged. Thence the force marched on Cabul, reaching that place on 17th September, after some final fighting at Maidan, but only to find it in the hands of General Pollock. With this incident terminates the separate command of General Nott, and although criticism has been directed against the excessive caution he showed on several occasions after the Afghan assault on Candahar when he might be considered outmanœuvred, it does not detract from the fact that he held his ground during the six most critical months in Afghanistan without any extraneous aid, and that when the aid came he had defeated all the forces which the chiefs could bring against him, and was practically master of Southern Afghanistan.

We must now retrace our steps to describe the preparations made by the Government of India on the first receipt of the news of the disaster at Cabul, and the advance of the main avenging army under General Pollock, who, as has been said, reached the Afghan capital a few hours before General Nott. Before the full extent of the catastrophe was known in India, some steps had been taken with the view of opening communications with Jellalabad and reinforcing the garrison of that place. A brigade was sent forward to Peshawur in December, 1841, and in the following month it was reinforced by another brigade from

Ferozepore, but the efficiency and confidence of this corps were largely diminished by the uncertainty of the Government policy, the hesitation of those in command, and the demoralisation of the native soldiers, whose fears, worked upon by the Sikhs, led them to tarnish their military reputation in their desire to avoid entering the dreaded Khyber Pass. These facts explain the mishap that befell the force under Brigadier Wild, which, on attempting to reinforce the small garrison of the fort of Ali Musjid, a few miles within the Khyber, was repulsed with such loss that any subsequent renewal of the attempt with the same means was seen to be so hopeless that the small force in garrison there was withdrawn. It was hard upon the heels of this disaster that General George Pollock, an officer of creditable service and attainments, who had been specially selected for the command on account of his knowledge of native troops, reached Peshawur and devoted himself to the restoration of the moral confidence of the sepoy regiments. In this task, inglorious but difficult, he completely succeeded, and after two months' exertions he commanded a force which might be led with some degree of confidence against the most formidable Afghan tribes. So complete was his success in this respect that, within a week of his receiving the necessary reinforcements in cavalry and artillery, he advanced towards the Khyber, which the Afghans had placed in the best possible posture of defence. An error of tactics might have nullified superior armament and discipline, and revived with increased force the trepidation of the sepoys; but General Pollock left nothing to chance in his attack upon the Khyber. He attacked the Afghans, who mainly consisted of the Afridi clan, on their right flank and on their left, and, combating them in their own fashion, he expelled them from the heights, thus obtaining the command of the pass. The result of this first action of the war decided the subsequent course of the campaign, for it restored the confidence of the Indian soldiery, and led them once more to believe they were invincible. A few days after General Pollock recovered possession of Ali Musjid, and on 5th April, 1842, he reached Jellalabad, where he formed a junction with "the illustrious garrison" of that place, and the subsequent delay of four months was due to the indecision on the part of the Government of India as to whether there was any necessity to advance to Cabul and inflict a signal punishment on Akbar Khan. It is probable, as Kaye says, that if there had not been English prisoners in the hands of the Afghans the inducements to an inactive and inglorious policy would have prevailed, and that the relief of the Jellalabad garrison would, however inadequate, have been deemed sufficient compensation for our military discomfiture and dishonour.

While these events were in progress at the seat of

government in India and at the gateway of Afghanistan, the restored monarchy of the ill-fated Sudozai family had come to an end. After the destruction of the English force, which was supposed to be the sole buttress of his power, Shah Shuja was left by Akbar Khan with the empty name of king and the more tangible possession of the Bala Hissar. The intrigues of which the last court held by a Durani monarch was the scene possess no practical interest, and even at the time of their occurrence they failed to prevent Afghanistan reverting to the Barukzais, or to delay the advance of the English army. After four months' uncertainty and confusion they ended with the murder of the prince who formed their central figure. Rarely did Shah Shuja venture to leave the shelter of the Bala Hissar, but on 5th April, 1842, he was induced to pay a visit to, one of the chiefs, and was shot near the city wall. Thus, almost at the same moment as General Pollock was forcing his way through the Khyber, perished ignominiously the Afghan prince who for more than thirty years had been so intimately associated with the first phase of English policy in Afghanistan. Opinions have differed and will differ as to the character and conduct of Shah Shuja, but those who knew him best were the most satisfied as to his capacity. The charges against his good faith during the crisis at Cabul are more difficult to meet and probably can never be settled, but too harsh a verdict should not be passed on a prince who believed that he had been deserted by his English allies. In any case, Shah Shuja was proverbially unlucky. From his first appearance in public life his affairs had been attended with misfortune, and in the East it is deemed calamitous to be associated with one born under an unlucky star. Shah Shuja did not possess the genius or the reputation to compensate for the inherent badness of the policy which first sent English troops into Afghanistan, and which made us attempt to force a king on the people of that country.

After General Pollock's arrival at Jellalabad there was a delay of several months while Lord Ellenborough, who succeeded Lord Auckland as Governor-General, was making up his mind as to sanctioning an extension of military operations in Afghanistan. Lord Ellenborough's timidity showed the effect produced by the destruction of the Cabul brigade, and the unreasoning dread of keeping any troops west of the Khyber was reflected in the order of retirement which he wrote on 29th April. Fortunately for the military reputation of the Indian Government it was couched in sufficiently uncertain language to justify General Pollock asking for more explicit instructions, and on 4th July Lord Ellenborough wrote a second despatch authorising General Nott to retire by way of Ghuzni and Cabul, and General Pollock to advance as far as Cabul to assist his brother officer's withdrawal. There is scarcely any reason to doubt that this latitude would not have been given to the commanders but for the presence of the English prisoners, whose release was deemed essential even by those who pronounced an advance to Cabul unnecessary. Negotiations for the release of the prisoners were begun in April, immediately after the advance to Jellalabad; but they produced no result, as the prisoners were removed for safety to the Bamian Pass, where they remained until the middle of September, when, by bribing their custodian, they succeeded in making their escape to the British army. The death of General Elphinstone during his confinement terminated the career of the man who was mainly responsible for all the disasters of the war. The sufferings of the prisoners have been admirably described in the narratives of Lady Sale, Sir Vincent Eyre, and others.

On 23rd August, more than four months after his arrival at Jellalabad, General Pollock resumed his advance on Cabul, and on 8th September he had occupied the Jugdulluck Pass and expelled from it the Ghilzai levies, who hoped to repeat their earlier triumph over the force of General Elphinstone. But in this expectation they were disappointed, and the ease and completeness of the English success restored the belief in the superiority of discipline over brute force. But Akbar Khan felt bound to make an effort on his own account to oppose the English advance on Cabul, and he accordingly hastened with all the fighting men he could collect to attack General Pollock's force before it had made its way through the passes. The decisive action of the campaign took place at Tezeen on 13th September. The Afghans occupied a strong natural position, their numbers were very considerable, and they fought with great determination and gallantry; but all their advantages and efforts failed to alter the result, which was a decisive and glorious victory for the English army. With the defeat at Tezeen the Afghan powers of resistance collapsed, and two days after it was fought Akbar Khan had fled to the Hindu Kush, and Cabul was in our possession. A fortnight after this success Istalif was taken and Charikar destroyed in expiation of the destruction of the Goorkha regiment, while, with a view to leaving some mark of our vengeance on Cabul itself, the Grand Bazaar was destroyed so far as it was found possible to injure so substantial a building.

These retaliatory measures consummated, the English army of vengeance began its return march from Cabul on 12th October, and so far as it was possible for a later success to wipe out and obliterate the memory and effect of early disaster, it may be said that Pollock and Nott had redeemed the errors and misfortunes of Elphinstone and his colleagues. The withdrawal was effected without loss or difficulty, and it was only when well within the Khyber that the predatory tribes ventured to make an assault, not altogether unsuccessful, on the rear-guard. At the same time as our forces were withdrawn the Government of India issued a proclamation defining over again the policy it intended to pursue towards Afghanistan, and enunciating the principles upon which our policy has been more or less shaped ever since. The two most important passages repudiating the action of Lord Auckland read as follows: "To force a sovereign upon a reluctant people would be as inconsistent with the policy as it is with the principles of the British Government, tending to place the arms and resources of that people at the disposal of the first invader, and to impose the burden of supporting a sovereign without the prospect of benefit from his alliance. The Governor-General will willingly recognize any government, approved by the Afghans themselves, which shall appear desirous and capable of maintaining friendly relations with neighbouring states."

After this solemn and emphatic repudiation of the policy which was associated with the attempt to revive the Sudozai dynasty in the person of Shah Shuja, it was only natural that people's minds should turn to the imprisoned Dost Mahomed, who had governed the most important part of Afghanistan without extraneous assistance, and who had repeatedly professed his desire to serve the English. As soon as the English army had left Afghanistan, he, with all other Afghan prisoners, was released and allowed to return to his own country. After an honourable reception by the Sikh durbar at

Lahore, which may have borne fruit in the temporary alliance of 1849, Dost Mahomed, in February, 1843, regained Cabul, where he found that events had shaped themselves in favour of his unopposed recovery of ruling power. Opinions differ as to his real sentiments towards the English. Mohun Lal, who was a staunch advocate of the Sudozai cause, alleged that he was hostile to us, and even privy to the Cabul massacre, but his own solemn and positive declarations were to the effect that he had held no communication with his son Akbar or the other chiefs in arms against us. If he was naturally somewhat elated at the success of his people in delivering their country, his policy after his return to Cabul gradually reverted to that he had enunciated to Sir Alexander Burnes before the English Government had committed itself to a false policy and an effete cause.

With the events recorded in this chapter terminated the first act in the evolution of English policy in Afghanistan. An unreasoning fear, based on ignorance of the geography and political condition of the intervening countries, had made the at that time visionary scheme of an attack on India by Russia assume the aspect of a practical project. In his minute Lord William Bentinck had shown how the plan of campaign might have worked out, but the practical experience of warfare in Afghanistan proved that the obstacles of nature, the inadequacy of supplies, and the human resistance to be encountered, rendered the feat one of many years' accomplishment, and not of a single war. For this knowledge, which was the only practical result of our first Afghan wars, there can be no doubt that the loss of thousands of lives and millions of money, aggravated by the stigma attached by the first military reverse to the reputation of the East India Company, was too heavy a price to pay. But the worst consequence of our premature and immature action in Afghanistan was that it produced a most unfortunate reaction, and that it instigated the Government of India to adopt a policy of inactivity and indifference, which was prolonged long after action was required and might have been safely resorted to, and the influence of which has not been completely shaken off to the present day. It has been said that the worst consequence of our policy was that it led the Afghans to hate us for the unnecessary injuries we inflicted upon them, but, serious as was that consequence, its graver and more durable effect was to dishearten English statesmen, and to deprive our policy of that element of courage which is essential to success. Lord Ellenborough, whose high spirit could not be lightly impugned, regarded with a lively apprehension, not far removed from panic, operations west of the dreaded Afghan passes, and long after the annexation of the Punjab this sentiment retained undiminished force. It is only in our time that the progress of railways up to and beyond the old frontier of India and the immense improvement effected in rifles and artillery have shown that war in Afghanistan can be carried on with an approximate certainty of success. The dread which deterred us for forty years from taking up the question has now given place to the sure conviction that whenever the necessity arises we need not be prevented by any overwhelming sense of its magnitude from applying the remedy that the situation may seem to demand.

Chapter V

THE WARS WITH THE SIKHS

THE opinion of Sir Charles Metcalfe was quoted in an earlier chapter to the effect that our power in India was based in his time to a great degree on the native belief in the invincibility of the armies of the Company. That belief was rudely shaken by the incidents of the Afghan war, and curiously enough the brilliant campaigns that followed in the Punjab did not re-establish the reputation that had belonged to the English in the days of Hastings and Bentinck. The armies that fought at Sobraon and Chillianwalla were far superior to those that won Wandiwash and Porto Novo, but the reverses in the Afghan passes had broken the glamour of eighty years' unchecked military success. Lord Ellenborough had done everything possible to remove the traces of the reverses that were his predecessor's misfortune as much as his fault. He had evacuated Afghanistan amid a series of military successes, he had conquered the great province of Scinde by means of his general, Sir Charles

Napier, and the victory of Meeanee, and he had suppressed the inclination of Maratha insubordination on the field of Maharajpore. Still Lord Ellenborough's administration, justly or the reverse, is generally considered to have been a failure, and his recall in 1844 was the culminating misfortune in his brief connection with India. His successor, Sir Henry Hardinge, was a gallant soldier who had distinguished himself in the Peninsula and at Ligny, where he lost his left hand, and who after the peace had entered political life. He was destined to fill the high positions of Governor-General of India and of commander-in-chief[1] at home, in succession to his old chief, the Duke of Wellington.

Appointed to India in the summer of 1844, he was instructed by the Court of the East India Company to spare no effort to maintain the peace which existed in India. His instructions concluded with the following words: "It has always been the desire of the Court that the government of the East India Company should be eminently just, moderate and conciliatory, but the supremacy of our power must be maintained when necessary by the force of our arms." Sir Henry Hardinge was destined to provide further exemplification of the truth that the sincere wish for peace is no preventive of the necessity of undertaking wars for the defence of threatened territory and rights. Of his three

[1] In this capacity his principal achievement was to found Aldershot.

years in India, the first alone was peaceful, and in that year he extended the educational policy introduced by Lord William Bentinck. After that his residence in India was chiefly in the camp, for Sir Henry Hardinge was before everything else a soldier, and the first campaigns with the Sikhs were conducted under his personal supervision, although the nominal command was held by Sir Hugh Gough. On one memorable occasion he asserted his supreme authority as Governor-General to prevent his military associate from committing what seemed to him a rash and precipitate attack.

The Sikh wars were undoubtedly provoked by the Sikhs themselves, and if the Government of India had been left unmolested it would long have adhered to the clauses of the treaty of 1809, which forbade interference in the domestic affairs of the Punjab. The death of Runjeet Singh in the first stage of the Afghan war had led to a diminution of the cordiality of the relations between the English and the Sikhs, but as the latter had no wish to strengthen their hereditary enemies, the Afghans, no rupture occurred during this period, and it is even possible that one might have been fully averted if the family of Runjeet Singh had produced a capable successor. The excesses of the Lahore Court, the seizure of the reins of power by the Khalsa army, and the successive assassinations of Maharajas and ministers, constituted a state of chaos, marked by rapine and debauchery, that was a menace to the neighbours of the Punjab. Notwithstanding the provocation, the Indian Government remained firm in the resolution to abstain from all intervention. The murder of Runjeet's son and successor, Shere Singh, occurred before Sir Henry Hardinge's arrival, and the child Dhulip had also been placed on the throne. During the first twelve months after his arrival ten of the leading nobles or sirdars were assassinated openly or by secret means. The climax of confusion was reached when the Rani, widow of Runjeet and mother of Dhulip Singh, induced the Khalsa army to march for the British frontier on the specious plea that if they crossed the Sutlej the Company's sepoys would rise to join them. This move was really due to her own fears, and was not popular with the men who undertook it.

On the 11th and 12th December, 1845, the Sikhs crossed the Sutlej, and thus began a war which the British had steadily refused to precipitate even under provocation. English troops had been stationed for some time near the frontier, in anticipation of trouble, and within a week of the invasion the Anglo-Indian army attacked the Sikhs in their entrenched position at Mudki, and inflicted upon them a signal defeat. This battle, fought on the 18th December, was so decisive in establishing the superiority of the European soldier over the Sikhs that sanguine expectations were formed of a speedy termination to the struggle. It was on this occasion that Sir Henry Hardinge, waiving the privileges of a governor-general, served as second in command under Sir Hugh Gough. Among the officers killed was Sir Robert Sale, who had commanded the Jellalabad garrison.

The hopes raised by the victory of Mudki were considerably diminished by the second and more stubbornly-contested battle of Firozeshah, fought three days later. The Sikh camp was exceptionally strong, and the confidence of the Khalsa army had in no way been shaken by the earlier reverse. The main force, under Sir Hugh Gough, had to wait for some hours for the arrival of Sir John Littler's division of 5,000 men and twenty-four guns, although Gough wished to attack without waiting, and was only overruled by Hardinge's assertion of his superior civil power. The desperate nature of the encounter shows that without Littler's co-operation a repulse would have been more than probable. The attack on the camp began at three in the afternoon, but it was dark before the centre attack, led by Sir Henry Hardinge in person, gained part of the enemy's position, while the flank attacks were either repulsed or miscarried. The battle was resumed at sunrise, and after some hours the fight was won. There was a good deal of confusion during the engagement, and scarcely any battle in our history in India presents more material for criticism and controversy. Our losses were very heavy, and among the officers was the gallant Major Broadfoot, the hero of

Jellalabad. The battle of Firozeshah intensified the anxiety with which the progress of the Sikh war was regarded, but curiously enough the temper and confidence of the Company's sepoys greatly improved after this rude ordeal.

After these two severe battles both sides were employed in bringing up fresh troops, and the campaign re-opened in February, 1846, with the measures necessary to capture Sobraon, where nearly 50,000 Sikhs, with eighty or ninety guns, were assembled in a fortified camp for the defence of the passage of the Sutlej. A detached corps, under the command of Sir Harry Smith, gained a decisive success over part of the Sikh army at Aliwal (6th February, 1846), when, besides many killed and wounded, the Sikhs lost fifty-two guns. The survivors joined the main Sikh army at Sobraon, while Sir Harry Smith joined the Anglo-Indian army outside.

The attack on the Sikh position at Sobraon, one of the most remarkable achievements of British and native troops in Indian history, was fixed for the 10th of February. There had been some difference of opinion as to its feasibility, but in the morning of that day a heavy bombardment of the Sikh camp began from twenty siege mortars. After two hours of this fire, which seems to have produced less damage than was expected, the order to attack the entrenchments was given to the infantry. The two divisions to which this task was entrusted were both repulsed, but they rallied, and in the end gained the interior of the enemy's position. The cavalry, led in single file through a gap in the entrenchments—a feat unique in military annals—arrived to aid the infantry, and the struggle was carried on, while the Sikhs, stubbornly resisting, were driven back on the bridge. The bridge soon collapsed beneath the weight of the fugitives, many of whom were drowned in the river that they had crossed with every anticipation of victory only two months before. The Sikh loss was probably not less than 10,000 men, and sixty-seven guns were left on the ground. The native regiments behaved splendidly, and an additional cause of congratulation was furnished in the fact that "the Sikh artillery exceeded in calibre anything known in European warfare, and possessed a longer range."

The Anglo-Indian army encamped one week after the battle at no great distance from Lahore, when negotiations for peace were commenced by the most influential sirdars, acting in the name of the infant Dhulip. The Treaty of Lahore, which concluded the first Sikh war, was signed on the 8th of March, and ratified the following day. Perhaps the most striking passage of the closing scene was the surrender of the Koh-i-Nor by the young Maharaja, whose father, Runjeet, had acquired the diamond from the fugitive Shah Shuja by the stratagem of exchanging turbans. By the treaty the Sikhs surrendered the territory between the Sutlej and the Beas, paid a war indemnity of a million and a half, and reduced their army to 20,000 infantry, 12,000 horse, and a proportionate number of guns. The Sikh power was further undermined by the detachment of Kashmir, under Ghulab Singh, who paid us a sum of three-quarters ot a million. Some criticism has been directed against the treaty on the ground of its moderation, but considering the severe losses of the war, and the extent of new territory that would have had to be administered in the event of annexation, moderation here meant prudence.

In December, 1846, a new arrangement was concluded at Lahore, whither the Governor-General, now created Lord Hardinge, proceeded in person. Lal Singh, the favourite of the Rani, had been removed from his office and placed in confinement in India some weeks earlier for treacherously encouraging an insurrection in Kashmir. By the arrangement in question the Rani was removed from power, a Council of Regency and a British Resident were appointed to carry on the government for the eight more years of Dhulip's minority. The first Resident at Lahore was Sir Henry Lawrence, and the arrangement worked fairly well for the year and a half that led up to the rising at Multan in 1848, which was the signal for the second Sikh war.

Lord Hardinge's governor-generalship terminated soon after the second Lahore arrangement, and it will be best remembered for the first struggle with the Sikhs. In January, 1848, he handed over the government of

India to his successor, the Earl of Dalhousie, and as he did so he declared that "it would not be necessary to fire a gun in India for seven years to come." His confidence was based not merely on his recollection of the great victory of Sobraon, but on his redistribution of the British forces in India, which left a permanent garrison of 60,000 men guarding the line of the Sutlej. The completeness with which the prediction was falsified must be held as conclusive proof of the danger of attempting to make any political prophecies at all. Lord Hardinge had achieved very considerable successes, and it could not have been expected of him to declare spontaneously that he considered his work only half done in the Punjab. He offered his successor the seven years of peace which Bentinck and Metcalfe together, alone among English rulers of the peninsula, had up to that enjoyed, and in doing so we cannot doubt that the professional spirit of the soldier conceived that he was offering the most acceptable gift to his civilian successor. Little did Lord Hardinge think that that successor was destined to be the most remarkable conqueror among English rulers of India after Clive and Warren Hastings.

The Lahore arrangement of December, 1846, was only the temporary cure for a deep and dangerous malady. The attempt to control the Sikh chiefs entrusted with the regency of the Punjab by means of a British Resident, and to put an end to the plotting of the

Rani, was destined to failure, because the Sikh power was far from being crushed or the spirit of their leaders broken. English authority was to provide a remedy for the evils of a dissolute court and chaotic condition of affairs in the country, by verbal or written orders, at a moment when it did not possess the power to enforce them. But the want of the available power never prevented Englishmen in India from speaking with the confidence of the lords of the country, and the orders of the Lahore Resident were as curt and imperious as if they were issued in Calcutta or Bombay. It would be idle to inquire whether a more indulgent attitude for Oriental caprice and the depravity of a corrupt society such as the one led by the Rani would have averted the second crisis in the Punjab. It is probable that at the most it would only have deferred for a few years the necessity for our active intervention, and that delay would but have given us the appearance of condoning a long list of culpabilities and crimes. In any case we may write with a sensation of pride that it was not the way of the English.

A very few weeks after the arrival of Lord Dalhousie in India the British Resident, Sir Henry Lawrence, sent a demand to Mulraj, governor of the town of Multan, for an explanation of some of his proceedings as a great trading merchant, and also for a statement of his accounts as a servant of the state. After some delay Mulraj, sooner than comply sent in his resignation, which was accepted, and two English officials, Mr. Vans Agnew and Lieutenant Anderson, were sent with a small escort to occupy the fortress of Multan, and take over the administration of the province in the name of a new Sikh governor. As Mulraj made no opposition to the occupation of the fortress, and gave in his own submission to the English officers, 18th April, 1848, there must always be an element of doubt in deciding whether the events which followed were part of a plot or accidental. On their way back to their camp the two Englishmen were attacked and wounded. With some difficulty the escort succeeded in carrying them off, and in taking shelter in a mosque. Letters were at once despatched to Lahore and Bunnu asking for assistance. The next day the guns from the fort began to fire on the mosque, and in a little time the place was battered to pieces. Then the Sikhs and the crowd broke in, to find Vans Agnew sitting on the bed of his wounded and helpless comrade. As the ruffians did their work Vans Agnew uttered the memorable words, "We are not the last of the English."

Meanwhile the call for help had sped on its way, but Lord Gough at Firozepore would not incur the risk of advancing over two hundred miles of desert to Multan, and no blame can attach to him for refusing. The second letter to Van Cortlandt at Bunnu produced a different result. It was opened by his assistant at Dera Ghazi Khan, Herbert Edwardes, who, gathering such force as he could collect, some 400 men in all, hastened to the rescue. It was not his fault that none were left to rescue. Mulraj advanced to meet him with an army ten times as numerous as his small force and a formidable artillery, but Edwardes kept the Sikhs at bay by mingled activity and audacity, describing himself as "a terrier barking at a tiger." Soon some Mahomedan chiefs, glad to have a chance of fighting their religious rivals, came to his assistance, and he beat Mulraj in two pitched battles, compelling him to retire into Multan. But Edwardes had no means of capturing that fortress without siege guns, and none were available until a force tardily moved forward was collected before the fortress in September. In the meanwhile the Rani had been sent for safety to Benares, but this step did not diminish the excitement in the Punjab nor restrain the Sikhs from making one more bid for independent power. Perhaps they were the more confident as to the result because they had succeeded in forming an alliance with the Afghans.

The siege of Multan was not many days old when the Sikh subsidiary force, under Shere Singh, went over to Mulraj, and the British, instead of attacking the fort, found themselves assailed in their own camp. Up to this moment Lord Dalhousie had not directly intervened in the conduct of the question, but the delay in taking Multan caused him to assume the personal direction of the campaign. The decision he came to was to occupy the Punjab and to make it a British province. In a public speech he declared, "If our enemies want war, war they shall have, and with a vengeance." In order to be near the scene of action, Lord Dalhousie left Bengal for the Sutlej, but the command in the field was taken by Lord Gough, who had participated with Lord Hardinge in the first Sikh war. It is the fashion to sneer at the impetuosity of this gallant Irish soldier, but this is not the place to defend him against his critics.

The prevalent feeling among military men was that the power of the Sikhs had been broken at Sobraon, and that the second war with them would prove but a military promenade. History censures the over-confidence, but after all the sentiment arising from signal victories like that named is natural and unavoidable. Over-confidence often entails discomfiture, but we must remember that belief in one's self, one's race and country, which is the foundation of over-confidence, is essential for Imperial triumphs and sway. Lord Gough advanced in the full anticipation of easy and complete success. The encounters at Ramnuggur and Sadulapore showed that the Sikhs had still a great deal of fight left in them, and that the war was not going to prove a mere holiday. The first great battle of the campaign was fought on 13th January, 1849, at Chillianwalla north-west of Lahore, on what became the Great Trunk Road, and more recently the railway.

The battle of Chillianwalla is generally termed the most severe and doubtful in British history in India. It is usual to speak of it as a defeat, and to find relief for the admission in abuse of Lord Gough. But it was only a drawn battle, and may be held to have exactly realized the description. Each army gained an advantage in different parts of the field, and both occupied the same positions on the day after the fight. But, if the result was doubtful, it cannot be disputed that if the success of the attack by Colin Campbell's brigade, which gained the heart of the Sikh position and captured thirteen guns, had been equalled by the second brigade of Pennycuik's division, the battle of Chillianwalla would have ranked as one of the most brilliant and complete victories in British annals. The narrow margin by which victory escaped from his grasp shows that there was no great error in Lord Gough's plan of attack, and the blame should rightly fall on the troops, and not on the general. The news of Chillianwalla, with the long list of killed and wounded in the unlucky 24th regiment, created a panic in England. The Duke of Wellington, despite his eighty years, talked of going out himself, but sent Sir Charles Napier in his place, and Lord Gough was formally superseded by the conqueror of Scinde, a soldier whose impetuosity was quite as marked as Lord Gough's. But in those days India was not so near as now, and before Napier could reach the scene Lord Gough had brought the war to a triumphant end and exposed the injustice of his official treatment.

The capture of Multan on 22nd January was the first incident in the second phase of the campaign. It released an army of 17,000 troops with a powerful artillery force, which hastened to join Lord Gough. After Chillianwalla the Sikhs had retired to Goojerat, where they concentrated all their force, including a contingent of Afghan cavalry under Afzul, the father of the Amir Abdur Rahman. On the other hand, Lord Gough had increased his force to a greater strength than it possessed at Chillianwalla, and especially in artillery, among which were some of the heavy guns that had bombarded Multan. Early on the 20th February, 1849, the British attack on the Sikh position at Goojerat commenced with an artillery fire, which was kept up for two hours. The fire of ninety guns compelled the Sikhs to evacuate a nullah which covered their position, and then the British infantry advanced to the attack. One position was carried after another, and as the Sikhs were driven out of their last lines the British cavalry, which had been held in reserve, was let loose on the fleeing foe. Fifty-three guns out of a total of sixty were captured, and the Sikhs suffered very heavily in killed and wounded, while the British loss was comparatively small.

The great victory of Goojerat should silence the critics of Lord Gough. Lord Dalhousie determined to turn it to account by "prosecuting the war to the entire defeat and dispersion of all who are in arms against us, whether Sikhs or Afghans." He entrusted the pursuit to Sir Walter Raleigh Gilbert, who with 12,000 lightly equipped troops pressed the fleeing Sikhs hard, and never halted until he had crossed the Indus and driven the Afghans through the Khyber Pass. The native imagination was much impressed by this fact, and the saying went through the bazaars that the Afghans had come through the passes like lions and had run back again like dogs. The closing scene of Sikh independent military power was more dramatic and dignified, and it cannot be better described than in the language of Colin Campbell, afterwards Lord Clyde, who witnessed the scene.

"On the road to Rawal Pindi we passed the greater portion of the Sikh army with its chiefs, who had laid down their arms the day before. They were without food, and also without ammunition. The high priest, or Gooroo, who took the chair on the right of the general (Sir Walter Gilbert), after laying down his arms said to him in a loud and firm voice, 'The injustice of the English drove me to take up arms. They confiscated my property in the Jullunder Doab, amounting to five lakhs annually. Poverty, starvation, and want of ammunition have obliged me to surrender. These wants have brought me here. But for these wants we should have again tried the fortune of war. I do not regret what I have done, and I would do the same to-morrow if it were in my power.' There was nothing cringing in the manner of these men in laying down their arms. They acknowledged themselves to have been beaten, and that they gave in because they were starving. Each man, as he laid down his arms, received a rupee to enable him to return to his home. The greater number, of the old men especially, when laying down their arms, made a deep reverence or salaam, as they placed their swords on the ground, with the observation, 'Runjeet Singh is dead to-day.'"

The facts justifying and necessitating the annexation of the Punjab were so plain and unanswerable that the elaborate and diffuse minutes explaining the decision in terms of regret and apology seem quite unnecessary and almost insincere. The Sikhs were the aggressors, and after Sobraon we should have been within our rights in annexing the Punjab. The effort to give continued life to the Punjab under its own Maharaja did not weaken the claim established by the Sikh aggression of 1845 and the fortune of war. The scenes of disorder during the brief interregnum showed that the compromise on which we had counted for averting the responsibility of annexation would not work, and the open insurrection of the Sikhs in 1848 left no practical alternative to adding the Punjab to British India. The young Maharaja, Dhulip Singh, was provided for with adequate generosity by receiving a pension of fifty thousand pounds a year.

Having annexed the Punjab, Lord Dalhousie provided for its administration by creating a new board of control composed of three members. It was quite an experiment in Anglo-Indian administration, and that it proved successful was entirely due to the master mind of Lord Dalhousie. The board served the double purpose of giving a new shape to the government of the Punjab, and of putting the Lawrence brothers in their places. Sir Henry and John Lawrence were masterful men, who would have assumed the whole direction of affairs and of Government policy in the Punjab if there had not been a superior master mind in the person of the Governor-General. Having conquered the Sikhs, Lord Dalhousie had to conquer his principal subordinates, and there is nothing finer in the history of dictators than the firm but gentle manner in which he made them wheel into line.

The board (Sir Henry Lawrence, John Lawrence, and Mr. Charles Mansel) did its work well, but the credit must not be given solely to the Lawrences. Lord Dalhousie gave them "the best men in India," and the magnitude of the success achieved was the sum of local achievements by sub-commissioners and district officers. But even that statement detracts from the merit of the real pacifier of the Punjab, Lord Dalhousie himself. It was his policy alone that was carried out, despite the obstructiveness of Sir Henry Lawrence, arising to a great extent from injured vanity. John Lawrence, more practical or more amenable to the ascendancy of Lord Dalhousie, was a useful lieutenant, and when the Governor-General abolished the board of control in 1852, he received his reward in being appointed the first chief commissioner of the Punjab.

The principal achievement of Lord Dalhousie's policy, which was exclusively his own doing, and which Sir Henry Lawrence did his utmost to undo, was the taking away from the sirdars of the province of their military jaghirs. These men held their lands by military tenure, and constituted the main strength of the Khalsa army. They were our inveterate enemies. It was they who made the war in 1845, and rose in insurrection three years later, and it was morally certain that they would again revolt on the first opportunity. Sir Henry Lawrence would have dealt gently by them. Lord Dalhousie resolved to crush them by confiscating their property. His orders were given in peremptory and unmistakable language. "Nothing is granted to them but maintenance. The amount of that is open to discussion, but their property of every kind will be confiscated to the State. Let them be placed somewhere under surveillance, but attach their property till their destination is decided. If they run away our contract is void. If they are caught I will imprison them, and if they raise tumult again I will hang them as sure as they now live and I live then." That was the language of a true ruler, and no one can dispute that that measure, above every other, kept the Punjab quiet during the great ordeal of the Indian Mutiny.

THE MARQUIS OF DALHOUSIE.

[*To face page* 172.

Chapter VI

LORD DALHOUSIE'S GOVERNMENT

THE conclusion of the struggle with the Sikhs and the consequent annexation of the Punjab gave at the beginning a character of aggrandisement and expansion of the Empire to the governor-generalship of Lord Dalhousie which it never lost to the last day of its seven years' continuance. The enlargement of the area of direct British responsibility was due to other causes than the declared hostility of the neighbours of India, and was effected by other means than those of war and conquest. But it is natural to place first those annexations which were accomplished by force of arms. That of the Punjab, the most important and valuable of all, has been described. It fixed the western frontier of India very much where it has remained ever since. As a conquest it was matched by an enlargement of territory on the eastern frontier which was scarcely less significant, and which in the course of time was destined to prove but the prelude to direct contact with China.

If it is correct to say that in the struggle in the Punjab the Sikhs were the aggressors, and brought their fate on their own heads, it may be declared with still greater confidence that the second Burmese war was caused by the arrogant defiance of the ruler of Ava. The first war with Burma in the time of Lord Amherst had resulted in the annexation of the coast province of Arrakan. The right of trade and residence had also been conceded at Rangoon, and a British Resident was received in the capital. These concessions were made under the Treaty of Yandabu in the year 1826. In 1837 the king who signed the treaty died, and a change of dynasty occurred. The new ruler devoted all his efforts and energy to the removal of what he considered the most offensive stipulation in that treaty, the presence of a British envoy in his capital. By an attitude of insult and menace he succeeded so well as to render life at Ava intolerable for an English officer, and the Resident withdrew down the river Irrawaddi from the capital to Rangoon. This success increased the confidence of the Burmese authorities, who followed it up by adopting at Rangoon a system of exaction and extortion, practised at the expense of the British residents. The Government of India, without a representative at the Burmese capital, had no means of obtaining redress, and twelve years' impunity emboldened the Burmese officials to such a degree that they were on the point of driving the merchants away from Rangoon just as effectually as they had driven the Resident away from Ava.

Things were in this extreme condition when the British community at Rangoon made an appeal for the protection of the Government in the form of a petition to Lord Dalhousie. In this document, presented in the month of September, 1851, they said: "Affairs have now arrived at such a crisis that unless protected your memorialists will be obliged to leave the country, and doing so must sacrifice their property. Neither life nor property is safe, as the Governor of Rangoon has publicly stated to his dependants that he has no money to pay them for their services, and has granted to them his permission to rob the inhabitants, and to get money as they best can." No responsible ruler of India could listen to such a demand for protection based on well-authenticated facts with deaf ears, and Lord Dalhousie took up the question with a lively sympathy with the wrongs of his fellow-countrymen, and a resolute intention to see that they were righted. At the same time it did not appear as if the matter would attain the proportions of war. The wrong was so clear an infraction of the treaty, the amount of compensation for actual loss inflicted was so small, only about a thousand pounds, and Rangoon was so accessible to attack from the sea, that it was confidently expected that the presence of a few ships of war would suffice to bring about a satisfactory arrangement. And such, no doubt, would have been the case but for the unfathomable depths of Burmese ignorance and presumption.

Three ships of war were accordingly sent to Rangoon, but, instead of inducing the Governor to make amends, this display of force roused his indignation, and led him to insult the Governor-General's representative and to increase the burdens he imposed upon the foreign merchants. The demonstration having failed, the decision was come to at Calcutta to employ force, and orders were issued for the preparation of an expedition to Burma. In the organization of the expedition Lord Dalhousie displayed a rare thoroughness and providence. So far as care for the comfort and health of the troops went, no war had been undertaken at that time with a superior organization or more accurate provision. But some mistakes, for which Lord Dalhousie could not be held responsible, marred the commencement of the enterprise. A native regiment—the 38th Bengal Infantry—was ordered to take part in the expedition, and when the men protested against the order it was found that they were in the right, because the terms of their enlistment specially exempted them from service beyond the sea.[1] There were other unpleasant matters that need not be referred to here. At last, after some little delay that might have been avoided, the British expedition occupied the mouth of

[1] The high-caste races of India consider that a voyage beyond the sea destroys their caste.

the Irrawaddi, and was ready to attack Rangoon in April, 1852

The defences of Rangoon were represented by an immense pagoda, or fortress temple, the dimensions of which may be gathered from the fact that it contained a garrison of 18,000 men Among these men were the household troops, called "The Immortals," in their golden, or more probably gilt, armour It was declared with some exaggeration, as the result showed, that the garrison would all die at their posts, because the king held the wives and children of the married soldiers as hostages for their conduct, and because the unmarried soldiers were chained to their posts Our troops—5,500 in number—suffered considerably from the heat and the fire of the Burmese cannon in the pagoda, when orders were given to carry the place by assault This desperate step seems to have struck the defenders with a panic, and as the British troops made their way in at the front gate they fled through the back gate Some prisoners, including women and children chained to the Burmese guns, were taken, but the defiance of the Governor remained unabated, for he sent in a letter advising the English "to retreat while they could"

The war, in which the Burmese had no possible chance of success, was thus continued through the ignorant obstinacy of the ruler of Ava and his advisers There remained no alternative to the further prosecution of the war in the direction of the Burmese capital

The port of Bassein, the second commercial emporium of the Irrawaddi delta, had also been seized, and the possession of Martaban, near the more important modern port of Moulmein, completed our occupation of the coast-line; but the Lord of the Golden Foot recked nothing of such distant losses. The expedition was accordingly conveyed up the river to Prome. Here the Burmese army was attacked and defeated, and as the king continued to utter only threats of defiance, the question of a further advance to the capital itself was raised. The Court of Directors gave its sanction to prosecuting the war to the bitter end, but Lord Dalhousie, foreseeing that the difficulty would be not to advance and conquer, but to retire from the Upper Provinces, resolved to attain his ends in a different way. The king would not negotiate for peace; the Governor-General contented himself with making a simple but precise notification to the effect that the Lower Provinces of Burma had become British. The annexation of the great province of Pegu cut off the Upper Provinces from the sea, and brought in a fresh revenue which more than compensated for the expenses of the whole war. In his proclamation, Lord Dalhousie warned the king that if he molested the borders, reprisals would be made, and, if necessary, his remaining territories would be invaded and annexed. To his friends the Governor-General declared that he held Upper Burma in the hollow of his hand.

The need to close it did not arise for another thirty years, in the time of Lord Dufferin, but Lord Dalhousie deserves the credit of having forseen its probability by writing, "the necessity of absorbing Upper Burma will come some day."

Having annexed the Lower Provinces, measures had to be taken to provide for the administration of a region and population that did not know what the meaning of the word government was. The Burmese officials were nothing more than robbers, and the people had been accustomed from time immemorial to being robbed. Lord Dalhousie took as much pains in devising a new system of government for his Eastern conquest as he had done for his Western, only the conditions were harder in Burma than in the Punjab. He paid four visits between 1852 and 1854 to Rangoon, and he found in Sir Arthur Phayre a coadjutor not less able and energetic than John Lawrence. To Lord Dalhousie belongs the credit of having laid the foundation of the remarkable prosperity of Burma, which, in the coming century, will probably attain dimensions, through the opening up of China, of which at present the world has little conception.

These conquests, to which for the sake of completeness that of the little hill state of Sikkim must be added, were effected outside the boundary line of British India. Those that have now to be described were annexations within that line—territories that had been left a nominal independence by formal treaty, magnanimity, or indifference. The direct cause of most of these later annexations was the enforcement of the right of lapse—that is to say, where a chief left no heirs, and where the privilege of adoption had not been exercised, or, if exercised, had not been recognized, the state in question passed to the supreme Government. Up to the time of Lord Dalhousie, the right of lapse had not been exercised; but it was indisputable that such a right was vested in the Government. It had not been exercised because the East India Company had not shaken off all the traditions of its early commercial character. It showed a tenderness for native royalties, or quasi-royalties, and it was very content that they should relieve it of some part of the uncongenial task of providing for a backward and impoverished population. This feeling had begun to pass away in the time of Lord William Bentinck, but another twenty years were to expire before the Company could bring itself to deal firmly with the privilege of adoption as practised among the native princes, who had undoubtedly presumed too much on the goodwill and generosity of the English. In isolated cases the right of adoption had done no harm; but its frequent repetition in states, where the disappearance of all blood-heirs was proof positive of the degeneracy of the race and the corruption of the Government, only served to intensify the evils of misgovernment which were becoming the scandal of India. Lord Dalhousie's view of the matter was set forth in the following words :—

"No man can deprecate more than I do any extension of the frontiers of our territory which can be avoided, or which may not become indispensably necessary for considerations of our own safety and of the maintenance of the tranquillity of our own provinces. But I cannot conceive it possible for any one to dispute the policy of taking advantage of every just opportunity that presents itself for consolidating the territories which already belong to us, by taking possession of states which may lapse in the midst of them ; for thus getting rid of those petty, intervening principalities which may be made a means of annoyance, but which can never, I venture to think, be a source of strength ; for adding to the resources of the public treasury, and for extending the uniform application of our system of government to those whose best interests we sincerely believe will be promoted thereby. The Government is bound, in duty as well as in policy, to act on every such occasion with the purest integrity and in the most scrupulous good faith. When even a shadow of doubt can be shown, the claim should be at once abandoned."

The principle at the root of uncontrolled and uniform adoption was, that the government of a state might be placed in the hands of a blood stranger with just the same indifference as attached to the transfer of property. The Hindu chiefs did not wish to die childless because they would be deprived of what was considered a proper and duly ceremonious funeral, with which their spiritual welfare was closely associated; and consequently the practice of adoption was introduced to save families from the extinction to which abuse and degeneracy would soon have consigned them. So long as the English rulers did not think very deeply of their responsibilities in India, or were absorbed in the every-day work of political combination and the struggle with enemies far more numerous and powerful than themselves, no great anxiety was displayed as to how the chiefs utilised the privilege of adoption, or as to what were its practical consequences. Still, the Company in 1834 had begun to think a little more seriously of the matter, and it laid down the principle that adoption was "an indulgence that should be the exception and not the rule, and that it should never be granted but as a special mark of favour and approbation." Every year afterwards saw an increase of the opinion that the government of a people could not be lightly transferred from hand to hand as if it were a mere case of chattels. Hindu chiefs might well be left the right to adopt heirs to watch their funeral biers, or even to continue the name and preserve the property; but the cares of government, the interests of the subjects, were not to be thus lightly passed from hand to hand.

The Company had also to think of its own rights and interests while it scrupulously respected those of others, and while the Afghan war was still in progress, it declared that it would "abandon no just and honourable accession of territory or revenue." It was clear that the assent of the paramount state was necessary in all cases of adoption, so far as the government of the state was concerned, and as it was necessary, the right of veto was implied. The principles underlying the question had been well threshed out before Lord Dalhousie arrived in India, and the question itself had reached a phase preparatory for some new departure, if not definite solution. Lord Dalhousie's part in the matter was to give a decided and uncompromising turn to the question by putting an end to an artificial system. It was not to the good of any one that it should be prolonged; the time had come to end it. Even if the adopted heirs had been generally model princes, the hour of suppressing the privilege would surely have arrived. It came a little the sooner because even the supporters of the system could not find a word of praise or protest to utter on behalf of the individuals affected.

The first case that presented itself for solution was that of Sattara, a Maratha state which we had ourselves created at the close of the war in 1818. When the

Raja had to be deposed in 1839 for misconduct, his brother was appointed by us in his place, but at the same time he was informed that, as he had no children, the principality was very likely to lapse to the British on his death. At the best, "the question was one to be left entirely open for consideration when the event occurs." The Raja, after some years, applied for permission to adopt an heir, but the request was refused. On his death-bed the Raja took the matter into his own hands and adopted an heir. This happened in 1848, very shortly after Lord Dalhousie arrived in India. It was distinctly a case for the application of the principles that have been set forth; and the attempt of the Raja to force the hand of the British Government, after it had refused to entertain his request, was a point that kept it firm in the intention to make no concession, although the Governor of Bombay, Sir George Clerk, leant to the view that, as the adopted son was undoubtedly the Raja's legal heir, it might be well to recognize the adoption in full in this instance.

The decision of the Supreme Government was brief and unqualified. The adoption in its political sense would not be recognized, and the state of Sattara lapsed to the British. In its private and personal significance the adoption was pronounced valid, and the heir received the family estate and jewels of the Raja. As the Sattara case regulated the procedure followed in all subsequent cases, it may be as well to quote some of the arguments employed by Lord Dalhousie and the Court of Directors in coming to their decision. Lord Dalhousie said :—

"In my conscience I believe we should ensure to the population of the state a perpetuity of that just and mild Government which they have lately enjoyed, but which they will hold by a poor and uncertain tenure indeed if we resolve now to continue the Raj, and deliver it over to a boy brought up in obscurity, selected for adoption almost by chance, and of whose character and qualities nothing whatever was known by the Raja who adopted him, nothing whatever is known to us."

The decision of the Court in London was not less emphatic :—

"The result of our deliberation is that concurring with you in opinion we are fully satisfied that by the general law and custom of India a dependent principality like that of Sattara cannot pass to an adopted heir without the consent of the paramount power, that we are under no pledge, direct or constructive, to give such consent, and that the general interests committed to our charge are best consulted by withholding it. The pretensions set up in favour of the adopted son of the Raja being wholly untenable, and all claims of collaterals being excluded by the fact that none of them are descended from the person in whose favour the principality was created, the ex-Raja Pertab Singh, it follows that the territory of Sattara has lapsed by failure of heirs to the power which bestowed it, and we desire that it be annexed to the British dominion."

Five or six minor lapses, of which the most important was that of Jhansi, occurred during Lord Dalhousie's tenure of power. They do not present any special features, and were decided promptly and without difficulty in accordance with the principles enunciated. It is necessary to point out that it was only intended to apply these principles to small dependent states, and not to large quasi-sovereign states. Lord Hardinge had indeed attempted to apply them to Indore, the state ruled by the Holkar family, but Lord Dalhousie stated in the most emphatic and public manner that he applied them only to "subordinate states" and "dependent principalities." In a very special degree was Lord Dalhousie in favour of dealing leniently with "the old Rajput states," which represented the India of antiquity, and what might be described as the national life of the country.

If the Sattara lapse was important as furnishing the first instance of the application of certain principles, that of Nagpore was the most remarkable, on the ground of the extent of territory and considerable population affected. The state of Nagpore, in Central

India, had been the scene of some of the stormiest episodes during the development of Maratha power, and its prince was one of the chief leaders of the Maratha confederacy. During the campaign of 1817–18 the Raja was the patron of the Pindaris and our declared enemy. He fled at the close of the war, and the throne of Nagpore was left vacant. We might have then annexed it, but Lord Hastings preferred to create another puppet state, which should owe its existence to our generosity. Petty principalities were then in favour as a means of averting the necessity of direct government. During the minority of the prince whom Lord Hastings placed on the throne, Nagpore was well governed by an English Resident, and flourished; but, after his majority, the administration was neglected, and the state acquired an evil reputation as the worst governed in India. Things went from bad to worse under a prince who thought only of "the pleasures of dancing and singing," according to his own confession. He died unregretted in 1853, without an heir, and without having adopted one. His refusal to adopt an heir seems to have been due to his recognition of the fact that he had not the right to take this course, the succession being restricted to "the heirs male of his body lawfully begotten."

As a consequence of these circumstances a lapse was declared in Nagpore, which then became part of the British Empire. Lord Dalhousie showed great generosity and forbearance in his treatment of the Ranis and dependents of the removed family. Good pensions were assigned to all with any reasonable claim, and the Bhonsla fund was established for their permanent relief. The spoliation of the Nagpore palace, one of the chief charges afterwards brought against Lord Dalhousie, has no foundation except in the imagination of his assailants.

Another Maratha chief, a pensioner, however, and not a ruling prince, furnished a second striking instance of the lapse of a pension but not of a territory. The case is specially interesting on account of its introducing to us the person who will live with infamy in history under the name of Nana Sahib. In 1818 the Peishwa, the hereditary minister to the House of Sivaji, who had eventually grasped its ruling power, surrendered to Sir John Malcolm, who promised that he should be paid an allowance of £80,000 a year. It was intended that this sum was to be a purely personal allowance, to be paid only during the life of the deposed Peishwa Baji Rao. Baji Rao lived on until 1851, and his adopted heir was Nana Sahib, who acquired, without dispute, the treasure and personal estate of his father. The Government also left him the jaghir or estate of Bithoor, in the North-West Provinces, which it had conferred on Baji Rao. But the payment of the pension was discontinued. It is known that Nana Sahib cherished as a grievance its discontinuance, but he had no justification for expecting its continuance, and there was absolutely no reason for the Government to pay it.

Two instances of interference in Mahomedan states may fairly be put alongside those described, which occurred in Hindu territories. They were the detachment of the Berars from the Nizam of Hyderabad's dominion, and the memorable annexation of Oude. With regard to the former case, it arose out of the inability of the Hyderabad executive to meet punctually the claims it had accepted for the maintenance of the force known as the Hyderabad Contingent. The general finances of this state were brought to a condition of hopeless confusion by a system of mingled extravagance and incompetence, which neglected the resources of the state, paid extortionate interest for temporary advances, and never thought of adjusting expenditure to revenue. Disputes were endless between the supreme Government and the Government of Hyderabad, and as far back as 1843 the former began to threaten that it would have to take over territory for the support of the Contingent. In 1851 the arrears had swelled to three-quarters of a million sterling; and although the Nizam made an effort to, and did, reduce this total two years later, Lord Dalhousie came to the decision that there was no remedy for the evil short of a cession of territory. In 1853 he accordingly sent Sir John Low with the draft of a treaty ceding the Berars to the British in his pocket, never doubting that the Nizam would promptly assent to the loss of this territory as the price of ending an interminably unpleasant matter. But there are depths in Oriental minds that the European can never fathom. The demand for the Berars in its original form was met by an emphatic refusal. Sooner than surrender that part of his state, the Nizam would yield the whole. There was something dignified and affecting in this attitude of a prince whose worst faults were an ignorance of arithmetic and the desire to maintain an ostentatious splendour on inadequate means. Lord Dalhousie seems to have been touched; at least, for the only time in his career, he modified his policy. The treaty of cession was altered to one of assignment. Nearly fifty years have intervened, and the Berars are still assigned to us and governed by English officials. But the title of the Nizam to the sovereignty of the Berars remains as unimpeachable as ever.

The second annexation at the expense of a Mahomedan state was more important in itself and in its consequences. The kingdom of Oude was the greatest dependency of the Emperor of Delhi north of the Ganges. In the early years of the century it had been converted into a self-governing kingdom with our co-operation, and the only conditions made for our protection were that the king should make the prosperity of his subjects his chief object, and that he should, when necessary, follow our advice. The king wilfully neglected his duties, and a very short time after Lord Wellesley raised him to the throne that Governor-General admitted that he saw no remedy for the misgovernment in Oude short of its annexation. Things went from bad to worse under the same ruler, until in 1831 Lord William Bentinck felt bound to warn the king, despite his age, that unless an improvement was promptly effected the entire management of his country would be taken over, and he himself "transmuted into a state prisoner." It is probable that the last word should have been "pensioner."

This king died in 1837, and Lord Auckland took advantage of the occurrence to make a fresh treaty, emphasizing our right of control and preparing the way, as it were, for entrusting the administration to British officers. A still more definite step was taken by Lord Hardinge on the eve of his departure from India. He gave the king two years' grace to reform his administration, and, failing an improvement, "the British Government would be forced to interfere by assuming the government." Lord Dalhousie did not carry out the threat, although there was ample justification for annexation. He at first contented himself with giving the king another warning, but the lenience of the policy pursued was interpreted as an act of condonation.

The British Residents at Lucknow, some of them notoriously friendly to native states, reported in the strongest terms on the anarchy prevailing in Oude, and on the necessity of terminating it by annexation. At last, in 1854, Sir James Outram was directed to prepare an express report on the condition of Oude, with reference to the point as to whether the king had turned the respite allowed him by Lord Hardinge to profitable account. Outram's report was not merely a simple negative, but the most emphatic condemnation of the misgovernment in the kingdom. In his letter to the Court of Directors, Lord Dalhousie summed up the whole question in the following remarkable sentences:—

"For tolerating so long this total disregard of the obligations of solemn treaty, and for all the ills and human suffering which has sprung therefrom, the British Government is heavily responsible. It cannot indeed be charged with indifference to the evils whose existence it perceived, or with neglect of all exertions to palliate or remove them. For from the date of the treaty (1801) to the present day the records of Government exhibit one unbroken series of acts of counsel, of complaint and of condemnation on the part of the Government of India and its representatives at Lucknow. By official notes, in friendly letters, through the mouth of the Resident, and at formal personal interviews, the Governor-General has urged from time to time upon the notice of the Ruler of Oude the wretched internal condition of his kingdom, and throughout all that period at frequent intervals words of indignant censure have alternated with earnest remonstrances, with warning and with threats. But the Government of India has never taken the one measure which alone could be effectual by withdrawing its countenance from the Sovereign of Oude and its troops from his dominions. It is by these aids alone that the sovereigns of Oude have been enabled for more than half a century to persist with impunity in their course of oppression and misrule. Their eyes have never seen the misery of their subjects; their ears have never been open to their cry. Secure of the safety of his person —secure of the stability of his throne—each successive ruler has passed his lifetime within the walls of his palace or in the gardens round his capital careful for nothing but the gratification of his individual pleasure. Were it not for the support which the Government of India is known to be bound to afford the king against all domestic as well as foreign enemies, were it not for the constant presence of British troops at Lucknow, the people of Oude would speedily work their own deliverance, and would impose upon their ruler the effectual check of general revolt by which Eastern rulers are best controlled. Colonel Sleeman thus bears his testimony to this statement: 'I am persuaded that if our troops were withdrawn from Oude the landholders would in one month march over them all and pillage the capital of Lucknow.' I submit to the Honourable Court that the time has come when inaction on the part of the British Government in relation to the affairs of the kingdom of Oude can now be no longer justified and is already converting our responsibility into guilt."

The practical result of this despatch was that the Court decided in favour of annexation and requested Lord Dalhousie to give effect to this decision before he left India. In February, 1856, the formal proclamation of annexation was issued because the king refused to abdicate, declaring that he was the good friend of the English and that he would go to England to lay his case before the Queen. The execution of the policy decided upon was not rendered the more agreeable by the fact that this statement was undoubtedly true, for the alliance with the English had been. the sheet-anchor of the Lucknow ruler from the time that Warren Hastings put down the Rohillas; nor does it appear that there was any wilful intention to misgovern on the part of the Oude rulers, but rather an indifference and neglect of the duties of their position and a curious conviction that the British were not in earnest and that their admonitions did not cover any serious purpose. Oude was the last of the numerous and remarkable annexations effected during the period of Lord Dalhousie's rule. While recognizing that the obligations in each of the cases of annexation were more or less imperative for such procedure, it cannot be denied, and it implies no aspersion of Lord Dalhousie's wisdom and success, that the effect of so many annexations following one another with scarcely a break was to create a feeling of apprehension among the native princes, who could only appreciate, not the motives or the limitations set forth in official documents of the policy, but its results. The Oude decision attracted the greater stir because it was the chief Mahomedan state, or shared that position with Hyderabad, and also because it was generally regarded as the ally of the English.

Although addition of territory formed so large a part, and perhaps the most prominent feature, of Lord Dalhousie's rule, it would be a very great mistake to conclude that he was only an absorber of native states. He carried out many reforms, and he indicated others which were retarded by the Mutiny and only carried into effect at a later period of history. It has been computed that he added nearly forty million new subjects to the British Empire; and as he had to devise a new system of administration for that number of people, this work alone would have constituted a fit labour for the whole life and undivided attention of an ordinary mortal. But with Lord Dalhousie it was only one occupation among many employments. Among his creations was that of the non-Regulation Province, which admitted of the government of newly-annexed regions in accordance with the local laws and customs as far as was compatible with British law and order, under the supreme control of the Governor-General in person.

Among his great material works must be placed the introduction of railways and the telegraph. His celebrated Railway Minute of 1853 laid down the policy and sketched the line of action that have been ever since pursued. He instituted the system of guarantee which first attracted British capital to India, and of which the modern necessities of that country now require a development. He bestowed as much care and thought on the improvement of India's communications by sea as well as by land. He rendered navigation more secure by the provision of lighthouses and the improvement of harbours. He also threw open the ports to trade, lowered the tolls and abolished the conditions approved in an earlier age for fettering the trade of foreigners. Owing to these measures, in a large degree, the trade of India increased by seventy-five per cent. during his governor-generalship. He also founded the Public Works Department, and was the first to set aside a definite portion of the revenue for works of utility. Finally he established a cheap system of internal postage, and he increased the revenue by twenty-five per cent.

A few closing words may be given to the question of his military policy, more especially because he has been charged with having neglected some simple precautions, and because some critics of his government have attributed to that neglect the outbreak of the Mutiny. A recent writer,[1] speaking with all the advantage derived from his following so many historians and commentators on the great struggle, declares that "the preponderance of the native army owing to its increase, consequent on the great extent of Lord Dalhousie's annexations," was a cause of the Mutiny, and he goes on to compare Lord Dalhousie's policy, to that of the proprietor of a newly-acquired mansion,

[1] General McLeod Innes in *The Sepoy Revolt.*

who insists on heightening it into a palatial edifice without thinking of the foundation. What are the facts? No one deprecated more strongly than Lord Dalhousie "the preponderance of the native army," or pointed out more clearly its evils and consequences. He reduced the number of the native army by 7,000 men, and it was not his fault that the removal of English regiments for the Crimean war weakened the European garrison. Nor should it be forgotten that he either increased or introduced new elements of great value into the native army, such as the Goorkha regiments and the Punjab Irregular corps which provided a source of strength in the hour of trial. If space admitted, a complete defence of Lord Dalhousie's military policy, based on his own minutes, could easily be made. Here it must suffice to say that Lord Dalhousie's annexations did not lead, as alleged, to an increase of the native army, but to its reduction, however slight.

Chapter VII

THE INDIAN MUTINY[1]

MORE than twenty-two years before the first outbreak of the Sepoy Mutiny, in 1857, Sir Charles Metcalfe had written that British power in India reposed on the belief in its invincibility; and he went on to ask the question, What would become of it should the native army, which was its chief prop, ever turn upon its masters? He answered his own question with an interrogative "What?" Seven years after the words were written the reputation of the British arms for invincibility was destroyed in Afghanistan, and remarkable as was the vindication of military power displayed afterwards in Afghanistan itself, as well as on the fields of Scinde, the Punjab and Lower Burma,

[1] The vast and complicated subject of the Indian Mutiny has been treated in an infinite number of works, from the imposing six volumes of Kaye and Malleson to the little single volume of *The Sepoy Revolt* by General McLeod Innes. All that may be attempted in the present work is to give a connected and sufficiently comprehensive description of the great struggle for the information of the general reader.

the old idea of the invincibility of our arms could never be revived. The spell worked at Plassey and Buxar had been broken. The alarmist writings of Sir Henry Lawrence and General John Jacob some time after the Cabul misfortunes were but the repetition of Metcalfe's warnings in more detail. They were not heeded. Nor is this surprising. The triumphs that marked the closing chapter of conquest in India, the stress of government that followed on the heels of those triumphs, left no leisure for visionary anticipations, while they also seemed to provide the refutation of pessimistic predictions. On the eve of quitting the country, Lord Dalhousie had written that our empire in India is based on our power, and on belief in our power, and he of all men was the last to doubt our strength.

Notwithstanding the abundant evidence available according to English ideas of our power at the moment of the fall of Sebastopol, belief in its reality had been considerably shaken in India. The opinion of the bazaars was far more affected by the Russian capture of Kars, and the withdrawal of a considerable portion of the English garrison from India for the struggle with Russia, than by the successes in the Crimea or the terms of the Treaty of Paris. Among the sepoys themselves spread the view that they were the chief buttress of British power in the peninsula. They totalled up their numbers, and they saw that they numbered ten to one of the depleted white garrison of their country, while in discipline and armament they were in no respect inferior. The self-confidence of the sepoy army was the foundation on which designing men worked and plotted for their own ambitious ends; but it must be remembered that if that self-confidence had been destroyed by prompt and effectual measures on the part of the military authorities at the very outbreak of the mutiny, as might have been done, the intriguers of whom the sepoys were the tools would have been left stranded and exposed to the penalties they had merited. With these preliminary observations the narrative of events may be resumed.

Lord Dalhousie was succeeded by Lord Canning as Governor-General, and immediately afterwards, in consequence of Persian aggression against Herat, under Russia's instigation, a considerable Anglo-Indian expedition had to be sent to the Persian Gulf. The troops employed on that expedition were still absent when the first acts of insubordination were displayed by the sepoys. But the principal influence of the Persian war on the Indian Mutiny was of an indirect rather than a direct character. Reference has been made to a native regiment having refused to take part in the Burmese war, because by the terms of its enlistment it was not to serve across the ocean, and to the admission of its being in the right. The war in Persia created a fresh necessity for the employment of native troops beyond the ocean, and in consequence Lord Canning brought in new regulations for the recruiting of the regiments, to the effect that the men were all to be liable for general service in or outside India. There is no doubt that this change produced a profound and unfavourable impression on the sepoys, who were then largely recruited from high-caste races. At the moment when the native troops were most impressed with a sense of their own power and importance, this arbitrary change produced a feeling of irritation and resentment, but perhaps its worse consequence was to strengthen the belief in English weakness by making it appear that native troops were needed, not only in, but also outside of, India. The discontent of the native army might, perhaps, never have attained the dimensions of a general movement if there had not been a contributory development of political passion and aggression on the part of certain classes among the population of the country. They, too, would never have dared to carry their hostility to the lengths they did but for the manifest discontent of the sepoy army, which was perceptible long before the new cartridges were mentioned. The one class acted on the other. The gravity of the movement was caused by its dual character of a military mutiny and a political insurrection.

If the causes of the Mutiny were several, those at the root of the insurrection were still more numerous. The appropriation of territory on the cessation of pensions by the application of the principle of lapse had not merely excited the distrust of a considerable body of the ruling princes of the second grade, but was the direct cause of the enmity of the three ablest and most important adversaries we had to encounter during the whole struggle. They were the Rani of Jhansi, her adviser and henchman Tantia Topi, and Nana Sahib. The hostility of the Emperor of Delhi and of the younger members of the Mogul family was probably increased by the annexation of Oude, which destroyed the only Mahomedan kingdom of any importance in northern India. But for its cause we need not look further than the natural revulsion against a state of protection and tutelage by the titular ruler of the greater part of the peninsula. The Mogul Emperor was not the direct inciter of the insurrection, but he was the head to which the disaffected looked for countenance and encouragement in the effort to make the movement imposing and national. The disaffected knew they must have a leader, and none could appear better than the Emperor of Delhi. His name could not fail to attract support to the cause, and there is no doubt that he and the Mogul princes were willing to lend their names to the desperate venture, because they saw a chance of releasing themselves from the control under which they had been bound since Lord Lake released the Mogul family from the Marathas. The hopes of the Moguls were very natural. Their co-operation with the mutineers is not to be classed with the black acts of Nana Sahib.

While the Mahomedans looked to Delhi, the hopes of the Marathas turned to Bithoor, where Nana Sahib appeared to the majority of his race as the rightful Peishwa. Probably the true centre of the intrigues which disseminated reports over India that the rule of the British was destined to come to an end with the centenary of Plassey, and that the native troops held the white garrison at their mercy, was to be found in his palace. It is certain that his name and influence excited the Marathas to revolt in the second phase of the Mutiny, while personal jealousy of his pretensions was a strong motive force in restraining the great Maratha chiefs like Scindiah and Holkar from joining his party. The Brahmins, who formed the better-cultured and official class of the country, were solid in their sympathy and support of the movement because it would have restored their old ascendancy. The measures of the English in curtailing the privileges of caste by compelling high-caste sepoys to cross "the black water," and of adoption by depriving it of its political effect, were blows at their power and prestige which they could not be expected to accept without retort if the chance offered. The chance did seem to come when the pampered sepoys of the Company became discontented, and not only discontented but convinced that they held the fate of the existing Government in their own hands. To the keen intellect of the Brahmin leaders it seemed as if the British had themselves created the very force that was destined to destroy their power; but their ignorance of war led to their overlooking the fact that numbers alone do not constitute superiority, and that the resources of the English were not confined to the inadequate garrison in the country. The main springs of hostility having now been indicated, it only remains to say that after the commencement of the struggle some mistakes were made, which added to the number of our difficulties and of our opponents in the field. Among these was certainly the alienation of the talukdars, or landed proprietors, of Oude, who, originally friendly to the British, were gradually turned against them by a succession of measures culminating in Lord Canning's Confiscation Act.

The principal causes of the Mutiny were then as follows: (1) the weakening of the European garrison by the withdrawal of regiments for the Crimea and by the absence of other troops in Persia; (2) the dissatisfaction of the sepoys of Bengal with the General Enlistment Act; (3) the conviction of the sepoys that they were masters of the situation; (4) the revived hopes of the Moguls; (5) the bitter hatred of a few leaders like the Rani of Jhansi and Nana Sahib; and (6) the deep-rooted antipathy of the Brahmins. A brief consideration of all those causes will suffice to show that the old idea that the Indian Mutiny was caused by the introduction of greased cartridges cannot be sustained. If there had been no new cartridges at all, there would still have been a mutiny, and it would have run its course very much as it did. The new cartridges served the purpose of the intriguers by giving them an additional lever in exciting the sepoys to mutiny. They provided them with a signal or an emblem ; but if there had been no cartridges at all, it cannot be doubted that some other excitative would have been found. The manufacture of the cartridges only began in January, 1857, the first acts of insubordination were committed in February, and the Mutiny proper did not commence till 10th May. The outbreak was slow and deliberate, not instantaneous or impulsive, as it would have been if dictated by the horror of contamination at even the thought of biting the cartridge, for none were actually bitten by the great majority of the sepoys. But while the belief in the act of contamination was a splendid incentive, from the rebel leaders' point of view, to the indignation of ignorant and credulous sepoys, it is possible that their chief motive in availing themselves of this story about the Government's intention to destroy their caste was to hurry on the outbreak before the proposed change from the old musket to the new rifle could be put into effect. The supposition that cow's fat was employed in the preparation of the cartridge did not in the least deter the few native troops that had been armed with the new rifle from employing the denounced ammunition against the English. As this fact is not to be refuted the objection of the sepoys to the cartridges must have been largely factitious. At one moment they objected to them because they were told to see in them a trick and insult from the English; in the next they were ordered to use them, when a large number were captured in several arsenals, among others that of Cawnpore, to the best effect against the English, and in both cases they acted according to instructions.

The very first outbreak occurred in Calcutta itself among the retainers and followers of the ex-King of Oude, who had taken up his residence at Garden Reach, and whose supporters still clung to the idea that he would come by his own again. Their view was to profit by the coming trouble, so that they might again set up the good old system of plunder at the expense of the subject people, and of amusement in the palaces of Lucknow. They proposed to make a very effective beginning by the capture of the arsenal at Fort William, and such was the state of confidence in which the whole British community was lulled that they might have succeeded in their plan if Major Orfeur Cavenagh had not discerned that mischief was brewing and garrisoned Fort William with half an English infantry regiment. The rising of the Oude retainers came to nothing, and their schemes died out like a flash of damp powder. The first serious business occurred a few weeks later at Barrackpore, the chief cantonment of Lower Bengal, which had been in 1827 the scene of the most signal suppression of a mutiny recorded in history. The 47th Native Infantry had then presumed to show insubordination, and the battalion had been annihilated on the parade ground.

Towards the end of January reports were current that the brigade of four regiments at Barrackpore was much agitated by rumours spread by native emissaries to the effect that the English were about to forcibly convert all natives to Christianity. Then came the story about the cartridges, although they were still in the magazine or the factory. The disaffection showed itself in incendiary fires. Telegraph offices and officers' bungalows were burned down. It was not at Barrackpore itself that the first blow was struck. Berhampore was another cantonment one hundred miles north of Barrackpore, and close to the important city of Moorshedabad, the capital of the Nawab Nazim. Despite the fires at Barrackpore, some of the offending troops were sent thence to Berhampore, and what might have been expected followed. The crisis was probably hastened by the attitude of the commanding officer, but it could not have been averted. During the night of 27th February the infantry regiment at this station rose in mutiny, but the brigadier Mitchell succeeded in bringing down a native cavalry regiment and some guns in time to prevent serious mischief. A truce was concluded, and then followed the necessary court of inquiry. The offending regiment was disbanded, but not for some weeks later, after the outbreak at Barrackpore. The situation had not been improved at that place by the news from Berhampore. The general there declared that "we are living on a mine ready for explosion," due to the work of "some designing scoundrels." The explosion was caused by the removal of the offending regiment at Berhampore back to Barrackpore for the express purpose, although the men knew it not, of being disbanded.

On 29th March the sepoy Mungul Pandy attacked an English officer, and his comrades, although they did not aid him, refused to arrest him. The scene, so far as bloodshed went, was confined to the self-wound inflicted by Mungul Pandy; but it provided the evidence that the sepoys had broken loose from the restraint of discipline. On 31st March the 19th regiment was disarmed and disbanded without resistance. On 8th April Mungul Pandy[1] was hung, and some time afterwards the native officer who had declined to arrest him shared his fate. On 6th May the 34th regiment, of which Mungul Pandy had been a private, was formally disarmed and disbanded For that moment the situation at Barrackpore calmed down; or, perhaps, it would be more correct to say that the interest of events in other quarters deprived it of its importance.

At the end of April, part of the 3rd Cavalry mu-

[1] Our soldiers called the mutineers, from his name, pandies.

tinied at Meerut, with the result that eighty-five of the troopers were arrested preliminary to a court-martial. What ensued will be seen a little later. At Lucknow—or, rather, in their camp some miles outside it—the 7th Irregulars, an ex-regiment of the King of Oude's forces, displayed a spirit of insubordination and defiance. Sir Henry Lawrence resolved to disarm it, and the deed was done quickly and well. But it produced little or no effect. All the regular native regiments at Lucknow were tainted with disaffection, and it was clear that the people of Oude were ripe for revolt. All that could be done was to take timely precautions for the worst, and this Sir Henry Lawrence did with a thoroughness, energy, and skill that could never be surpassed, and that largely contributed, in their degree, to the preservation of our position in India.

These preliminary and minatory outbreaks culminated in the mutiny at Meerut on 10th May, 1857, with which event, followed the next day by the capture of Delhi, the Mutiny is generally considered to have commenced. There is no doubt that, if the lesson of the various outbreaks during the first four months of the year 1857 had been taken to heart, a general disarmament of the Bengal army would have been effected, and the peril would thus have been materially diminished. But two motives, neither unnatural nor open to censure, hampered the putting in force of repressive measures. The officers of almost every regiment believed in and answered for the fidelity of that particular unit. The generals in command, while not guaranteeing the fidelity of any regiment, were convinced that there would be no general mutiny. The events at Barrackpore, Berhampore, and Lucknow had not opened their eyes. The ablest men in the country were agreed that, at the worst, it was only a passing storm that need not lead to any alteration of their regular arrangements. But, while extending condonation to the indifference and apathy with which the symptoms of coming trouble were received, the same tolerance cannot be displayed towards the apathy of the general at Meerut when he had to deal with an overt state of mutiny. Nor is such a plea ever likely to be admitted at the bar of History in favour of General Hewitt, because the consequences of his inaction were far-reaching. To the hesitation and inaction shown at Meerut on 10th May, more than to any other single event, must the spread of the Mutiny and its development into a general revolt be attributed.

The arrest and committal for trial of eighty-five troopers of the 3rd Cavalry regiment at Meerut have been mentioned. It had been followed by acts of incendiarism, which went on while the court-martial was sitting. In the result the whole eighty-five were found guilty, and each man was sentenced to ten years' imprisonment, although some were reduced to half that term. This was on 8th May; and on the following day a parade was held for execution of the sentence. As Lord Canning justly remarked, this was an indiscretion which only tended to irritate the whole native force present during the long ceremony of degradation. Meerut was the most important cantonment in India. It had been made the headquarters of the artillery of the Bengal army, and the force there included English artillery and cavalry as well as infantry. The excuses that were valid elsewhere for cautious action, or for deferring action, on the ground that the garrison was composed exclusively or mainly of native troops, did not apply to Meerut. General Hewitt possessed an English force that made him master of the situation. That he did not employ it to good and decisive effect must be deemed an unpardonable act of incompetence and imbecility.

If we are to judge from the subsequent reports published, no one in the Meerut cantonment expected the mutiny of the native regiments which declared itself in the evening of Sunday the 10th May. It began with the release of the condemned troopers by their comrades; it was followed up by the release of seven or eight hundred felons from the common gaol; and the signal for a general revolt was given by the murder of Colonel Finnis, while exhorting his men to return to a sense of duty. The murders of other English men, women, and children followed. But the interest in the Meerut affair does not lie in the manner in which it developed, but in the failure of the English officers to crush it with the overwhelming force at their disposal. The assembly of the troops was slow; and although Colonel Finnis had been killed at seven o'clock, it was nearly ten when the English troops marched down on the native cantonment. When they arrived there, darkness had fallen, and all the sepoys had disappeared. But incendiaries were at work, and the scene was soon illumined by the burning houses of the English community. During the night the released felons massacred the helpless English residents, while the sepoys were hurrying on to Delhi, and the English troops did nothing. Even during the next day nothing whatever was done, either to punish the criminals or to pursue the mutinous soldiery, and at eight o'clock on that very morning the mutineers entered Delhi with the tale that the English at Meerut had been destroyed.

The seizure of Delhi was accompanied by the massacre of all the English in the place. The details of horror need not be given. Some of the regiments on the ridge outside the city mutinied and killed their officers; others remained staunch for a time. During this period of doubt and suspense the heroic destruction of the Delhi magazine occurred. The possession of the magazine was vital for the Europeans in Delhi; it was vital also for the mutineers, as on its stores depended their ability to hold what had been won. The officer in charge was Lieutenant George Willoughby, and he had with him eight other Englishmen and a native force whose fidelity was known to be dubious. Willoughby prepared for defence; he also prepared for the destruction of the great magazine committed to his charge. And the moment arrived for the execution of the latter project. The train was fired, the magazine went into the air with hundreds of rebels, and five of its heroic defenders were never seen again; but of the four who escaped for a time Willoughby was one. Five days later the remaining English in Delhi, chiefly women and children, were butchered by the troops from Meerut. Some of the officers on the ridge and a few fugitives from the city escaped, after incredible suffering, to Meerut. Every one felt that the cause of the loss of Delhi was the inaction and incompetence displayed at Meerut, and the loss of Delhi entailed the conversion of the struggle into one of national importance because it meant that the Mogul Emperor had assumed, or had been unwillingly invested with, the titular lead of the movement. But while the conduct of those at Meerut filled their countrymen throughout India with indignation, the splendid deed of Willoughby inspired admiration and revived hope in the ultimate triumph of the English. It was the first act of heroism on a large and striking scale in a struggle illustrated by more numerous acts of heroism than any other chapter in our story.

Delhi lost, the importance of the blow became clear to every one, and the first object of Government was to recover it. For that end every effort was to be strained by order of the Governor-General, who pressed his views upon the Commander-in-Chief Sir George Anson; but the latter saw only the difficulties of the task, and declared that he did not possess the means. Urged by the exhortations of Sir John Lawrence as to the perils of delay, as well as by those of Lord Canning, Anson did at last give orders for a move towards the Mogul capital on the 23rd May, or nearly a fortnight after the rising at Meerut. All persons in authority assumed that the recovery of Delhi was "a matter of certainty," and that a terrible example might be made of it. Three days after the first movement Anson died on the march, and the command passed into the hands of Sir Henry Barnard. The advance was renewed the day after Anson's death, and without waiting for the siege-train, the non-arrival of which had been one of the chief excuses for delay. Meantime the strong force at Meerut preserved the ignominious inaction it had shown on the fatal Sunday. Nothing would induce General Hewitt to move hand or foot. He was waiting for the concentration of the English forces, and, curiously enough, the natives believed from its inaction that the Meerut force had been wiped out of existence by the mutineers. At length the greater part of the force at Meerut, under the command of Archdale Wilson, did move out on 27th May towards Delhi with the view of joining the main body under Sir Harry Barnard. The first fighting fell to its lot. The sepoys from Delhi attempted to defend the passage of the Hindun. They were defeated on 30th May, but the next day they returned to the attack with reinforcements from the city. They were again beaten, but saved their guns, and the small English force had suffered loss in the fighting and still more from the heat. The successes on the Hindun furnished the evidence of what might have been done by the Meerut force if it had pursued the mutineers on the night of 10th May. On 7th June the two forces united and began the last march on the Mogul capital.

The mutineers were found to have fortified a strong position with thirty guns at Budlee-ka-serai, six miles outside Delhi. The guns of the sepoys were heavier than ours, and they made a stout defence. It was only when the infantry got close enough to charge that the superiority of white valour asserted itself. The sepoys were forced to retreat with heavy loss, leaving their thirty guns in our hands. The victory was rendered more complete by the prompt advance which placed us on the same day in possession of the ridge that looks down on the city. The spectacle served to reveal something of the true difficulty of the task to be achieved. The strength of Delhi was only realized when it became a question of its capture. It was clear that the Governor-General's wish to strike a quick and effective blow there was not within the bounds of feasibility, and that the exaction of a terrible revenge must be left for a future occasion. Difficult as the task was seen to be on the morrow of the battle of Budlee-ka-serai, no one foresaw with sufficient clearness that the siege would cover a period of nearly four months.

The mutiny at Meerut and the following capture of Delhi were the signal for the general rising to break out. It has been said that these occurrences were a little premature, and that the engineers of the movement had contemplated a single general revolt on 23rd June, the anniversary of Plassey. Leaving that question aside as one of those that can never be satisfactorily answered, it is certain that the possession of Delhi signified an immense accession of power and prestige to the enemies of the British Government. The fact that the Mogul Emperor had in some degree identified himself with the movement was a direct stimulant to all the Mahomedans of northern India, who foresaw in his success the recovery of their ancient predominance. And it was from the Mahomedans that we encountered the most stubborn opposition, both at Delhi and at Lucknow, which represented the two great centres of overt opposition. The loss of Delhi produced a scarcely less deep impression among our Hindoo opponents, who saw in the loss of the imperial city a sure indication of our impending doom. The weakness exhibited at Meerut had, therefore, this unfortunate and irretrievable consequence, that it encouraged the mutineers and insurgents to believe in their success at the very moment that firmness and celerity would have discouraged them and led them to think that the English dominated the situation. For it must be borne in mind that up to 10th May not a single success had attended the efforts of the rebel cause. Looking back with our accumulated knowledge, we are able to declare that the action of the authorities generally was marked by hesitation, over-confidence, and a reluctance to admit the general defection of the sepoys; but, on the other hand, the mutinous soldiery had nothing to boast of or to provide them with consolation. Several offending regiments had been consigned to oblivion, and the ringleaders, such as Mungul Pandy, had been swung from a tree. A continuance of that course would indubitably have led to the collapse of the movement. Meerut and Delhi changed the whole situation, and its immediate consequences were seen at Lucknow.

Before the end of May English regiments had begun to arrive at Calcutta: the 84th from Rangoon, and the 2nd Madras Fusiliers from Madras, under the command of Colonel James Neill, perhaps the greatest soldier revealed by the Mutiny. The difficulty was to move these troops up the river in sufficient time to save the several cantonments from being overwhelmed, while, as yet, the rebellion remained in what has been called a state of suspension. Of these cantonments, Benares and Cawnpore were the most important. On 4th June Neill had arrived at Benares, and preparations were at once made to disarm the sepoys. Neill was the first man to turn with uncompromising firmness to the task of suppressing the mutiny. He was not a sepoy officer, he had no faith in "the black faces," and he was resolved to establish once and for all the superiority of the white race. What he did at Benares was earnest of the work he did all through the grave crisis of the year 1857, until he met his death heroically at Lucknow. When he arrived at Benares, he found counsels of moderation and proposals of propitiating the sepoys in favour, and it was pointed out to him that there were 2,000 sepoys as against 30 gunners, half a battery, and the 250 infantry he had brought with him. He proposed immediate action, and the disarmament of the natives within two hours of his arrival. His views, urged with much force and confidence, prevailed. The disarmament was effected, however, not in the orderly manner contemplated, but by the well-directed volleys of grape shot from the guns of Captain Olpherts' battery.

Above Benares, in the fork of the rivers Ganges and Jumna, lies the important city and fort of Allahabad. The arsenal of Allahabad was the most important base on which British power reposed in the heart of northern India along the main route of communication from Calcutta to Delhi. The garrison of Allahabad was exclusively native, but fortunately it was quartered in a cantonment two or three miles distant from the fort. Such, however, was the faith of the English officers in their men that it was proposed to move one sepoy regiment into the fort. Fortunately the civilian authorities saw more clearly than the military, refused to trust the regiment, and, instead, collected the European community in the fort. On 6th June, inflamed by the news from Benares, the regiment reported to be so faithful mutinied, and killed sixteen officers. There were fifty invalid soldiers in the fort, and these and the armed civilians succeeded in disarming those of the sepoys who formed part of its guard. The whole native city rose in emulation of the sepoys, and every white person and even every native Christian were massacred amid circumstances of indescribable cruelty. But the fort was safe, thanks to timely precaution, and in a few days Neill, the pacifier of Benares, had arrived to establish security and exact vengeance. His measures here were marked by the same resistless energy that had triumphed at Benares. He assumed the offensive to cover the withdrawal of the women and children to Calcutta, and he continued it with the full intention to crush the rebels, and, if necessary, to destroy their city with the fort guns. The rumour of his intentions spread, and the threat sufficed to clear the city of its inhabitants. Then followed in the surrounding villages the first measures of that great Retribution for the murder of English women and children which was to continue for two years. The master race had been aroused to a degree of ferocity and bloodthirstiness in no respect inferior to the rage and hatred of the natives. But we were not the aggressors. The rebels had begun the slaughter. They could not expect us to be backward in the death-dealing struggle which they had initiated. If they did, they were destined to complete disillusionment.

While these events were occurring at Benares and Allahabad, others of still deeper import were in progress at Cawnpore and Lucknow. The exact progress of events at the former place may be left over for description in connexion with the final tragedy, with, however, the observation that Sir Hugh Wheeler, in command there, very chivalrously disregarding his own needs, sent on to Lucknow the only reinforcement of fifty English infantry that ever reached him.

At Lucknow Sir Henry Lawrence was in supreme civil and military command. He had no misconceptions about the gravity of a peril which he had long foreseen. Even before the news of Meerut he had begun his preparations for the defence of the Residency in anticipation of the worst, and he alone throughout India was in no sense taken unawares.

It was well that this was so, for the loss of Lucknow in addition to Delhi would have much aggravated and gravely compromised the situation. The disarmament of the 7th Irregulars already mentioned was followed by preparations for the defence of the Residency into which the whole of the European community was gradually drawn, while the detached position of Mutchi Bhawn, commanding a bridge over the Goomti, was also held by a detachment with guns. The remaining sepoy regiments were collected in the cantonment of Murriaon, north of the Goomti. The position of the Residency on elevated ground above the river was advantageous. It possessed considerable facilities for defence, and above all a secure and copious water supply. Having fortified the Mutchi Bhawn, and placed in it a garrison of some English troops, with all the Sikh and other sepoys on whom he thought he could depend, Lawrence pushed on his measures for the provisioning and defence of the Residency. He was still engaged in this task when the sepoys at Murriaon mutinied on 30th May, the day before the battle won by Wilson in front of Delhi. Those who mutinied were fired upon and scattered; but some of the native regiments did not mutiny, and all the Sikhs over whom Sir Henry Lawrence exercised a special ascendency remained faithful. One regiment of Sikh cavalry, which would have been useless at Lucknow, was moved down with some other troops to Cawnpore. In addition to the native troops, with their colours, who took part in the defence of Lucknow, were a certain number of army pensioners who rallied to the Government. Up to this point it had seemed as if the English garrison would be isolated in a sea of native treachery and hostility; but the defence of Lucknow was the first instance of the loyalty and devotion shown by some races, and especially the Sikhs, to our cause. During the four weeks following the dispersion of the sepoys at Murriaon nothing of importance happened at Lucknow. The crisis only arrived with the news of the surrender and massacre at Cawnpore on 27th June.

After making sure of the position at Allahabad, Neill learnt that the command of the force destined to effect the succour of Cawnpore had been entrusted to Sir Henry Havelock, who had just returned from Persia. Havelock arrived at Allahabad on 30th June, and the advance began the next day; but three days later a messenger arrived from Lucknow with news of the Cawnpore massacre. At Cawnpore the sepoy force numbered 3,000, and the Europeans, including the officers attached to those regiments and invalids, about 300. Sir Hugh Wheeler detected the signs of coming trouble, and took steps for the safety of the Europeans. He prepared a position on the river bank, which, if not the best, seemed to him the best, and he appealed to Nana Sahib of Bithoor for active co-operation. Believing in his friendship, Wheeler asked him to provide a guard for the treasury and magazine. On 22nd May this was done, and at the same time the Europeans withdrew into the prepared position in a state of confusion verging on panic. The actual mutiny did not take place until 4th June, by which time Nana Sahib and the sepoys had effected an understanding. The treasury was sacked, the magazine seized, and the whole force prepared to march for Delhi. Had this plan been carried out, the name of Cawnpore would never have become infamous. But Nana Sahib induced the troops to remain with him. The attack on the weak, improvised entrenchments began on 6th June, and continued with scarcely any intermission in the bombardment for three weeks. The heroism of the defenders of that miserable entrenchment has never been surpassed, and the loss they inflicted on the assailants was immense. But the provisions soon gave out, and the result, failing aid from Calcutta, was never in doubt—at last, on 25th June, Nana Sahib offered terms—"a safe passage to Allahabad" for all in no way connected with the acts of Lord Dalhousie, a curious limitation that inspired confidence instead of raising suspicion. Two days were spent in negotiation, and on the 27th the Europeans left their position for the river bank, where they were to find the boats that were to convey them to Allahabad. No sooner were the Europeans in the boats, than orders were given by Nana Sahib and his friend Tantia Topi for the massacre. In the midst of the massacre Nana Sahib ordered no more women or children to be killed, and about 120 were taken out of the boats alive. All the men were killed except those in one boat. Of the desperate attempt these fugitives made to escape no description here can be given. It must suffice to say that only two officers, Mowbray-Thomson and Delafosse, and two privates, Murphy and Sullivan, escaped to tell the story of Cawnpore. The final tragedy occurred after their escape, and can never be accurately described because it had no survivor. On the 15th July, when the avenging troops of Havelock had approached so nearly to Cawnpore that one more victorious rush would carry them into it, Nana Sahib ordered the butchery of the women and children, over 200 in number, for other captives had been made at Futtehghur, and when his own sepoys refused to carry out his orders he let loose in the Beebee-ghur, which was their prison, the butchers of the town. There had up to this been many murders and much treachery, but the Cawnpore tragedy was the first horror, and the Nana's treachery far surpassed that of any other leader. Even at this lapse of time it is difficult to write of the Cawnpore butchery with calmness, and the Memorial Well will stand for ever, let us hope, as a warning against over-confidence in India.

The fall of Cawnpore isolated Lucknow, and warned Sir Henry Lawrence that the period of inaction was over. He might, however, congratulate himself on having been left undisturbed far longer than he could have expected. The approach of the mutineers was signalled the next day, and, after withdrawing his small force at Murriaon, Sir Henry moved out a portion of his troops to encounter the enemy. He took this step partly as a feeler of the fidelity of his own natives and of the efficiency of the enemy, and partly to gain a little more time to complete his measures of defence. The encounter occurred at Chinhat (30th June); and although the troops were disheartened by the miscarriage of their food supplies, the early phases of the battle promised a considerable victory. The sepoys detected, however, the one weak spot of the position, and making a flank attack under the cover of a wood, placed the column in a position of such danger that no means of extrication offered save a prompt retreat. During the retreat some of the native soldiers deserted to the enemy, who pressed the pursuit and effected an entrance at several places into the city of Lucknow, where they were welcomed by a rising of the populace. On the following night the garrison was withdrawn from Mutchi Bawn, which was blown up, and the whole force was then collected in the Residency, the garrison of which consisted of 1,000 Europeans and 700 natives, chiefly Sikhs. The non-combatant population numbered 600 Europeans and 700 native Christians. Of the former, 240 were women and 320 were children. The supplies were ample. Meat lasted throughout the siege, and the grain held out for many months longer and for the rescuers as well as the besieged.

The credit for the successful defence of Lucknow was due to the energy and timely precautions of Sir Henry Lawrence; but he was not destined to share in the glory of a defence which his measures had rendered possible and hopeful. Two days after the whole force had collected in the Residency a chance shell burst in his room, thus ending his brilliant career. It was while he lay wounded on his bed that he uttered the memorable and modest words that he "had tried to do his duty." His last thoughts were to complete with words of advice and exhortation the defence of the position which passed to General Inglis. The civil and political charge was left to Major Banks; but when he was killed a little later, all authority was concentrated in the hands of General Inglis.

It would be futile to attempt to tell the story of this ever-memorable siege in a few lines. Beginning on 1st July, it continued until the 25th of September, and during those twelve weeks the attack with heavy guns and mines was almost unceasing. Although for various reasons the state of the garrison at the moment of relief was almost desperate, the mutineers, aided by the efforts of the vast population, had not scored a single success. The loss of the garrison had been heavy, but only one breach had been effected, and there the assault had been repulsed, and only one battery had been silenced, to resume its fire, after a few days, on the blowing up of Johannis' House, by which it was commanded. The full dramatic effect of the defence of Lucknow was brought out by the circumstances of its relief by the force under the command of Sir Henry Havelock.

We left the reinforcements, which began to be steadily moved up from Calcutta by Lord Canning from the commencement of May, at the moment when some of them had reached and secured Allahabad under Neill on 10th to 12th June. But notwithstanding the imperative necessity of rescuing Cawnpore, where Sir Hugh Wheeler was in desperate straits through the non-arrival of the troops, on which he had been counting daily for more than a month, no further advance was possible until the arrival of the rest of the force, placed under the command of General Havelock. This corps was to consist of the two regiments first sent up the river, and of two others which had just arrived from Persia, while the Governor-General was beginning to count on filling their places with the troops on their way to China, which he had taken steps to divert at Singapore. But it must be remembered that it was the very hottest season of the year, and that the means of communication and of transporting troops were exceedingly slow and defective. Still on 30th June Havelock began his advance above Allahabad, only, however, to call a halt a few days later, when the bad news came in from Cawnpore. Havelock resumed the advance in person on 7th July. His force consisted of 1,400 English and 560 native troops. He had twenty English volunteers as cavalry, besides 95 natives. The bulk of the natives were Brasyer's Sikhs, who had largely contributed to the defence of Allahabad. The first battle of this brief but memorable campaign was fought on 12th July at Futtehpore, about half way along the Grand Trunk Road to Cawnpore. The second and third battles were fought on 15th July—the first at Aong, and the second at Pandoo Nuddee. They were all signal successes, owing to the resistless impetuosity of the English infantry, inspired by the hope that there were still living fellow-countrymen for deliverance. On the very day of those engagements the massacre of the women and children was perpetrated. In the first of these battles the native cavalry had shown either doubtful faith or doubtful courage, and had been disarmed; and, after the third, Havelock had no more than 1,100 English and 300 Sikhs left. Still he pressed on, and on the 16th he fought and won the three actions which gave him possession of Cawnpore. Between the 7th and 16th July his force had marched 126 miles under a tropical sun, and won four battles over greatly superior forces. The devotion and fortitude displayed by this small body of troops can never be surpassed, but they had arrived too late to save. Even their vengeance was inadequate, for the arch-fiend, Nana Sahib, and his chosen colleagues had escaped.

The recovery of Cawnpore was the essential preliminary to the relief of Lucknow, which was believed to be in greater straits than was the case. Havelock leaving 300 men under Neill to defend an entrenchment at Cawnpore, transported his force of less than 1,500 men, including fresh troops who joined in the latter part of July, across the river Ganges—here a mile and a half broad—and began his first advance towards Lucknow on 29th July. The very next day he had to fight two severe actions with the mutineers at Oonao and Busherut Gungee. His losses were considerable; but a still more terrible enemy revealed itself in an outbreak of cholera, and on the day after his victory he received the bad news from Neill of the mutiny of the regiments at Dinapore, whom the authorities had very culpably neglected to disarm. At the same moment that his force was materially reduced in numbers, his communications were thus threatened and his hopes of reinforcement destroyed. He accordingly was compelled to retreat to Mungurwar, opposite Cawnpore. On 12th August he was further obliged to recross the Ganges, and it was not till 20th September that he was again in sufficient strength to resume the advance. During those five weeks he defeated the Nana's troops, captured Bithoor, and found himself superseded by Sir James Outram, only, however, to be left in the command by the chivalrous forbearance of that officer, who thus well deserved his name as the Bayard of India.

Havelock's second advance began on 20th September with a force of nearly 3,200 men, of whom 2,400 were British infantry. After a three days' march, attended by one day's severe fighting, the force reached the Alum Bagh, on the southern side of Lucknow, and four miles distant from the Residency. While Havelock rested his men at the Alum Bagh on 24th September, the cheering news arrived of the storming of Delhi. The operations of the 25th resulted in the entrance of the relieving force into the Residency by the Bailly Guard Gate after desperate fighting, during which Neill was killed. The junction of the two forces removed the greatest peril at Lucknow, and Havelock proceeded to occupy the Residency and an extended position down the river to the Chutter Munzil. After the relief Outram assumed the command.

Leaving aside such minor incidents of the struggle as the arrest of the Mahomedan intriguers at Patna by Mr. William Tayler; the defence of "the small house" at Arrah by Vicars Boyle; its relief by Vincent Eyre, and even the more important passages at Agra, we may turn to the siege of Delhi, which had been brought to a victorious conclusion almost simultaneously with the relief of Lucknow. We left that part of the story with the arrival of the British force on he Ridge after the battle of Budlee-ka-serai. After some talk of attempting to seize Delhi by a *coup de main*, it was decided to entrench a position and await reinforcements, of which many were expected, as by this time the loyalty of the Punjab was felt to be assured. During the month of June the force on the Ridge was increased by reinforcements to a strength of 6,500 men, but the mutineers also obtained large accessions, as the first impulse of all Mahomedans was to move to Delhi.

One passage of the measures taken under the supreme direction of John Lawrence for the concentration of the Punjab forces for the capture of Delhi deserves mention, as it furnishes evidence that the great organizer was no statesman. He proposed, on 12th June, to call in the Amir Dost Mahomed, to surrender to his charge Peshawur and the district west of the Indus, and to promise him that river as a permanent frontier. If this advice had been followed, we should have alienated the Sikhs, and added an Afghan peril to all our other dangers. That John Lawrence should have made the suggestion to the Governor-General must be pronounced a strange aberration of judgment; but that he refrained from accompanying his despatch with the protests of Herbert Edwardes and all the other Punjab officers that he had received, can only be termed an autocratic abuse of power that verged on the unscrupulous self-assertion of an official despot. Lord Canning ignored the recommendation of the leader of his civil service.

The pacification of the Punjab by the disarmament or the destruction of the sepoy regiments, the raising of fresh regiments among the Mahomedans of Moultan and the Afghan hills, and the employment of contingents from Cashmere and the cis-Sutlej states whose loyalty was conspicuous, may be held to have been complete by the end of July. As the result of these measures John Nicholson and his movable column of nearly 2,000 men were allowed by Lawrence, who yielded in this reluctantly to the pressure of his lieutenants, to march for Delhi, and with their arrival early in August the siege entered upon a more active and hopeful phase.

Early in July General Barnard died of cholera: his successor, Reed, was soon afterwards incapacitated by illness, and the command then passed to Archdale Wilson. After the arrival of Nicholson, the British force numbered 8,000 strong, while the defenders of Delhi mustered at least 30,000. During the last fortnight of July and the first fortnight of August the enemy carried on a very vigorous offensive, making repeated attacks upon the Ridge. These were all repulsed with heavy losses, and vigorous counter attacks were made from different points. The approach of the siege train for which the main attack had been deferred induced the mutineers to send out a large force in the hope of cutting it off, but Nicholson was detached with a mobile force to bring it to action, and inflicted on it a severe defeat at Nujufgurh on 25th August, capturing nineteen of the rebel guns. The batteries were not ready to begin their fire until the 11th and 12th September, by which time the besieging force had been increased to 14,000 men, less twenty-five per cent. in hospital. After two days' battering, breaches were declared practicable in the Cashmere and Water Bastions, and these points, with the Cashmere Gate, which was blown in by our engineers, formed the objectives of three of the columns entrusted with the assault. A fourth column under Major Reid, who had held Hindoo Rao's House, the most exposed point of the attack during the siege with the Sirmoor Goorkha battalion, was to endeavour to enter the city by the Lahore Gate. The first three columns completely succeeded, but the fourth was repulsed owing to Reid being severely wounded, losing an eye. The reserve fifth column came at a critical moment to the aid of the first under Nicholson just as that gallant leader was seriously wounded.

The positions captured on 14th Sept., at a loss of sixty-six officers and 1,104 men killed and wounded, were held, thanks to the stout-hearted counsel of Nicholson, Neville Chamberlain and Baird Smith. The advance into the city was resumed on the 19th, and on the 21st the whole city, with the person of the old Emperor, was in our possession. On the same day two of the princes who had jeered at the English prisoners from the palace windows when the Meerut mutineers put them to death, were captured outside the city and shot by Hodson, of Hodson's Horse, with his own hand when there seemed to him to be a risk of their being rescued. The recovery of Delhi, followed a few days later, as has been seen, by the relief of Lucknow, marked the turning point in the great struggle. Up to these incidents it had been for us a question of absolute existence, and no one could foretell the result. At least the native leaders might be pardoned for thinking that they had a good chance of driving the English out of the peninsula. But after these events, the scene changed. The struggle was far from being over, but the issue could no longer be deemed in doubt. The remainder of the intended China expedition had arrived, and troops were being despatched from England.

The second and most obstinate phase of the struggle centred round Lucknow, whither the sepoys who escaped from Delhi fled. Outram and Havelock, in their extended position at the Residency, and the Alum Bagh, which was held for the purpose of keeping open communications with Cawnpore, were still in a certain sense besieged by the immense native force in the city of Lucknow. Only desultory fighting occurred; and when the supply of provisions was found to be ample, all anxiety was removed. In the meantime Sir Colin Campbell, who had arrived in India to assume the com-

MEETING OF COLIN CAMPBELL, HAVELOCK, AND OUTRAM AT LUCKNOW.

Reproduced by permission of Glasgow Corporation.

[To face page 231.

mand-in-chief, was collecting a force at Cawnpore with the view of dealing finally with the rebels at Lucknow. Early in November he had an available force of 5,000 men, after leaving 1,000 men as a garrison at Cawnpore. Owing to his rejection of the advice of his chief engineer, Major Goodwyn, who adopted Havelock's original plan of campaign, Colin Campbell found the enemy well prepared to receive him, and was compelled to fight several fierce actions, in which he suffered considerable loss. He reached the Alum Bagh on 12th November, and from the 14th to the 18th he was engaged in the operations necessary to establish a junction with Outram and Havelock, and afterwards to withdraw the garrison from the Residency. Communication was established between the besieged and the relieving force by Dr. "Lucknow" Kavanagh, who very bravely made his way in disguise through the rebel lines and position, and provided Sir Colin with valuable information. For this deed he received the Victoria Cross. There was some stiff fighting, but the result was completely satisfactory, and on 27th November Colin Campbell began his march back to Cawnpore, leaving Outram to hold the Alum Bagh position with 4,000 men. During these operations the gallant Havelock died of the strain and hard work he had undergone since he left Allahabad. He had accomplished his task with admirable thoroughness and skill. His will always be the central figure in the suppression of the revolt, and the statement will scarcely be challenged, that if he had been given the supreme direction of the war, he would have brought it to a speedier and more brilliant conclusion than the slow and plodding Sir Colin. There were great possibilities about the heroic Neill, a comparatively young man; but in the aged Havelock the war produced if exception be made in favour of Sir Hugh Rose, its one tactician and strategist.

Colin Campbell arrived at Cawnpore just in time to save it from a menacing attack by Tantia Topi at the head of a formidable force, including a considerable part of the Gwalior contingent, which had revolted against the Maharaja Scindiah. His next step was to prepare the means for a final attack on Lucknow. The co-operation of Jung Bahadur, the Regent Minister of Nepaul, with a force of 10,000 men, had been secured for this task, and it was hoped to concentrate such a body of troops as would result not merely in the expulsion of the rebels from Lucknow, but in their practical annihilation. While these preparations were in progress, Outram, in his exposed position at the Alum Bagh, was subjected to not fewer than six severe attacks by an enemy sometimes ten times his strength. He succeeded in repelling every attack, and in the latter half of February, 1858, reinforcements began steadily to join him. A new army, under Brigadier Franks, composed of English and Nepaulese troops, advanced direct from Benares to invest the eastern side of Lucknow, while Jung Bahadur was coming down from the north rather more slowly than had been expected.

The whole army had practically collected in front of Lucknow on 5th March, 1858, when the attack began. To Outram was entrusted the conduct of the operations north of the Goomti, which demanded time and patience, while the other measures were to be subordinated to its progress. The general idea was to drive the rebels out of the city through the western side, which was not to be blocked, and then to pursue them with the very considerable cavalry force that had been collected for that purpose. The plan was an excellent one, and deserved to obtain complete success. It only miscarried to the extent of failing to achieve a complete triumph through Colin Campbell's caution in restraining Outram from turning a favourable opportunity to the best account, and also through the incompetence or ill luck of one of his cavalry commanders. The total force available at first was 19,000 men and 120 guns, but on the arrival of Franks and Jung Bahadur this was swelled to 31,000 men and 164 guns. By 9th March Outram had made sufficient progress to enable Campbell to begin the main attack south of the river. The enemy's position consisted of a series of detached buildings or palaces, each of which had to be stormed separately—and at this point it may be appropriate to recall the fact that the enemy consisted mainly of troops who had been trained by English officers, and whose whole career had accustomed them to the idea of victory. It was also perfectly clear to the mutineers that, so far as ultimate success went, they were fighting their last battle. If they could not hold Lucknow, they could not hold the open country; and, consequently, they fought with the courage of desperation. This was specially the case at the Begum Kothi, where the 93rd Highlanders and a Punjab regiment bayonetted between them 2,000 sepoys, and the famous Hodson ended his brief but brilliant career as a fighter and leader of fighters. Of him, and all the controversies his name has given rise to, let us say, *de mortuis nil nisi bonum.*

On 14th March Outram had done so well that he asked permission to force the iron bridge, which would have given him command of the western side of the city; but Colin Campbell, ever cautious and ever slow, sent back word that he was "not to do so if it would cause his losing a *single* man." In face of such instructions no move was possible, and Outram's force, with no serious obstacle in its front, and, practically master of the situation, was confined to an inactive *rôle,* while the last rebel positions in the city were being stormed at great loss. An end came to this street fighting on the 15th, and it was hoped that the next day a considerable success would be scored by cutting up the fleeing sepoys. But, in this matter, all the arrangements miscarried. The cavalry were first sent along certain roads on the assumption that the sepoys would take them, which they did not; a large number of sepoys escaped across the Goomti, and made their way through a gap in the encircling line of troops; and, finally, the failure of Brigadier Campbell, on the 18th March, to cut off the retreat of the bulk of the rebels to the westward deprived the victors of the fruits of their victory. Lucknow had been finally recovered, but the bulk of its defenders had escaped to carry on the struggle for many subsequent months.

At the moment when Colin Campbell was preparing for his final advance on Lucknow, Sir Hugh Rose, afterwards Lord Strathnairn, was engaged in the Central-Indian campaign, which made his name famous among Anglo-Indian generals. The Bombay and Madras armies had remained quite unaffected by the mutiny of the Bengal troops, and among the contingents maintained in several different forms in the native states that of Hyderabad, with the exception of one cavalry regiment, was conspicuous by its loyalty. But the forces of the Maratha chiefs Scindiah and Holkar declared for the rebels, although the chiefs themselves remained faithful, and the whole of Central India, with the exception of Bhopal, ruled by the loyal Begum, became a focus of hostility. Sir

Hugh Rose has been blamed for not commencing operations earlier than he did, but his instructions compelled him to wait for the column moving from Madras, under General Whitlock, which was to co-operate with him. In February, 1858, the campaign began with the capture of Saugor and other strong places, and early in March he forced the difficult Mundenpore Pass by some brilliant manœuvring, which completely misled the enemy as to his intentions. On 23rd March he reached Jhansi and laid siege to it. There were 11,000 men in the place; and a few days after his arrival news came that Tantia Topi was approaching with an army of 20,000 men from Calpi. Sir Hugh, without relaxing his siege operations, marched with only 1,500 men to meet Tantia Topi, whom he completely routed on the banks of the Betwa. It was a brilliant achievement, which would alone suffice to establish the reputation of the general who conceived and executed it. Three days later he carried the town of Jhansi by storm, and the Rani fled to Calpi, where she rejoined her defeated ally, Tantia Topi. This portion of the campaign concluded with the capture of Calpi; from which, however, both the Rani and Tantia Topi succeeded in making their escape.

For a moment it was thought that their course was run and that they would become hopeless and helpless fugitives. But the Rani had conceived a new and daring scheme. She had resolved to acquire possession of the strong fortress of Gwalior and to make it a fresh base of operations. On her approach Scindiah drew up his army to oppose her, but it refused to fire a shot, and Scindiah was obliged to flee to Agra. All his forces declared for the Rani, who proclaimed Nana Sahib as the Peishwa from the rock on which the fortress stands, thus making a sort of rallying cry to all true Marathas. On hearing this news, Sir Hugh Rose, who was on the point of disbanding his force, at once took the field again. On 16th June he captured the Morar cantonment, and on the following day he fought another successful engagement during which the Rani was killed. Fighting went on for several days, but on the 21st the fortress was carried by a *coup de main*, the credit of which is due to Lieutenant Rose, of the Bombay army. Tantia Topi succeeded in escaping, and was not finally crushed till the spring of 1859. He was betrayed by one of his hosts, who gave him up to Major Meade. After a short imprisonment, he was hung for his participation in the Cawnpore massacre, but before he died he was allowed to write out an account of his adventures and experiences, which forms the basis of most of our knowledge of what might be called the rebel case.

The final suppression of the Mutiny in Oude proved long and arduous, partly through the escape of the bulk of the mutineers from Lucknow, and partly because the talukdars were arrayed against us through Lord Canning's ill-timed Confiscation Act. After much severe fighting, accompanied by many successes and a few reverses, the campaign was brought to a conclusion, with the year 1858, by driving the last band of mutineers across the Rapti into the Terai of Nepaul. It was generally believed that Nana Sahib was among these fugitives, and a story was subsequently circulated to the effect that he had died of fever in the Terai. His re-appearance was periodically reported until at last, six-and-twenty years after the close of the Mutiny, a man was arrested in Central India as being the infamous Nana. Opinions differed as to his identity, but after a brief incarceration he was released for want of proof. There seems to have long existed, in well-informed native circles, a belief that the Nana did survive the Mutiny, and that he was concealed by some of his compatriots, in whose eyes he was the Peishwa. With this single exception, all the leaders of the Mutiny were satisfactorily accounted for.

In concluding this brief summary of the most severe ordeal through which any people ever had to pass in the maintenance of their authority over alien races, it is only necessary to dwell upon two main points —the causes of the Mutiny, and of its successful suppression.

The causes of the Mutiny were first, and, above all,

the over-confidence of the English officers and authorities. They carried the legitimate and essential belief in themselves to that inordinate degree when precautions are neglected and the rules of common sense are defied. By the clearest laws of human nature the natives could not be wholly content with a position based on the supremacy of the white race, yet the sepoys were assumed to be animated by a loyalty and devotion as great as those of our own countrymen. At the very moment when these views were prevalent the discipline of the sepoys had been relaxed by their having obtained the better of the Government in several disputes affecting their own status, and by their conviction that their support was indispensable to its existence. At the same time they had grown discontented with their own pay and position. The period of peace that followed the close of the second Burmese war promised to continue indefinitely because no enemies were left to be encountered, and peace signified the loss of batta—that extra pay which had been so long and so regularly enjoyed as to make it seem part of the fixed allowance. Another cause of discontent was the introduction of the General Service Bill, which altered their terms of service without regard for their prejudices and without giving them a say in the matter. These were the real irritants in the minds of the sepoys and the causes of their mutiny. The "greased cartridges," which had not even been distributed and which have been elevated into notoriety as the cause of the Mutiny, were an extraneous subject which served the turn of the intriguers by giving them a lever in working on the credulity and passions of the native soldiery. Every political agitation fixes on some badge or token as a signal for action. To some extent the "greased cartridges" were employed in working up the sepoys to a pitch of frenzy; but the allegation that the English intended to convert the natives to Christianity by force was employed just as freely and effectually. These excitations might have produced local scares and risings, but the great Mutiny can only be explained by the deeper causes mentioned, which had been in operation long before the introduction of the Enfield rifle was thought of.

The causes of the suppression of the Mutiny are clear and simple. They might be summed up in a single sentence—the superior fighting power of the British soldier. The struggle continued during the greater part of two years, and for that protracted period the endurance of the soldier was subjected to a rude strain by the climate and disease, as well as by the opposition of a well-drilled and well-armed enemy of at least ten times his strength in number. There were very few brilliant strokes of generalship to supplement the efforts of the men and the regimental officers who led them into action, and they were delivered by Havelock and Hugh Rose. As leaders who inspired their men with confidence, and who, once launched in pursuit of the foe, never gave him breathing space, Franks, Napier (afterwards of Magdala), and Hope Grant established their reputations. James Neill and John Nicholson, slain at Lucknow and Delhi, attained the position of popular heroes, and the soldier-statesman, Henry Lawrence, indicated by his example the way in which the rising he had foretold should be suppressed. Finally, the band of men who, under the nominal headship of John Lawrence, kept the Punjab in tranquillity and turned it from a grave menace into a tower of strength claim a share in the glory of the suppression of the great revolt.

The Empire owed the preservation of India then solely to the men of the mother country; and if the whole of the Peninsula had risen in one black mass of hostility, the result, although more dearly and more slowly won, would have been the same. But this conviction does not diminish the gratitude and recognition due to those who stood by us and eased our task in the hour of peril; and taking them in their order of importance, it seems that the loyalty of the Madras and Bombay armies entitles them to the first place in our enumeration. They had not been pampered and spoilt like the high-caste sepoy of Bengal, and they showed themselves true to their salt. In the second place, the loyalty of the Sikh nation cannot be over-praised or over-valued, and the memory of the dark hours of the Mutiny will long cement and strengthen a sympathy and spirit of comradeship subsequently shown in many a shock in the passes of Afghanistan and on the plains of China. The contingents supplied by the Maharaja of Cashmere, and by the Maharaja of Puttiala and the other cis-Sutlej Sikh states, rendered invaluable service in the field and in keeping open important routes of communication. Nor should the assistance rendered by the Goorkhas of Nepaul under Jung Bahadur be minimized. It was the result of the impressions produced by a visit to London, when the mountain chieftain went back to his eyrie in the Himalayas, declaring "England has no more faithful ally than I." Well he proved, when the hour came, that he was as good as his word. In the last place, let us not forget to mention the native statesman Salar Jung of Hyderabad, whose sagacity and example were not less valuable auxiliaries for the impression they produced on his co-religionists than was his direct service of the first magnitude in keeping the Deccan quiet during the crisis. There were minor contributories, but to mention them would seem to detract from the merit of those who took the foremost part.

The great Mutiny was a terrible ordeal, but British rule in India may have come out of the test purified as if by fire. Should a similar peril ever arise in the peninsula again, we can only hope and pray that our race will display the same great qualities that carried the day in 1857–8, and that we may find in that hour of danger and distress friends as staunch and true as those who stood by us in the dark moment when the banner of rebellion and fanaticism flaunted defiantly in our face from the palaces of Delhi and Lucknow, and when the mere handful of white faces in the midst of the hundred millions of Bengal and the north-west seemed like a ship among the breakers.

Chapter VIII

TWENTY YEARS OF PEACE

THE Indian Mutiny had decided the fate of the East India Company, and its disappearance had been facilitated, if not foreshadowed, by the change introduced into the Charter on the occasion of its last renewal in 1853. Whereas the previous renewals had always been for a specific number of years, which had latterly been fixed at twenty, the Act of 1853 stipulated that the Charter was only to remain in force as long as Parliament should see fit. The shock produced by the Mutiny on public and official opinion was so great that it was little marvel that the legislature decided, in spite of all that could be said in favour of the great Company, to proceed to summary execution. The decision could not be said to come altogether as a surprise. The change had long been considered desirable, and even respect for an institution which had done so much to promote the national dignity and fame could not blind people to the fact that a dividend-seeking corporation was not the proper body to discharge the duties of government among a vast alien and helpless population.

The Act for the better government of India, passed during the session of 1858, was received in that country in the month of October, and on November 1st, in the same year, Lord Canning formally proclaimed Queen Victoria ruler of India, and at the same time assumed himself the title and style of her Viceroy. The Queen's Proclamation was remarkable for the moderation of its language. The noise of strife had scarcely subsided, the cannon indeed were still speaking in Oude, when the Queen gave the Princes of India the assurance that they should not be disturbed in their possessions, for anything short of gross misgovernment, and that even where deposition should become necessary, the nearest or the most suitable relative would be appointed to the vacancy. This message of peace and security undoubtedly produced a great impression. It confirmed the loyal, and removed the apprehensions of the doubting and half-hearted. The rule of the Sovereign could not have begun better than by declaring itself the harbinger of peace, stability, and concord amid the wreck and ruin of a desperate internal war. It promised the natives of India religious tolerance, and immunity from interference, equality before the law, and admission to offices in the public service. What it promised to be at the moment of utterance has been verified and proved by the experience of more than forty eventful years.

The termination of the Sepoy Mutiny had scarcely been accomplished, when another mutiny occurred of what threatened to be graver import. To the Black Mutiny succeeded the White. Among the arrangements accompanying and forming part of the transfer of the government from the Company to the Crown was the incorporation of the Company's European troops in the regular British army. This change, however simple and inoffensive it may appear to us, was regarded by the officers and men composing the old East India Company's European establishment with supreme dislike and dissatisfaction. It no doubt signified some material loss, for the Company had been a very generous master, but the men themselves affected to take umbrage only because they had not been previously consulted in the matter, and accorded the usual right of option. They represented that they could not be transferred in this manner without having a say in the matter, and that they should have been first disbanded, and then re-enlisted, which would have given them a title to a fresh bounty. Their grievance was based on a pecuniary loss and an infraction of form, and probably it was not without some justification. But the lengths to which the European soldiery of the defunct Company carried their discontent far surpassed the limitations imposed by propriety and discipline. At a moment when the storm in India had scarcely ceased to ruffle the waters, part of the British garrison showed itself disposed to follow the bad example of the sepoys and to turn on its own fellow-countrymen. At Allahabad and several other places, a collision was only avoided with difficulty, and, as the only way out of the trouble, the Government granted the men their discharge, but refused to pay them any bounty for re-enlistment. Not fewer than ten thousand men had in this manner to be sent back to England.

The difficulties of the situation were far indeed from being confined to military troubles. Every class in the European community was ready to declare that it had a grievance against the Government when new taxes to meet the necessities of the situation had to be imposed. Not less resentment was aroused by the laudable and indispensable efforts made in the Queen's Proclamation and also in all Lord Canning's utterances, to bridge the chasm existing between the English and native communities. Time was needed to remove the bitter feelings among the former, and the sense not so much of hatred itself, as of the conviction that it lay under a personal ban of hatred and suspicion in the latter. But Lord Canning, as the statesman charged with the execution of his Sovereign's declarations, could not wait on events; he had to make a beginning, and at least to indicate the way that those who followed in his steps should pursue. He naturally incurred much opprobrium at the time, but in the light of history Lord Canning's reputation for statesmanship will be enhanced by the moderation of his policy as conciliator, and by the dignity of demeanour with which he bore the taunts and attacks of his own countrymen. A more malignant document has rarely been penned than the petition from the Calcutta community demanding his recall.

The difficulties of the new situation in India were far more formidable than mere opinions and prejudices. They consisted of monetary troubles which cannot be evaded, and must be overcome. An empty exchequer, a diminished revenue with limited and uncertain chances of expansion, were not encouraging facts in grappling with the difficulties and incubus of debt left by the terrible struggle through which India had passed during the space of two years. Even the reorganization of the indispensable peace garrison, which was henceforth to contain a far larger proportion of European soldiers to natives than before, entailed an increased expenditure, which had to be provided for by new taxation, or a re-adjustment of old. In this situation the difficulty was rendered greater because there was a dearth of men as well as of means. The Indian services had been prolific of talent, but curiously enough they had never produced a born financial genius like Mr. Gladstone in England, or Akbar's minister, Todar Mal, in India. The occasion demanded a financier, and did not admit of delay until he could be discovered among the older representatives of the Company's *régime*, or the new competition wallahs. Lord Canning consequently wrote to

England for the assistance that he wanted, and it was sent out to him in the person of Mr. James Wilson. Mr. Wilson was the first Financial Member of Council, and the example he left has proved an animating influence with all his successors. The work he accomplished in less than two years, before he was struck down by the climate and over-work, was colossal. He reorganized the whole customs system, introduced an income tax and a licence duty, and created a State paper currency. By his efforts a good beginning was made in the direction of providing a revenue, but little or no progress was possible on the side of expenditure, owing to the immense sums expended on the army. His successor, Mr. Samuel Laing, effected a considerable reduction in the army expenditure in the last year of Lord Canning's rule, and brought an equilibrium in the financial position of the country within sight.

The army question was important from another point of view than its effect on financial matters. In the arrangement and new disposition of the garrison considerations of future security were necessarily bound to play a large part. The old faith in the sepoys could never be restored, and it was clear that considerations of safety imposed a close regard to what might be held a safe proportion of European to native troops. In the time of the Company the natives had been six times as numerous as the Europeans, and included a powerful artillery force. There was consequently no difference in the armament of the two forces, and they were on a par in all respects for purposes of warfare. It is true that on the eve of the Mutiny, the white troops had received the Enfield rifle, and the sepoys had not. That was the only difference between them, and the deficiency was more than made up by the fact that the bulk of the artillery was native. The new Anglo-Indian army, of which the foundation was laid before Lord Canning left India, was to be composed of one-third Europeans, and two-thirds natives, while, as a further precaution, all the artillery was to be European. The old high caste sepoy of the army before the Mutiny practically disappeared, and in his place Sikhs, Pathans, Dogras, and Goorkhas were recruited in large numbers. The lines then introduced have been closely followed ever since, and the present native army of India may be considered independent of, and unaffected by, those waves of anti-English feeling which must always occur in a community so mixed and so impressionable as that of Hindostan. At the same time the number of European officers with each native regiment was materially reduced from about twenty-four to seven or eight, and herein undoubtedly lurks a grave defect and possible peril. They were to be drawn from officers of the royal army who volunteered to serve in the staff corps formed in each of the three Presidencies.

The eventful rule of the last Governor-General—and first Viceroy—of India came to an end when the reorganization of Anglo-Indian administration had been carried to a point that left the result clear and assured. Both in the trying time of the Mutiny, and the more tranquil but scarcely less critical period that followed, during which he had to contend with his own exasperated countrymen, and to restore confidence generally in the community, Lord Canning bore himself with a calmness and dignity worthy of the best traditions of his country. In the suppression of the Mutiny he played his part gallantly and well, and it may be truly said of him that not one of the great actors in the drama made so few mistakes, and when the cannon had ceased to sound, he alone saw what was the right course to pursue. The name of "Conciliation Canning," applied almost as a taunt, will preserve his fame, while the fact that he gave his life to his work and country adds a touch of pathos to his story. A few months before he left India his wife, who had shared the toils and perils of the Mutiny, fell a victim to fever; and a few months after his own return to England, in 1862, he died from a decline produced by his ceaseless labours during the six years of his rule in India. Like his predecessor, Dalhousie, he was a victim of his untiring devotion to his work and duties, and in that sense he may be said to have given his life for his country in one of her greatest hours of peril.

Lord Canning's successor was the Earl of Elgin,

whose name will always be honourably remembered in connection with our position in China as the negotiator of the Treaty of Tientsin. When the Mutiny was at its worst, he had supported Lord Canning in his demand for the diversion of the China Expedition in 1857, and had himself gone to Calcutta to offer his services. His selection as the next Viceroy was consequently natural and appropriate. He arrived in India in time to take over charge from his predecessor (March 12th, 1862), but his brief tenure of office was quite uneventful, although it is proper to note that he continued the policy of conciliation toward the people of India initiated by Lord Canning. His death in November, 1863, brought to a sudden close a career that seemed to have little more than commenced.

Up to this point the Governor-Generals and Viceroys of India had, since the time of Warren Hastings with one or two dubious exceptions of brief duration, been chosen from great politicians or soldiers at home. The members of the Company's service had not been held eligible for this exalted office, and perhaps it was due to the desire not to create jealousy among them that the great prize of all was not permitted to dangle before their eyes as a bait. Sir Charles Metcalfe, indeed, had enjoyed the privilege of "officiating" as Governor-General during a whole year, and had thus been afforded the opportunity of completing the reforms of Lord William Bentinck. But this case was regarded as an exception, and not as a precedent. It was fully intended that the supreme position in India was to be reserved for a notability in English political life. Events, however, were to prove in one special case too strong for this resolution.

The reputation of John Lawrence had been raised to such a height by the events of the Mutiny, that the ordinary rules did not seem to apply to his case. He was called by his admirers "the saviour of the Punjab," and some did not hesitate to term him "the saviour of India." To a remarkable degree he had been associated with the Punjab from the time of Lord Dalhousie, and the recent death of the old Afghan ruler, Dost Mahomed, had again directed attention to the situation on the frontiers of that province. Already there were rumours of coming trouble in Afghanistan, and this fact finally decided the Government of the day to nominate Sir John Lawrence as Lord Elgin's successor. It will always be considered a curious phenomenon in the manner in which public reputations are built up, that John Lawrence, who advocated abandoning Peshawur in the crisis of the Mutiny, and who wished to make the Indus the frontier of India, should be regarded as the great authority on the Afghan question which he detested, and which he would have declared non-existent by ignoring it.

The viceroyalty of Lord Lawrence is generally described as uneventful, and if this means that he did less definite work, and made a slighter impression on history than most of his predecessors or successors, the description is certainly correct. Considering his reputation and experience, his period of rule was distinctly disappointing. He did not attempt to grapple with any of the difficulties of the situation, or the defects of the administration, and bad as was the financial position on his arrival, he left it worse at his departure. Two terrible famines—those of Orissa in 1866, and of Bundelkhund in 1868–9—strained the resources of the Government, and showed how unready it was to deal with such difficulties. The loss of life was appalling, owing to the inability to convey rice into the famine districts.

Lord Lawrence's one war was with the hill state of Bhutan, which lies on the southern side of the Himalayas, parallel as it were with the larger and more powerful state of Nepaul, from which it is separated by the territory of Sikkim. The relations of Bhutan with Tibet invested its affairs with special importance, and our first collision with it, in the time of Warren Hastings, had resulted in the despatch of a mission to the land of the Lamas. The Bhutanese are a lawless race constantly engaged in civil war, and their favourite recreation was to carry on raids into our territory. These had become so frequent and daring, that a punitive expedition had been decided on, when the Mutiny occurred to delay it. The final outrage was an insult to an English officer sent to make an arrangement for improved behaviour by the hillmen, but compelled to sign an ignominious treaty instead. An expedition was accordingly sent into the country, and after some difficulty terms of peace were imposed on the Bhutanese. They were thought at the time far too lenient, and there is scarcely room to doubt that the time must come sooner or later for the annexation of Bhutan.

During Lawrence's viceroyalty, the affairs of Afghanistan were in a very disturbed state, and he consistently regarded them with the calmness and lack of interest that would have been appropriate if Afghanistan had been in a different planet instead of being a neighbour. The succession of Shere Ali had been disputed by his brothers, and a savage civil war broke out which promised to overwhelm the Amir, who had been formally recognized by Lord Elgin. Shere Ali accordingly sent a request to Lawrence, as the man who had signed the treaty with his father, for some arms, but met with a refusal. As a consequence Shere Ali was defeated and fled to Herat. Then his brother Afzul, father of the present Amir, on occupying Cabul asked to be recognized as Amir, but Lawrence refused to recognize him as more than Amir of Cabul, at the same time recognizing Shere Ali as Amir of Herat. This see-saw business was not statesmanship. It filled all the Afghan chiefs with disappointment and enmity, and it brought what was supposed to be British policy into contempt. Yet it was precisely what might have been expected of one who wished to retire behind the Indus, especially as Lord Lawrence's chief characteristic was obstinacy. Of him, more than of most men, it might be said—

> "He who is convinced against his will,
> Is of his old opinion still."

The consequences of his policy were to be reaped later on, and even to-day they have not all been garnered.

The next Viceroy of India was the Earl of Mayo, a genial Irishman possessing in the fullest degree those national qualities which require a large scene for their effectual display and general appreciation. With the quickness of his countrymen he grasped the details of a subject without difficulty and almost by instinct, and he possessed the statesmanlike capacity to adapt his means to an end, and to harmonise the separate measures of his administration with the requirements of his whole scheme of policy. No one in manner or spirits could have been more typically Irish, yet no one could have possessed greater business capacity or a clearer appreciation of the truth that, while sentiment may be an animating force, hard facts dominate all situations in the affairs of men. Yet it must always be counted to his credit that he introduced into Anglo-Indian life, and especially into that part of it affected by the relations between Europeans and natives, a cordiality and a frankness that had never previously existed. To say, however, that Lord Mayo was the most genial of Viceroys seems to imply a diminution of his merit as compared with other Viceroys, who never possessed and could not practise that charm of manner which is the rarest gift of Heaven, and this difference was especially noticeable in the successor to Lord Lawrence.

The appointment of Lord Mayo was regarded at the time of its being made as a hazardous experiment and as an excessive reward for an untried man. His rapid and complete success soon silenced his critics and vindicated the judgment of Lord Beaconsfield, then Mr. Disraeli, who had made the appointment. Lord Mayo threw himself into his work with remarkable thoroughness, sparing no pains in mastering details and in qualifying himself for his difficult task. His report on the defencelessness of Aden, which he declared was in no sense deserving of the name of a fortress, showed his Government before he had set foot in India that he was thoroughly in earnest in his resolution to grapple with the difficulties and duties of his high station. Speaking of his trouble in dealing with the deficit, which was a chronic feature of Indian finance at that time, he wrote: "It is a hard task, but I am determined to go through with it, though I fear bitter opposition where I least expected it. I have put my hand to the work, and I am not going to turn back, and I will kill before I die some of the abuses of Indian administration."

Lord Mayo's work may be conveniently divided under

three heads, the revenue and expenditure, foreign policy, and the relations with the Native States of India. It may be best to take the financial question first, because it is the least known and appreciated.

Notwithstanding the efforts made by successive Finance Ministers, the annual deficit had for some time exceeded three millions sterling when Lord Mayo assumed office. At the end of his first year he had succeeded in establishing an equilibrium (£50,782,413 expenditure as against £50,901,081 of revenue); in his second year he attained a surplus of 1½ millions (£49,930,695 of expenditure as against £51,413,685 of revenue); and at the end of the third year he had increased the surplus to over 3 millions (£46,984,915 of expenditure against £50,109,093 of revenue). This remarkable improvement, which has never been fully appreciated by his countrymen, was rendered all the more remarkable by the fact that it was due to economy and reform in expenditure, and not to an increase of the revenue, which might have taken place without conferring any claim to merit on the part of the ruler.

While Lord Mayo was grappling with the difficulty in the early stages of his rule he wrote, "the waste of public money is great, and I have been obliged to take strong measures," and he traced much of the mischief to the number of treasuries. At all costs he declared that the finances must be placed upon a sound and stable basis, and his first reforms were of the drastic nature required to secure a surplus. He cut down public works by nearly a million a year, and other departments by half as much more, and at the same time he raised the income tax from 1 to 2½ per cent. These extreme steps were necessary to save the immediate situation, but more carefully organized reforms were needed to effect a durable amelioration of the financial position. It would be impossible to give the details of the reorganization of accounts which he effected, and of the attendant reforms in system, regularity, and economy that followed. Briefly put, an overhauling of all the departments took place, with the result that many abuses were removed, and much waste put an end to. But the radical reform which he effected was to require all the local governments to establish an equilibrium in their own local finances, and to abandon their old practice of making the central government bear and supply their deficits.

The greater portion of the diminution of expenditure occurred under the head of the army, and in this direction he effected not merely much economy, but material reductions. These reductions did not apply to the European army, which he considered not a bayonet or a sabre too strong. He brought about a considerable lowering in the cost of its maintenance by diminishing the number of regiments and increasing the strength of each regiment, so that it did really consist of a full establishment. In this and other ways he reduced the cost of the European garrison by over half a million a year.

With regard to the native army a reduction was found possible of the Madras establishment, which resulted in an economy of £178,000, and of the Bombay army, by which £77,000 was gained annually. In this manner a considerable sum was saved to the Exchequer, at the same time that there was no diminution of numerical strength or efficiency. His policy had been, while providing for the defence of the peninsula, "to save the people of India from contributing one farthing more to military expenditure than the safety and defence of the country absolutely demand."

As an erroneous opinion might be formed from the statement made that Lord Mayo's first economy was to reduce the expenditure on public works by nearly a million, it will not be out of place to supplement it with some reference to the fact that he carried out, or at least commenced, many public works with the view of providing against, or diminishing, the loss entailed by famine. By work on canals and irrigation, as well as by developing the railway system, he showed that he was in no sense indifferent to useful and necessary public works. He wrote in one of his despatches:—"By the construction of railways and the completion of great works of irrigation we have it in our power, under God's blessing, to render impossible the return of those periodical famines which have disgraced our administration, and cost an incredible amount of suffering, with the loss of many millions of lives."

Lord Mayo is best known, however, for his external or foreign policy, and especially for his relations with Shere Ali, the Amir of Afghanistan. The Durbar at Umballa in 1869 marked what might be called a turning point in Anglo-Indian history, for from it dates the Afghan and Central Asian policy, pursued with more or less consistency ever since. Reference has been made to Lord Lawrence's policy while Afghanistan was a prey to civil war among the sons of Dost Mahomed. Very shortly before Lord Mayo's arrival Shere Ali had succeeded, by the military ability of his son Yakoob Khan, in driving his rivals out of the country and in re-establishing his authority. In March, 1869, he came to have his famous interview with the Viceroy. He wanted support in various ways, and a regular annual subsidy, but Lord Mayo had no power to grant any of his requests. Notwithstanding, he managed so skilfully in the task of propitiating the Amir that Shere Ali returned to his country convinced that his true policy was to work in harmony with the British. This was very important, for at that moment Russia had established herself firmly in Tashkent, and was on the point of despoiling Bokhara of the city of Samarcand, the far-famed capital of Tamerlane.

Lord Mayo described the policy he wished to see pursued in the following general recommendation :—

"Surround India with strong, friendly, and independent states, who will have more interest in keeping well with us than with any other power, and we are safe." At the same time Lord Mayo advocated coming to a friendly understanding with Russia, and he took advantage of the return of the late Sir Douglas Forsyth to Europe to ask him to travel home by way of St. Petersburg, with the view of making informally some representations on the subject of Central Asia. The result of these negotiations was to obtain for the first time an admission from Russia that Afghanistan lay outside her sphere of influence, and that the Oxus, generally speaking, should be regarded as the northern frontier of that country. Lord Mayo not only laid down the lines on which all our subsequent policy has been conducted, but he obtained on paper the recognition of the very arrangement existing to-day.

Lord Mayo also commenced the delimitations of frontier between Persia on the one side, and Afghanistan and Baluchistan on the other, which were to remove the uncertainties and perils of disputed boundaries. North of the Himalayas he established some sort of relations with Yakoob Beg, the Mussulman adventurer who had driven the Chinese out of Kashgar, but Sir Douglas Forsyth was sent on the first occasion in a private capacity, and failed even to see Yakoob. Two years later he was deputed by Lord Northbrook as his official representative, but no practical advantage in either politics or trade followed from this second visit to Kashgar.

There remains only to describe the third subject associated with the name of Lord Mayo, viz. his relations with the great feudatories of India. The Mutiny had certainly invested with greater reality their relationship to the supreme power, and the presence of a Sovereign made the expression of their fealty and obedience more natural and sincere, but no overt step had been taken towards making them our friends. The Queen's Proclamation, followed by the creation of the Order of the Star of India, to which native princes and statesmen were admitted, had formed a hopeful beginning, but the time had arrived for taking a further step forward. This he did in a speech of remarkable friendliness and fervour to the Rajput princes, who represent the hereditary nobility of the country. He urged them to undertake reforms, and to think of their subjects' welfare by telling them—"If we wished you to remain weak, we should say, Be poor, and ignorant, and disorderly. It is because we wish you to be strong that we desire to see you rich, instructed, and well governed."

At the same time he made it the cardinal point of his policy to show that under no circumstances would he annex native territory; and while he often had occasion to deplore native misgovernment and the personal excesses of native rulers, he steadily adhered to his resolution that the true remedy was the slow one of improving the whole class of princes by education, and not by inflicting chastisement on the offending individual. With the object of promoting education among the princely and noble classes he founded the Raj Kumar College in Kattiawar, and the Mayo College at Ajmere for Rajputana. The good work accomplished by these institutions cannot be over-estimated. To them is mainly due the higher sense of duty that characterises the princes of India now as a body when compared with their predecessors of the Mutiny period. Our own task has been lightened at the same time that the princes have been brought to attach a higher importance to the efficient discharge of their own duties and responsibilities.

At the same time that there was a movement on the part of the feudatories towards the Crown, there was a return movement on the part of the Crown towards India. That country had been very rightly called her brightest jewel, and Queen Victoria fully realized from the first day of her assumption of personal authority the importance of the charge, the opportunities of beneficence that it offered, and the addition that it furnished to her dignity and importance. An indication of these sentiments was furnished in the time of Lord Mayo by the visit of the Duke of Edinburgh to India during the winter of 1869–70. It undoubtedly stimulated the loyalty of the princes of India, and

THE MAHARANA OF UDAIPUR.

[To face page 268.

we must never forget that with Oriental friends or foes sentiment counts for much more than it does with us.

At the very moment when Lord Mayo seemed on the point of completing the reforms that he had set on foot, and carried far towards completion, his career was cut short in a tragic and sudden manner. Among other objects of reform Lord Mayo wished to ameliorate prison life in India, and especially in her penal colonies. In the Andaman Islands the death rate among the convicts averaged ten per cent., and although 8,000 of the most desperate criminals in the whole country were there congregated, this state of things could not be allowed to continue. Murders were common among the convicts, and the ravages of disease were increased by the scarcely restricted importation of spirits. Lord Mayo took in hand the reform of this costly and dangerous establishment. He sent a strong man to administer it, but the task proved so heavy that Lord Mayo decided to visit the islands with the view of stimulating the work. He accordingly arranged to include a visit to the Andamans in a tour to Burma that was intended half for necessary personal supervision and half for a much-needed holiday.

He landed at Hopetown, the port for the Andamans, on February 8th, 1872. He spent the whole day in a personal examination of the chief island, and it was dark when he proceeded to the pinnace to return to the man-of-war that had brought him. As he proceeded along the jetty a man who had been tracking the party all day sprang from behind and buried a knife in the Viceroy's back. While the English officers and others seized the murderer, the present Sir Owen Burne, who was Lord Mayo's private secretary, was helping his chief out of the water, into which he had fallen. For a moment or two the hope was entertained that the blow was not mortal, but in less than five minutes from his being struck Lord Mayo fell down dead. As if to make the incident more ghastly in its details Lady Mayo was on board the war-ship awaiting the return of her husband. The perpetrator of this bloody and senseless crime was a Pathan fanatic who had vowed to avenge his own wrongs, as he considered them, by killing a prominent English official. It was the hand of destiny that brought one of the most gifted of our Indian rulers within reach of his cruel knife.

Lord Mayo's successor was the Earl of Northbrook, whose viceroyalty was rendered remarkable by the visit of the Prince of Wales, now King of Great Britain and Ireland and Emperor of India, to India. The famine of 1874 in Lower Bengal was almost as severe as that of Orissa, in the time of Lord Lawrence, had been, and strained the resources of the State. The organization of relief was better managed, and furnishes Lord Northbrook's chief claim to be remembered favourably as an Indian ruler. With regard to external affairs he continued the policy of his predecessors, and appointed frontier commissions to define the Persian borders on the east. He was also so completely satisfied with his own Afghan policy, that he called Shere Ali "the staunchest ally of the British Power in Asia."

Among notable events of his four years in India may be named the deposition, in 1875, of the Gaikwar of Baroda for attempting to poison the British Resident, Colonel Phayre, in 1874, and the surrender by Maharajah Scindia of a man whom he declared to be the infamous Nana Sahib of the Mutiny. However, an investigation dispelled this belief, and the miserable, chattering object surrendered by Scindia was pronounced to be not identical with the sleek and portly pensioner of Bithoor. Curiously enough the affair strengthened a suspicion that the Nana was not dead in 1874, and that some of the chiefs were sheltering him from pursuit. The plotting and arrest of the Wahabis of Patna, attended by the murder of Justice Norman, was another striking event of this period. But the principal event of all was the visit of the Prince of Wales, who landed at Bombay on November 8th, 1875, and left the same port three months later, on February 12th, 1876. The tour of the Heir Apparent produced immense enthusiasm throughout the peninsula, and undoubtedly strengthened the bonds connecting the princes and peoples of India with the rest of the Empire.

Chapter IX

OUR LAST AFGHAN WARS

LORD NORTHBROOK'S successor was Lord Lytton, who took up the post of Viceroy on 12th April, 1876, about two months after the departure of the Prince of Wales. The appointment of Lord Lytton, a poet and diplomatist rather than a man of affairs, was received with some of the criticism that had been bestowed on the earlier appointment of Lord Mayo, but for much of the work that devolved upon him Lord Lytton was qualified in a very exceptional degree. The princes and peoples of India did not need any further proof that Englishmen were practical and hard-headed, but it was something new for them to learn that the many-sided national character of the ruling race could be represented by a highly gifted genius of the school of Hafiz and Omar Khayyam. For much of the work that fell to his share those qualities were more appropriate than the dull sobriety of many of his predecessors and some of his successors. If there had been no rude shocks of war, the viceroyalty of Lord Lytton might have passed away in glorious pageantry, and left a memory of idyllic peace and pleasantry such as attached to the Court of King René of Provence.

For the first part of his mission no one could have been better equipped than Lord Lytton. For some time previously the want had been felt of a proper and effective title for Queen Victoria as ruler of India. In that country the style of Maharani was not sufficiently imposing to represent a supreme authority, and, as it was in very common use, the pre-eminence of the British ruler did not stand out clearly, and was even somewhat obscured. The visits of the royal princes to India had furnished evidence of the increased importance of that country in its relations with the Empire, and also of the increased interest taken by the Queen in its welfare. The feudal system might be considered to have come down in full force in India to the present time, and, consequently, it was desirable and even necessary that its head, the central figure on which all the rest depended, should have a title of unquestionable and visible supremacy. Among the papers in his portfolio of instructions Lord Lytton bore the document giving the heads of the proposal to create and proclaim Queen Victoria as Empress of India, for which, after some hesitation, the words Kaisar-i-Hind were selected as the most appropriate Indian translation. Several claimants came forward in later years to the credit of having originated this rendering in 1876, but the official who had first employed both terms in a public proclamation remained silent. In 1874, before there was any intention of making an addition to the royal style, General Sir Andrew Clarke, then Governor of Singapore and the Straits Settlements, issued a proclamation to the Malay chiefs in the name of the Empress of India, or Kaisar-i-Hind.

Lord Beaconsfield is entitled to the credit of having originated and carried out the change. In India it was certain to meet with approval and applause, but in England it was a hazardous experiment. It was a moment of much sluggishness of opinion at home as to the value of our possessions beyond the sea. The colonies were pronounced by prominent politicians an encumbrance, and India was deemed a heavy responsibility without any compensating benefits. On the other hand criticism of any addition to the style of the Sovereign could not have been more acute, and the use of the mere names, Empress and Imperial, seemed in some curiously constructed minds an attempt on the British Constitution. It is hard in these days of imperial activity and alertness to repress a smile of contempt at what was public opinion in this country during the triumph of littleness and self-effacement, that marked the epoch from the death of the Prince Consort to the Treaty of Berlin. The assumption of the style of Empress of India by Queen Victoria was the first re-

Photo by] [*Elliott & Fry.*

LIEUT.-GENERAL SIR ANDREW CLARKE, G.C.M.G.

[*To face page* 274.

action against these debasing and destructive tendencies, and from it may be dated the commencement of a larger Imperial life for the British races throughout the world.

Lord Lytton threw himself into the congenial task of making the Proclamation of the new Empress of India as effective as possible with all the ardour of his gifted imagination. The Imperial Durbar held on the historic Ridge above Delhi on 1st January, 1877, was the most gorgeous and imposing ceremonial ever held in India. For the first time her princes took their allotted places in the Empire, while the impression produced on foreigners was immense, because an unexpected union and solidity were revealed where disunion and secret hostility had been more than presumed. Much of the picturesqueness of the pageant was due to the initiation of Lord Lytton, whose speech to the assembled princes was clothed in language that breathed oriental fancy and felicity. The plain significance of the change was perhaps best brought out by the despatch, a few months later, of Indian troops to the Mediterranean at a critical moment in the Russo-Turkish War. The Indian Empire with all its military resources had become an integral part of the whole British Empire in a sense that had never previously existed.

The remainder of the year that witnessed the Imperial Proclamation and part of the next were saddened by an appalling famine in Mysore and Southern India generally, which cost an immense number of lives and an enormous sum expended on famine relief.

With these exceptions, attention during Lord Lytton's viceroyalty was mainly directed to external affairs. Many causes contributed to this result. The Russo-Turkish war had introduced a disturbing element among the fanatical tribes of Afghan race along the Indian frontier, and the Akhond of Swat, whose age added to his reputation for saintliness, went so far as to preach a Jehad or Holy War against the English. Revived interest had also been created in Russia's movements by the advance of an expedition into the Turkoman country and the occupation of Kizil Arvat in May, 1877. At the same time the Chinese had returned to Central Asia and were engaged in the task of conquering the ephemeral kingdom of Yakoob Beg. To none of these matters could the Government of India be indifferent, and soon it had its own special troubles with the ruler of Afghanistan.

The Umballa Durbar in the time of Lord Mayo had established relations on a friendly footing with the Amir Shere Ali. The first frontier negotiations between him and Persia had not weakened them, but the second negotiations about the Seistan border in 1875 failed to meet his expectations. More serious cause of umbrage was given, however, by our interference on behalf of his son Yakoob Khan, whom he had placed in confinement. His expectations of tangible aid from us in the form of a regular subsidy had been disappointed, and he resented advice from those who did nothing to strengthen his position. He resented it the more because he saw in the occupation of Quetta, in the spring of 1877, evidence that we were taking steps to dispense with his alliance and provide against his defection, whereas that forward move was really intended as our reply to the Russian advance from the Caspian. Even the friendly efforts of a special envoy from the Sultan of Turkey, who sought to induce the Amir to regard the English as his best friends, failed to produce any improvement in the situation. More than a year before the breach actually happened it was clear that Shere Ali's sentiments were the reverse of what they were at the time of the Umballa Durbar, although it was not known how far he had committed himself to Russia until after the discovery of the secret correspondence at Cabul in 1879. He had also been irritated against us by our reluctance to support his pet scheme of nominating his youngest son, Abdullah Jan, his heir in preference to Yakoob Khan. In 1877, and again in 1878, Shere Ali received Russian officers at Cabul, and entered into a formal alliance with the Tashkent Government, although Russia had in the meanwhile suffered some loss of prestige by the retreat of General Lomakine from Kizil Arvat, and the arrest of her march on Constantinople due to British action.

The winter of 1877–8 was marked by the Jowaki

campaign, which resulted in the pacification of the Kohat Pass lying south of Peshawur. The difficulty of preserving tranquillity on our Indian borders, illustrated by many costly expeditions, drew more attention to the importance of having a definite friendly understanding with the Afghan ruler. The criticism bestowed at home on the precautionary measure of occupying Quetta undoubtedly made the Government cautious in developing its Afghan policy. It was also delayed by the evident possibility of war breaking out with Russia. But in the summer of 1878 events marched so rapidly in Afghanistan that any further delay on our side became impossible. Before Parliament broke up in August, it was known that a Russian General had arrived at Cabul, and met with a public reception of undoubted significance. At the same time, reports came to hand of the movements of Russian troops in Central Asia, and especially of a fresh expedition against the Turcomans. Lord Lytton at once decided to depute an English officer of distinction as his envoy to Cabul, and selected General Sir Neville Chamberlain for the task. General Chamberlain was not only one of the most distinguished soldiers of the Mutiny period, but he had commanded several frontier expeditions with much success. He was also favourably known among soldiers for his moderation and tact. At this juncture, one of the chief motives underlying Shere Ali's policy was removed through the death of his young son Abdullah Jan.

Although the Government had resolved on requiring the Amir to receive the Chamberlain Mission, every one knew that his doing so was extremely doubtful. The conference at Peshawur in January, 1877, between Sir Lewis Pelly and the Amir's chief minister had left the impression that Shere Ali was completely alienated, and that reconciliation was out of the question. What was about to happen confirmed this impression. A letter was addressed to Shere Ali informing him of the intention to depute Sir Neville Chamberlain to his capital, and asking for his honourable reception. To this communication Shere Ali did not condescend to give an answer, and towards the end of November it was accordingly determined to send Sir Neville on his journey. His escort entered the Khyber Pass, but on reaching Ali Musjid, the first post held by Afghan troops, the commandant refused to allow it to pass and threatened to fire. The Chamberlain Mission was thus rendered futile on the very threshold of its undertaking, and Shere Ali offered a public affront to the British Government in marked contrast with his cordiality towards the Russian. There remained no practical alternative for bringing Shere Ali to a more reasonable frame of mind than to order the invasion of his country.

The defiance of the Amir did not find the Government entirely unprepared for the worst. Regiments had been warned for active service, and a plan of campaign had been drawn up for the attack on Afghanistan from three points at the same time. The largest force, under Sir Samuel Browne, was to operate against the Khyber, a second corps, under Sir Frederick Roberts,[1] against the Kuram, and a third, against Candahar *viâ* the Bolan Pass and Quetta, under Sir Donald Stewart. Complete and easily attained success attended the operations of the three columns. Sir Samuel Browne turned the Afghans out of Ali Musjid in the Khyber, and advanced to Jellalabad. Sir Frederick Roberts, after one fierce action at the Peiwar Kotal, reached the Shutargardan Pass and threatened Cabul with a flank attack. Sir Donald Stewart occupied Candahar without difficulty. No campaign could have been brought to a more rapid or more completely successful conclusion than the advance into Afghanistan in the winter of 1878–9. The Afghan powers of resistance seemed to crumble away at contact, and the loss incurred had been comparatively small.

When his armies were beaten Shere Ali fled from Cabul to Balkh, releasing his son, Yakoob Khan, from confinement before his flight, and leaving him to make the best terms he could with the English. For himself he retained the hope that Russia would come to his aid, and he sent several of his officials to Samarcand to

[1] The reader should refer to the graphic and interesting autobiographical work entitled *Forty-one Years in India*, by Earl Roberts.

inform General Kaufmann that the time had arrived to fulfil his promises to the ruler and people of Afghanistan. Yakoob Khan also wrote to the Russians assuring them of his fidelity, and there is no reason to doubt the truth of this statement, which is made on the authority of the present Amir. The sudden death of Shere Ali, who was considered by the Afghans to have gone mad, at Balkh in February, 1879, released the Russian authorities in Central Asia from the embarrassment in which their secret and treacherous proceedings had placed them, and Yakoob Khan, finding no help likely to come from north of the Oxus, decided to make peace with the English and thus avert the occupation of his capital. Negotiations for peace were accordingly commenced, and Yakoob complied with all the demands made upon him, which were embodied in the Treaty of Gandamak (May, 1879). He complied very readily, but time alone could show whether he possessed the power or the will to fulfil his engagements.

Among these engagements the most important was the reception of an English resident envoy at Cabul. No one seems to have entertained a doubt that the execution of this arrangement was perfectly feasible and well within Yakoob's power, and as he himself never expressed any reluctance or uncertainty, it is scarcely matter for surprise that we did not raise or imagine any difficulty. Sir Louis Cavagnari, the negotiator of the Gandamak Treaty, was accordingly appointed by Lord Lytton to the post of accredited British Resident at Cabul. He took up his residence in June at the Afghan capital, accompanied by a small staff of officers and an Indian escort. The Amir gave him a friendly welcome, and for some weeks everything progressed satisfactorily. But it soon became clear that Yakoob was not going to prove the strong ruler he was thought likely to be, and that his own position was exceedingly precarious. The Afghan soldiers had been summoned from many places to defend the capital and fight the English. Two regiments at least had arrived from Herat. They were naturally not animated by friendly feelings, and to make matters worse Yakoob had not the means of paying them regularly. The situation was consequently one of great and hidden peril. Nor must it be overlooked that the radical defect in the Gandamak Treaty was that, while it bound the Amir to do much, it conferred no equivalent advantages on him. If it had provided him with a regular subsidy he would have had the means at least of paying his troops, and gradually sending them back to their garrisons, and all might have gone well.

The secret history of the Cavagnari massacre at Cabul on 3rd September, 1879, will probably never be known, but all the available evidence exculpates Yakoob from active participation in the treacherous deed. The opinion held by the Afghans[1] themselves is that the affair was organized by the principal widow of Shere Ali, the mother of the favourite son Abdullah Jan, with the special object of dispossessing Yakoob of the throne, and this version is rather confirmed by the fact that this lady had some time before the outbreak of hostilities made an offer to the Government of India to poison her husband, Shere Ali, if it would guarantee the throne to her son Abdullah Jan.

Whatever the cause, the British world was startled by the intelligence early in September, 1879, that the whole of the Mission at Cabul had been massacred, and no other course was open to the Government than to despatch a punitive expedition. The second advance into Afghanistan had nothing to do with an aggressive policy on the part of the Conservative Government and Lord Lytton. If Mr. Gladstone had been Premier, and Lord Ripon Viceroy, at the moment, they would have acted in precisely the same way. Orders were at once issued for the reoccupation of Candahar, from which, as it fortunately happened, all our troops had not been withdrawn, and for the despatch of an army to attack and capture Cabul. The command of the latter force

[1] "The other version is that the mother of Abdullah Jan had given 3,000 sovereigns to Daoud Shah (the commander-in-chief) to incite the people to rebel against the presence of Cavagnari and to kill him, so that Yakoob should lose his kingdom. This account is credited by the Afghans at Cabul." *Abdur Rahman*, op. cit. vol. i. p. 152.

was given to Sir Frederick Roberts, and Sir Donald Stewart resumed the command at Candahar. General Roberts decided to march on the Afghan capital by the Kuram Valley and Shutargardan Pass, which had been reached by the force under his own command in the first campaign, and the result fully justified his decision.

No resistance was offered by the Afghans or the hill tribes on the Indian side of the passes, and on 30th September the whole force descended from the Shutargardan into the district at the northern extremity of which stood the town of Cabul, without any great natural obstacles intervening. The Afghan forces had gathered from all sides to oppose our advance at Charasiah, but Yakoob Khan escaped from their camp and came into ours, protesting his innocence of all participation in the massacre. It was the proceeding of an innocent man, as he could have easily made sure of his escape to Turkestan and Russian territory. He abdicated in favour of his son Moosa Jan, and was despatched to India pending a decision on his case. Such information as was procurable after the capture of Cabul was collected, and an attempt was made to prove him guilty. But the examination of the evidence soon established his innocence, and he was accorded a pension and an honourable place of residence in India, where he is still living.

In the meantime our arms had been attended with

uniform success in Afghanistan. General Roberts routed the main Afghan army at Charasiah, which he considers the happiest of his victories[1] (6th October), and on 9th–11th October occupied Cabul, where the massacre of the British Mission was avenged by hanging such of the assailants of the Residency as could be found, and by blowing up part at least of the Bala Hissar or Royal Citadel. Having established the superiority of our arms and punished, so far as possible, the offenders, the difficult question remained what should be our next step, and a wise decision was far more difficult to arrive at than may be supposed. One of the first conclusions forced upon us was that the central authority in Afghanistan was exceedingly feeble, and that the operations of war had practically destroyed it. Innocent or guilty we could not very well replace Yakoob on the throne, and his own abdication went to show that he had had enough of such dangerous honours as belonged to an Afghan ruler. His son Moosa was a mere child, and moreover he was in the hands of the fanatical party led by the priest Mushk-i-Alim. It was quite clear that there was no one to place upon the throne, and it naturally seemed imprudent to withdraw the victorious army until we could ascertain what was likely to occur after its departure. To have

[1] With 2,600 men, including 800 Europeans, he routed 10,000 Afghans, including thirteen regular regiments of Shere Ali's old army.

left Afghanistan in a state of disturbance would have been the height of folly, not merely for the preservation of our own interests in India, but because it would have furnished Russia with a plausible excuse for interference, and for reviving the schemes that she had entertained at the time of the Stolietoff Mission in 1878.

Moreover there appeared no reason to entertain any grave apprehension as to the consequences of keeping our army in Afghanistan during the winter. The opposition of the Afghans had either proved very insignificant or was thought to be crushed, and as there was no single chief with any visible claims to the throne, it was naturally enough assumed that there was no leader to combine the tribes against us. This reasoning seemed the more sound because the only two members of the Barukzai family with any claims to authority were far removed from the scene. Ayoob, the uterine brother of Yakoob, was at Herat; Abdur Rahman was a state prisoner in Russian Turkistan. It was, therefore, decided to maintain the occupation of the country during the winter, and to employ the interval in seeing what was the best step to take towards creating, or allowing events to create, a new government in Afghanistan. With the object of obtaining the best opinion on the subject, Lord Lytton appointed the ablest official at his disposal, Sir Lepel Griffin, to the post of Political Agent at Cabul.

The winter of 1879-80 did not pass off as tranquilly

as was expected, and Afghan hostility developed unexpected dangers. A fanatical priest, Mushk-i-Alim, and a soldier of fortune, Mahomed Jan, served as leaders of the popular movement in default of members of the reigning house. The tribes gathered from all quarters, attracted by the hope of repeating the achievements of 1841–2, but they were to find that they had to deal with a very different soldier from Elphinstone. At the same time the danger was far too serious to be treated with levity, and the Afghans might even claim that they had obtained a success in the Chardeh Valley when Massey's cavalry force was driven back by Mahomed Jan with the loss of one or two guns.

The position looked critical enough when General Roberts, after fighting on the hills for several days, evacuated the town of Cabul and withdrew all his forces into the cantonment of Sherpore, which he had carefully prepared as a defensive position. In this place he was perfectly secure against attack, and waited calmly until the Afghans had exhausted their fury, and his time to resume the offensive had arrived. The leaguer of Sherpore began on 14th December, and it ended ten days later with the repulse of Mahomed Jan's final assault. The Afghan loss in that attack was very heavy, probably not less than two thousand. With the view of establishing our military superiority in the country it was then decided that Sir Donald Stewart should march northwards with the greater part of the garrison at Candahar as soon as the spring was sufficiently advanced to admit of the movement.

In addition to raising the army at Cabul to such a strength as would place it quite out of danger, it was intended by this move to capture the fortress of Ghuzni, and to disperse the hostile forces collected in its neighbourhood. General Stewart left Candahar at the end of March, 1880, with a force of about 6,000 men. The column met with no opposition until it reached a point thirty miles south of Ghuzni. Here, at a place called Ahmed Khel, on 19th April, an Afghan force attacked the British while still in order of march. A desperate charge of four or five thousand Ghazis threw our troops into confusion, but after an interval of uncertainty the attack was repulsed. The Afghans lost over a thousand in killed alone, and there was no further resistance. Sir Donald Stewart reached Cabul on 27th April, and took over the command in chief.

The concentration of the British forces at Cabul was meant to be the prelude to an evacuation of the country. This intention would have been carried out, even if there had been no change of Government at home, but it must be noted that in the interval between the siege of Sherpore and the advent of Abdur Rahman, Mr. Gladstone had become Premier, and the Marquis of Ripon had relieved Lord Lytton of the Viceroyship. The excited language of the hustings led many people to believe that the Conservative Government of Lord Beaconsfield and its representative in India, Lord Lytton, were hungering for the annexation of Afghan territory, and that Mr. Gladstone's return to power was the only event to prevent its realization. There is not an atom of foundation for this belief, as no one could have been more anxious to withdraw from Afghanistan than Lord Lytton. He had even devised a plan which, whether it is praised or criticized, offered a feasible means of executing this wish and intention. He proposed to recognize different chiefs in different provinces, and with one of them, Shere Ali Khan Wali of Candahar, he had even concluded a definite convention. This attempt to carry out in Afghanistan a policy of *divide ut imperes* cannot be fairly judged, because it was nipped in the bud, not by the intervention of the new British ministers, but by the appearance on the scene of a fresh and important actor.

Reference has been made more than once to the Afghan chief Abdur Rahman, son of Afzul, and grandson of Dost Mahomed, who, at the time of Shere Ali's establishment on the throne, sought shelter in Russian territory, and received a pension and a residence at Samarcand. When General Kaufmann was intriguing with Shere Ali in the early stages of the war, he removed Abdur Rahman to Tashkent, as being at a greater distance from the frontier. The events of the winter 1879–80 made Abdur Rahman more than ever anxious to tempt fortune once more in his native country, and at the same time the Russians had no longer any strong reason for holding him back. It is impossible to say to what extent they helped him. The Amir represents that he received no tangible assistance from them, and merely states that he was grateful to them for the permission to depart. Be that as it may, he crossed the Oxus early in the year 1880, and was not long in collecting round him a considerable following, with which he established his authority over Badakshan, Kunduz and Balkh.

When the news of Abdur Rahman's arrival reached Cabul, it was at once seen that it would be advantageous if an arrangement could be come to with him to take over the government of Cabul. There was no eligible competitor on the spot, and if he would constitute himself Afghan ruler for the nonce, he would greatly simplify the withdrawal of the army and the execution of the policy of Lord Lytton. Accordingly a preliminary letter of inquiry, asking what were his plans and intentions, was addressed to him by Sir Lepel Griffin. To this the Amir made a diplomatic reply, but the letter encouraged him to come south of the Hindu Kush range. At the end of April, 1880, a formal suggestion was made that Abdur Rahman should take over the government of Cabul, which we were willing to place in his hands. Abdur Rahman's reply to this made it clear that, while he was willing to occupy and rule Cabul, that state alone would not satisfy him, and that while he was not loth to render services, he quite expected to receive benefits in return. It was a business-like communication, defining the principles which have regulated his policy ever since. Owing to the separate arrangement referred to about Candahar, Sir Lepel Griffin's reply, dated 14th June, had necessarily to make a limitation in that case, but with this exception he was prepared, on the part of the Government of India, to recognize him as ruler of the rest of Afghanistan, including Herat. The Amir would not of course consent to the severance of Candahar from his sway, but he saw the practical value of the conclusion of some terms with the English, and the negotiations continued. On 22nd July the Amir was proclaimed at Cabul, and when news came on the 29th of the battle of Maiwand, a three days' conference was held at Zimma between Abdur Rahman and Sir Lepel Griffin. At its close a written communication was handed to the Amir, setting forth the engagements we considered that we had contracted towards him, renewing the old promise of support against unprovoked aggression, and refraining from pressing the right for an English Resident at Cabul. No subsidy was given him, but a sum of nineteen lakhs, a quantity of artillery, and the forts and cantonment, were offered as a parting present. On 8th August General Roberts set out for Candahar, and two days later Sir Donald Stewart, after a brief interview with Abdur Rahman, left for Peshawur.

At the moment when we were negotiating with Abdur Rahman, the other Afghan chief of importance, Ayoob Khan, had appeared on the scene. Yakoob's younger brother had long ruled Herat when the war broke out, but he took no part in it until the spring of 1880. The principal cause of his taking action at all seems to have been jealousy of Abdur Rahman, or the more practical fear that his success would put an end to the chances of the Shere Ali branch of the family. But there is no doubt that the weakening of the British force at Candahar by the departure of Sir Donald Stewart greatly encouraged the Afghans of the West, and led them to think that a successful attack might be made on that place. Although rumours were prevalent, no definite or trustworthy news seems to have been received at Candahar about the approach of a large Afghan army from Herat. General Primrose, who had been left in command at Candahar, did, however, conceive it to be necessary to despatch a small force towards Girishk, on the Helmund, with the object of collecting information, and of giving confidence to the garrison in that place under the Wali, our nominee for Candahar.

This force made up a weak brigade of 2,300 men, including six companies of the 66th regiment and a battery of horse artillery, and was under the command of General Burrows. On 14th July the Wali's troops mutinied and went over to Ayoob Khan, but General Burrows was able to prevent them carrying off their guns. In consequence of this event, the English commander retired thirty-five miles nearer Candahar, while Ayoob crossed the Helmund with 12,000 men and thirty-six guns. Instead of promptly retiring on Candahar, General Burrows remained in an exposed position doing nothing, while his communications were threatened and even interrupted with his base. Somewhat alarmed at this possibility, and by rumours that Ayoob was on the point of occupying Maiwand, Burrows moved his force towards that place in the hope of being in time to forestall him. The two forces came into contact in the morning of 27th July, near this village. The Afghans were screened by a mist, and the English commander would not believe that they were in any great force. As a matter of fact, they outnumbered the British by nearly six to one, and possessed thirty-six guns, while the strength of their position, protected by a nullah in front, was very formidable. The British were completely outmanœuvred as well as outnumbered. None the less, the British regiment behaved so well that at first it seemed as if there would be no disaster. A panic seized some of the native troops, who fled in confusion, offering little or no resistance to the Ghazis, and the two regiments of native cavalry would not charge to assist the handful of European soldiers, who continued to fight to the bitter end. Our loss amounted to nearly 1,000 killed and 200 wounded, besides 330 followers killed. Two guns were lost.

Such was the fatal battle of Maiwand, the one military disaster that marked our two years' occupation of Afghanistan in 1878–80. It produced an immense impression, and although not so serious as was at first believed, when the reports spoke of the destruction of a British brigade, it revived and strengthened the old prejudice, describing Afghanistan as unlucky. The consequences of this reverse were not serious, and they were also quickly repaired. The tribes round Candahar indeed revolted, and for a time the town was besieged, but a considerable relieving force under General Phayre was prepared, and moved from the Bombay Presidency through the Bolan towards Afghanistan. Long before it could reach its destination another British force had struck the decisive blow, and retrieved Maiwand.

The news of that battle reached Cabul on 28th or 29th July. On the latter of those days[1] General Roberts

[1] I cannot deny myself the satisfaction of stating that, on that very day, I wrote a leading article recommending the same move, which appeared in the *Standard* of 30th July. "From this force (at Cabul) it would be easy to form a column for active service of 10,000 men. This move would possess many advantages, and it may be pressed upon the consideration of the authorities.

made an offer to lead a relieving column from Cabul to Candahar, and although some hesitation was shown this offer was accepted after reference to London. General Roberts's proposal once adopted was put promptly into execution, and on the 8th August he began his memorable march at the head of a picked force of between nine and ten thousand men. The distance he had to traverse was 300 miles, through a hostile and, for the most part, barren region, and the season of the year was that of the greatest heat. The army encountered no serious opposition at any point, and after a march of twenty-one days it reached the neighbourhood of Candahar and of Ayoob's camp in a strong position in the hills. The feat of conveying this force in safety and good condition, with supplies that never exceeded a sufficient quantity for five days, was rightly deemed remarkable, and established the reputation of General Roberts.

The battle which resulted in the complete defeat of Ayoob was fought on 1st September at Masra, seven or eight miles north of Candahar, the Afghan position being one strongly fortified on the hills above the old city of Candahar. After a stubborn defence the Afghans were turned out of the villages as well as of their entrenchments with heavy loss—estimated at 1,000

The spectacle of a British army advancing from one point of Afghanistan to another would produce a great effect on the tribes.

killed—and the greater part of their artillery was taken. Ayoob fled to Herat with the more disciplined portion of his army, while many of the irregulars escaped to join Abdur Rahman.

In consequence of these military operations the withdrawal of the British garrison from Candahar was indefinitely postponed, while the question of its permanent fate was deliberately considered by the Government. Very strong arguments could be advanced in favour of the retention of Candahar, but Mr. Gladstone's Government could not bring itself to sanction the step "because it would be going further in the direction of annexation than Lord Lytton had intended." While the final decision was postponed until the next year, a change in the surrounding circumstances contributed to mould it. The Wali, Shere Ali Khan, whose forces had deserted him before Maiwand, came to the conclusion that he did not possess the power to govern Candahar, and voluntarily annulled his convention with the British, preferring safety and a pension in India to the perils and uncertainties of an Afghan principality. When Parliament re-assembled at the beginning of 1881 the Candahar question was one of the subjects most closely discussed, and every effort was made to induce the Government to come to a decision worthy of our prestige and beneficial to our trade. The publication of the secret Russian correspondence found at Cabul, and General Skobeleff's capture of Geok Tepe about the same time were both calculated to arouse public interest in the question. But Mr. Gladstone, who was then in the act of condoning Majuba Hill, would not listen to the retention of Candahar.

Before the end of April, 1881, all the British troops had left Candahar, and Abdur Rahman moved down a force to take their place. He established a considerable garrison, because he knew that Ayoob would infallibly return from Herat to challenge his authority. Ayoob had been beaten by the English, but he was still a popular hero, and he possessed a considerable fighting force. The whole of the Shere Ali faction was also on his side because Yakoob's son, Musa Jan, was at Herat. The mollahs also declared for him because he was a Ghazi. A few weeks after the occupation of Candahar the two armies were in close proximity with each other on the Helmund, and in the first battle, fought at Karez near Girishk, on 20th July, Ayoob's forces were victorious, and some days later took possession of Candahar. As the news reached Europe it seemed that the power of Abdur Rahman had been subverted at the first shock. But the defeat was not as great as it was represented to be, and Abdur Rahman, hastening from Cabul with all the troops he could command, won a decisive victory over his rival on 22nd September. The battle was fought on the site of old Candahar, and lasted seven hours. The Amir attributed his victory to the cowardice of Ayoob, and to the return to their allegiance of four regiments which had abandoned his cause in the earlier action. Ayoob again fled westwards, but Herat was no longer available as a place of shelter, because the Amir had sent his governor in Turkistan, Abdul Kudus Khan, to attack it from the north. This attack was completely successful, and on 4th August Herat was wrested from Ayoob's governor. Ayoob was consequently compelled to flee into Persia, and the Shere Ali party, deprived of its natural leaders, lost its importance, and was no longer able to dispute for supremacy with Abdur Rahman.

The unification of Afghanistan under Abdur Rahman's sceptre was completed by a succession of victorious operations which culminated in the conquest of the long unconquered country of Kafiristan. In 1883 the Amir crushed the Shinwaris and the robbers of the Sala Khel tribe, causing two towers to be erected out ot the heads of the rebels killed in the several encounters. In other words he struck terror into the hearts of the worst marauders along the main route from Cabul to India. In 1884 Abdur Rahman attacked Maimena where the Governor, Dilawar Khan, refused to recognize his authority and maintained his independence. After a few days' siege Maimena surrendered, and Dilawar was put in prison at Cabul. A more serious affair was the Ghilzai revolt of 1886-7, which at one moment seriously threatened the Amir's position. It was caused first of all by the partiality of the Ghilzais to Ayoob Khan and by the intrigues of Mushk-i-Alim, and in the second place by the Amir insisting on their paying taxes. The fighting proved long and arduous, covering the whole of the region from Herat to Ghuzni, and Ayoob endeavoured to escape from Persia to take part in it. He was stopped on the frontier, and after some wandering in the Persian deserts gave himself up to the Government of India, who assigned him a small pension. He is still living in India, but not at the same station as his brother Yakoob.

The most serious affair of all was the rebellion of Ishak Khan in 1888. Ishak, son of Azim, for a few months Amir in 1868, was Abdur Rahman's first cousin, and had been left by him Governor of Turkistan when he came to Cabul in 1880. Ishak had sworn on the Koran to be loyal and true to Abdur Rahman. He posed as a very strict Mahomedan, and acquired a very considerable reputation as a saint. He also collected arms and money, and obtained the special sympathy and support of the Turkomans resident in his Governorship. He might have concealed his treachery for a further period if he had not heard that the Amir was seriously ill, and even dying. He then declared himself Amir by coining money with his own inscription; but he soon discovered that the Amir was not dying, and that he had only unmasked himself. On learning what his cousin had done the Amir sent a large army under his general, Gholam Hyder, who had made a reputation in the Ghilzai war, to attack Ishak, while his garrison in Badakshan menaced Balkh from the east. A keenly-contested battle was fought at Ghazni Gak, near Tashkurgan, on 29th September. After alternations of fortune victory rested with the Amir, chiefly through Ishak's cowardice, and Ishak fled to Russian territory, where he is still living on a small pension paid by Russia. After this battle the Amir went himself to Balkh to put things in order. He remained there two years, and, among other things, he built at Dehdadi (near Mazar-i-Sherif) "the largest and strongest fort" in his dominions.

The conquest of Kafiristan was the most remarkable of all the Amir's military achievements. He attacked this difficult country from four sides, and he selected the winter because the Kafirs would be less able to resist at that season. In a campaign of forty days, during the winter of 1895–6, his generals conquered the country, and removed the population to the Paghman province, near Cabul. The Amir has repopulated Kafiristan with military settlements, and has made its capital, Kullum, a strong fortress. The subjugation of the Kafirs seems to have been effected not only very successfully, but with much forbearance, and even generosity. The Amir now possesses a considerable Kafir contingent in his army.

Our last wars in Afghanistan, after overthrowing

the very unstable authority of the weak and capricious Shere Ali, have therefore resulted in the consolidation of Afghanistan into a stronger and more united state than it had ever been at any prior stage of its history. But our policy can claim no share in the credit for this result. It was the exclusive work of Abdur Rahman, who has proved himself one of the most accomplished rulers that any Asiatic country ever possessed. The old formula of our policy in Afghanistan ran in the words that it should be "strong, united, and friendly." Abdur Rahman has beyond all doubt made it "strong and united" for his own lifetime, and there is every reason to hope that his eldest son Habibullah, who has been carefully trained for the task of administration by his father, will prove a capable successor. Whether it is as "friendly" must remain an open question, which will be decided by our own policy as much as by the intentions of the Afghan ruler at the time when political and still more commercial problems may emerge from their present dormant phase and imperatively demand prompt solution.

Chapter X

THE LAST FIVE VICEROYS

IN the time of Lord Northbrook the political school in India, which had assumed to itself the title of Young Bengal, had begun to make itself obtrusive, but it did not assert itself very prominently until after the arrival of Lord Ripon, who was supposed to represent a Government that would concede whatever was asked of it. Of course this supposition was in the main erroneous, but Bengalese students and journalists took seriously what were merely the rhetorical flourishes of the hustings. Delegates were sent to England, the co-operation of Mr. John Bright was enlisted and easily obtained for public meetings, and the National Congress in India was established as an annual affair. Lord Ripon, representing the Gladstone Government, had to do something to fulfil, or at least to pacify, the expectations that its political programme had created. These were not satisfied by the general policy pursued by Lord Ripon in matters of internal administration, in the repeal of the Vernacular Press

Act enforced by Lord Lytton, and in freeing the trade of the country from its last remaining shackles. Lord Ripon revived and continued Lord Mayo's policy of the decentralisation of financial control and the development of local self-government; but something of a more sensational nature was wanted to show the native agitators that the Liberal Ministry was prepared to inaugurate a period of reckless and unqualified concession. The measure was found in the mischievous and unnecessary Ilbert Bill.

This Bill was entitled a Criminal Jurisdiction Bill, and it was directed against the status of the British community which had hitherto enjoyed an indefeasible right to a special jurisdiction and to trial by judges, or where necessary of juries exclusively composed of their own race. The measure named proposed to alter all this by a stroke of the pen, and to subject Europeans like natives to the Indian Code, and also to be tried by mixed juries and native magistrates. It was not an improvement of the status of the natives, and consequently it roused little enthusiasm in native circles. But it was a serious infraction and diminution of the privileges that the British community not unnaturally regarded as their inherited rights, and consequently its proposal was received with a storm of opposition and indignation that has never been surpassed. Even those who were least excited on the subject described the Bill as "probably innocuous, but perfectly unnecessary." The gravest fault in it was that it was a disturbing Bill, and any step that tends to disturb the delicate position of affairs in India is not merely a fault, but a crime.

The agitation against the Ilbert Bill was not confined to India. The opposition to the measure was not less emphatic in Parliament than among civilians on the spot, and Lord Ripon, alarmed by what threatened to become a general strike of the officials who alone rendered government in India possible, suspended the progress of the Bill. In London an attempt had been made by the Government to minimise the importance and significance of the agitation, but this attitude could not be kept up. Finally a compromise was decided upon. The Criminal Jurisdiction Bill became a harmless and useless addition to the Statute Book of India, shorn of the features which had made the Ilbert Bill a peril. None the less the accompanying agitation had been mischievous, and it had widened instead of narrowing the gulf between the European and native communities.

Lord Ripon had been sent out to India with instructions generally to undo everything that Lord Lytton had done in matters of frontier policy, and it must always be considered one of the most typical cases of historical irony that he was called upon to complete his predecessor's policy and even to do a great deal more. It is no secret that the first intentions of the

Liberal Ministry in 1880 were not merely to retire from Afghanistan, but to give up the Pishin Valley and Sibi which had been ceded to us by the Treaty of Gandamak. Several important personages would have gone further and evacuated Quetta, the occupation of which was pronounced to be the *causa teterrima belli*, and they might, but for Maiwand and the Russian advance east of the Caspian, have carried the day. Those events rendered it necessary to adhere to the terms of the treaty with Yakoob Khan, and some members of the Government were in favour even of prolonging the occupation of Candahar until it was seen how Abdur Rahman would progress in the consolidation of his power. The evacuation of Candahar was, however, carried out in the manner and with the consequences described in the last chapter.

When Lord Ripon was made responsible for the foreign policy of India, he found that the execution of the policy of indifference and inaction that had seemed so easy in England was not possible. Russia was rapidly bridging the distance from her frontier which had enabled the advocates of "masterly inactivity" to ridicule the Russian menace to India with a show of plausibility. A deaf ear could no longer be turned to the Amir's representations that he was in a difficult position, and that while he was willing to do our work, he expected to be paid for it. It was notorious that if we did not listen to him Abdur Rahman would not scruple to turn for consolation to his old paymasters in Turkistan. In the summer of 1883 Abdur Rahman had made himself master in his own country. He was ruler of Candahar and Herat as well as of Cabul. He was no longer an adventurer, but a Ruler established on his throne. In July, 1883, Lord Ripon decided to give him a fixed annual subsidy of twelve lakhs, or nominally one hundred and twenty thousand pounds per annum. The decision was a wise one. It deserves the epithet of heroic on the part of politicians who had sworn on the altar of Lord Lawrence's Masterly Inactivity that one of the things never to be granted was "a fixed annual subsidy." It is regrettable, however, that the Government neglected to make some arrangement with the Ameer to deter him from putting in force a prohibitive tariff, and thus strangling the foreign trade of India. We gave him much, and we asked for nothing tangible in return, which is never wise policy.

Lord Ripon's viceroyalty, therefore, was rendered important, not as was expected by our effacement in Afghanistan, but by our taking a very pronounced step towards establishing our influence in that country on a firm basis. Before Lord Ripon left India, events were to show that the decision had not been taken a moment too soon. In February, 1884, Russia effected an arrangement with the Turcomans of Merv for the recognition of her authority, and thus her hold was established over a place which she had repeatedly declared that she had no intention of annexing. This event entailed two important consequences. It became obvious to every one that our relations with the Amir should be strengthened, and that the boundaries of Afghanistan should be clearly defined. To secure the former object, an interview was arranged between the Viceroy and the Amir, but it was not carried out until after the departure of Lord Ripon. With regard to the latter object, various proposals were mooted, and pending an agreement between the Governments of Great Britain and Russia, it was proposed to demarcate the Afghan frontier ourselves, and notify Russia that we would not tolerate its infraction. Had this bold and proper course been taken, we should have saved ourselves much trouble and anxiety, besides greatly increasing our dignity. Instead of taking this step, an arrangement was concluded in August, 1884, for a joint Anglo-Russian Commission to delimit the Afghan frontier. The Amir was to depute an Afghan Commissioner to assist the British officer, but all decisions were to be left to the European officers, and behind them to their respective Governments.

The British Government appointed as its Commissioner General Sir Peter Lumsden, an officer of the highest distinction and character, who possessed a considerable personal acquaintance of the Afghans through having resided at Candahar during the Mutiny period.

It could not have made a better choice. On the other hand, Russia nominated Major Alikhanoff, a young officer of very inferior grade, who had made his reputation by visiting Merv as a spy. As the intention seemed to be to minimise the importance of the Joint Commission, some protest was made, and in place of Alikhanoff, General Komaroff, an officer of adequate standing was appointed Russian Commissioner. While General Lumsden was sent out from England, the Anglo-Indian force that was to serve as an escort proceeded under the command of Colonel (now Sir) West Ridgeway to the Herat province by the Nushki route through Beluchistan. Before the Commission had actually begun its work, Lord Ripon's viceroyalty had ended, and that of Lord Dufferin had begun.

Unlike many of his predecessors, Lord Dufferin went to India with an established reputation, to which the Indian Viceroyship in ordinary times could have added little. As a brilliant orator, a skilful Governor-General in Canada, a man who in letters and affairs had played a distinguished and versatile part, and added grace and dignity to whatever he undertook, Lord Dufferin had shown himself the worthy representative of the gifted race from which he sprang. High expectations were formed of his Indian rule in anticipation, and in the result they were not disappointed. Public opinion had soon tired of the wearying platitudes and unattainable

THE MARQUIS OF DUFFERIN AND AVA.

[*To face page* 308.

theories that had formed the stock-in-trade of the friends of Young Bengal, and which, in the attempted application of a small portion of them, had nearly set the whole peninsula by the ears. It was time to strike a higher and different note, and every one felt with confidence that in Lord Dufferin Mr. Gladstone had selected the right man to do it. Even before he left England the new Viceroy took occasion to say before an audience of the most influential persons associated with or interested in India that "in dealing with even a friendly Russia we should mainly rely on our own vigilance and valour."

Lord Dufferin arrived in India in December, 1884, by which time all the preliminaries were completed for the commencement of the delimitation, and our party was on the frontier waiting for the arrival of the Russians. But Russia followed a dilatory policy, and was no doubt thinking of how best she could benefit herself from the difficulties of the British Government through the position in the Soudan and the fall of Khartoum. With that object, M. Lessar, a French engineer who had become a Russian subject, was sent on a special mission to London to press the ethnological claims of Russia to a frontier coming down to the Paropamisus. While this agent was busy in London, the Russian Government decided to make a military demonstration on the Heri Rud and Murghab, with the object of inducing or compelling the Afghan forces to retire from their advanced positions, especially at Penjdeh. In consequence of this demonstration, General Lumsden was obliged to shift his camp farther south, and to a point farther away from Penjdeh, where Afghan and Russian troops were in closest proximity. In front of that place was a brick bridge across the Kushk called Pul-i-Khisti ; that is, the brick bridge. On 30th March General Komaroff attacked and routed the Afghan force that held the bridge. The Russian commander in his explanation stated that he had first called upon the Afghans to evacuate their positions—a demand that he had not the smallest right to make. The Afghans refused compliance, whereupon General Komaroff, after offering them every provocation to commence hostilities, marched against them in overwhelming strength of men and artillery. The Russians numbered at least 4,000 men, whereas the Afghans at Pul-i-Khisti were not one-tenth of that number. The Afghans fought courageously, and probably lost 200 killed.

This inexcusable attack, in defiance of all the laws of international relationship and even of humanity, was an open affront to the British Government. Even Mr. Gladstone was stirred to anger, and gave the House of Commons a fine oration about "the book which was open and could not be closed." But it was an occasion for deeds and not for words, and Mr. Gladstone was resolved not to go to war for the blood of a few Afghans. The Russian diplomatists, official and unofficial, had well gauged the depth of his indignation. They told their Government that Mr. Gladstone would not go to war, and they knew what they were talking about. It was one of those occasions when the country missed Lord Beaconsfield.

At the same time the position was rendered more embarrassing for the Liberal Premier by the fact that the Amir Abdur Rahman was at that very moment the guest of the Viceroy, and Lord Dufferin might not prove able or willing to bring the Afghan ruler to a frame of mind to overlook or feign indifference to the massacre—for it was nothing less—of some hundreds of his soldiers. The Amir says in his Autobiography, " But I was not a man to get excited, and therefore took the matter calmly as a lesson for the future." This guarded and vague statement is not very satisfactory, especially when read by the light of the very inaccurate and accusatory description he gives of the fight at Pul-i-Khisti, and of the part taken therein by English officers. Both General Lumsden and Major Yate have effectually refuted those charges, but it is a pity that the Amir should labour under such misconceptions. On the other hand, it is impossible not to sympathize with the general view he takes of British policy at that juncture, and not to share the contempt he expresses for the conduct of our Government when it received a slap in the face. The Amir then did not get excited, but left the British Government to do what it thought right. Lord Dufferin was consequently able to satisfy the authorities in London that the Amir would not on this occasion call upon them to fulfil their engagement to protect him against unprovoked aggression.

This was sufficient to enable the broken thread of the negotiations with Russia to be retied, and after a few months' correspondence the work of delimitation began in the autumn. An important change had in the meantime occurred. General Lumsden had either expressed his desire to return or had been recalled, and the Frontier Commission, diminished in numbers, was left in charge of Colonel Ridgeway. The Commissioners were not to attempt to decide any difficulties that arose, but to refer them in all cases for the decision of their respective Governments. They were to trace a workable frontier, while the efforts of the British Foreign Office were concentrated on obtaining fresh admissions from Russia as to Afghanistan being outside her sphere. It would be beside our purpose and beyond our space to enter here into the details of the disputes which arose about Zulficar, the Kushk Valley, and Khoja Saleh ; but it may be mentioned that M. Lessar, having done all he could in London to advance his ethnological frontier, proceeded to the Afghan frontier as Russian Commissioner to give it actual form. All these disputes, with the exception of the last, were settled on the spot without serious difficulty ; but when it looked as if the Khoja Saleh difficulty might develop into a second

Penjdeh affair, the British Government gave orders for the return of its representatives, which nipped the peril in the bud. Thanks to this firm action by Lord Salisbury's Government, the whole of the Khoja Saleh district was left to the Afghans. In October, 1886, the British Commission returned to India through Cabul, where the Amir gave it an honourable reception. In the following summer a protocol was signed by this country and Russia about this portion of the Afghan frontier. Only one trifling dispute about some pasture rights in the Kushk Valley has since arisen, and this was promptly and amicably settled in 1893 by Colonel Yate.

Afghanistan was not the only field of foreign affairs that attracted attention during Lord Dufferin's rule in India. Before he arrived at Calcutta our relations with Upper Burma, where King Thebaw maintained his tyrannical regime, had attracted attention and aroused anxiety. Our diplomatic relations with this despot were carried on in what was called a surreptitious manner, and trade languished throughout the whole of the upper valley of the Irrawaddi. Thebaw had developed into a drunken and ferocious despot, and constant petitions from Rangoon represented the situation as intolerable. His weakness matched his wickedness, and when the wild Kakhyen tribes burnt his frontier town of Bhamo he had no means of punishing them or protecting his subjects. It was not, however, until the autumn of

1885 that the question became serious through a dispute between the Burma Trading Corporation and the king; but the true gravity of the position was caused by French intrigue at Mandalay. The project for a commercial treaty with Burma was even placed before the Paris Chamber, and a report by M. Lanessan explained the efforts made by France to gain a footing in the country, which seemed at last on the eve of success. It was evidently necessary to stop this intrigue, not only in the interests of India, but of the friendly relations of England and France. When it was found that arms were being imported into Upper Burma, it became clear that no time should be lost. An ultimatum was accordingly presented at Mandalay, and an expedition was ordered to carry out the threatened punishment. Thebaw was as obstinate as he was helpless. Probably he was incapable of reform. The expedition crossed his frontier, Mandalay was captured, and Thebaw was deported to Calcutta, where he died some years later. On New Year's Day, 1886, Lord Dufferin issued his proclamation annexing Upper Burma, and thus was fulfilled Lord Dalhousie's prediction, thirty years before, that we held that country in the hollow of our hand. The annexation of this vast and fertile kingdom, with incalculable wealth and resources, which, even now, after fifteen years of our rule, are scarcely touched, was an historical event of the first importance, and would alone make Lord Dufferin's viceroyalty famous.

Several matters of interest occurred during Lord Dufferin's stay in India with regard to our relations with the Native States. In the first place, the strong fortress of Gwalior was, in 1885, handed back to the Maharaja Scindiah—a wise and generous step. As an equivalent we obtained possession of Jhansi. In the autumn of 1887 the Nizam of Hyderabad made a remarkable offer of sixty lakhs towards frontier defence against Russia. The Government did not think right to accept this offer in the form proposed, but it aroused much enthusiasm, and was the primary cause of the creation and organization of the Imperial service force representing the *élite* of the feudatory armies in the Native States. This force provides a material addition to our military strength in India, and has already on several occasions rendered valuable service in the field.

During Lord Dufferin's term the post of Commander-in-Chief of the Bombay army was held by H.R.H. the Duke of Connaught, who was present at the Durbar at Rawal Pindi. The fact was interesting as showing the increasing importance attached to Indian matters.

Perhaps the event that will be longest remembered with grateful feelings by the peoples of India in connection with Lord Dufferin's viceroyalty was one not directly associated with himself. The Fund for the provision of Medical Aid for Native Women, which will always be known as the Countess of Dufferin's Fund, instituted by that lady in 1885, conferred an immense boon on the women of India, who were condemned to suffer in silence from the incapacity or quackery of native doctors, or from the impossibility of any doctors at all being allowed into the zenanas. The provision of female doctors and nurses supplied a national want and every year increases the benefit enjoyed by the formerly helpless and neglected women of India. Many Viceroys have conferred benefits on the Indian community, but it was reserved for Lady Dufferin to bestow a blessing that will never be forgotten as long as gratitude endures.

Before leaving India, in December, 1888, Lord Dufferin made a tour, delivering a series of brilliant orations that will well repay perusal. All he modestly claimed for himself was that he had "done something towards enabling India to read her own thoughts, to discriminate between vain dreams and possible realities, to comprehend real wants as distinct from ideas which are neither needs nor wants, and which cannot be given to her." His work in India was rewarded with the title of Marquis of Dufferin and Ava,[1] the latter name, being added to record the memorable conquest of the country of which it was the most famous capital.

The next Viceroy was the Marquis of Lansdowne, who arrived in India at the end of 1888. During his

[1] The Amir Abdur Rahman, a keen judge of men, says in his Autobiography: "Lord Dufferin, who was such a statesman that a wiser and more clever ruler than he has never ruled in India."

government the Afghan question again became interesting, and passed through more than one critical phase of which the history still remains concealed in "secret and confidential" documents. Abdur Rahman's way of looking at things was so different from the views of our officials that a certain coolness became perceptible in our relations with him. He thought to enhance his own dignity by ignoring the Viceroy and dealing direct with the Imperial Government in London. He managed to send a personal letter to Lord Salisbury, but this irregular way of proceeding could not be tolerated, and he was told firmly but kindly that he must arrange matters with the Viceroy. With that object it was proposed to send Lord Roberts on a special mission to Cabul; but the Amir chose to take exception to our representative, on the ground that he had many enemies in Afghanistan, and that he was an advocate of the Forward Policy. He also objected to the size of his escort; but the real reason of his objecting to Lord Roberts was that he had heard that while he would give much to the Amir, he would also expect some tangible concessions in return. When Abdur Rahman evaded receiving Lord Roberts, our relations with him were threatened with a serious rupture, and for a brief period precautionary measures were enforced on the frontier. It was not, indeed, for more than two years after the refusal to receive Lord Roberts that they regained their former cordiality.

The Amir takes much credit to himself for the preservation of peace, but he omits to say that it was more threatened by his own warlike policy and incitements to his people to declare a Jehad or Holy War than by any projects on the part of Lord Lansdowne. We had helped him very materially, while his fiscal policy towards us could not have been more hostile, and his religious writings and proclamations were those of an enemy. We were entitled to ask for an improvement in the conditions under which the frontier trade languished. The movements of the Russians in the Upper Oxus region round the Pamirs did something to make him more amenable to reason. The collision at Somatash (July, 1892) between Colonel Yanoff and a small Afghan post of ten or twelve men, who were all killed, revived the memory of Penjdeh, and convinced the Amir of the necessity of being on good terms with the British Government if he was going to have a dispute with Russia.

Accordingly a fresh mission was arranged to proceed to Cabul under the charge of Sir Mortimer Durand, the Foreign Secretary. It arrived at Cabul in September, 1893, a few weeks before Lord Lansdowne's departure from India. The Durand Mission resulted in some important arrangements. A boundary was drawn on the map between British and Afghan territory. By this arrangement Chitral, Swat and other hill districts, including part of the Waziri country, were

THE MAHARAJA OF KASHMIR.

[To face page 318.

assigned to us, while the Amir acquired the right to annex Kafiristan. He also acquired an increased subsidy, eighteen lakhs in place of twelve. Thus the clouds were cleared away from the horizon of Afghanistan, and to give some proof of his friendly sentiments the Amir sent his second son, Nasrullah, to England in 1895. It is no secret, however, that he still clings to his old wish to be represented by a diplomatic agent in London, and perhaps a way may be found to gratify him without diminishing the dignity of the Viceroy, and at the same time by securing some counter benefits for our trade.

The desirability of clearly defining the limits of authority between India and Afghanistan had been made clear by events in Chitral, and also by the proved necessity of advancing the borders of Cashmere to Gilgit in one direction, and Hunza in another. This had been forced upon us by the movements of Russian officers. One of them, named Grombtchevsky, had succeeded in making his way across the Pamir to Hunza in 1888–9, and had gone so far as to promise its chief the protection of the Great White Czar. The reply to this piece of impertinence was the Hunza-Nagar expedition, which resulted in the easy conquest of the valley, and in showing what the Czar's protection was worth. A neglected postern door in the Indian frontier was thus effectually closed.

During the viceroyalty of Lord Lansdowne the late

Duke of Clarence, the eldest son of King Edward VII., visited India in the winter of 1889–90, and in the latter year the present Emperor Nicholas of Russia also made a tour through India. Minor troubles occurred in Manipore, a hill state bordering on Assam, where some English officials lost their lives in defending the Residency; Sikkim, with the Chinese, or rather, with the Tibetans; and in the Black Mountain, where General Lockhart began in 1892 the last series of frontier wars and expeditions, which continued for some years with scarcely any intermission. It is too soon to attempt any judgment on Lord Lansdowne's viceroyalty, and the opinion may even be hazarded that the future historian will find it extremely difficult to treat the governments of Lord Dufferin's three successors otherwise than in a group. But it would be an omission not to record that during Lord Lansdowne's term of power, Lord Roberts, as Commander-in-Chief, carried out the re-organization of the Indian army, which made it of unusual efficiency, and ready to cope with dangers which fortunately did not arise.

After nearly five years' stay in India, Lord Lansdowne was very ready to return home and resume his place in the political world. Some difficulty was experienced in naming his successor. A Liberal Ministry was in office, and bestowed the appointment on General Sir Henry Norman, latterly a governor of various colonies, but whose best service had been done in India, where he had been on the Viceroy's Council. Formerly he was a strenuous advocate of "masterly inactivity," and perhaps the idea was to revert, as far as possible, to a less active policy than that pursued by Lord Dufferin and his successor. However that may be, Sir Henry Norman, after holding the appointment for sixteen days, came to the decision, on personal grounds, to decline the office. A substitute was then found in the Earl of Elgin and Kincardine, son of the nobleman who, after concluding memorable treaties with China and Japan, died Viceroy of India a few months after his appointment. This choice was admittedly an experiment quite sufficiently justified in the result, and perhaps intended as a sort of tribute to the memory of his father who had rendered the State great service, and who had done something to strengthen Lord Canning's efforts to propitiate native opinion by continuing them.

The earlier frontier negotiations with Russia had settled the boundary from the Persian border to the Oxus, and Nature had provided an admirable and clear dividing line in the main stream of that river to at least as far at Kila Wamar; but above that place the claims over the Pamirs and the little khanates abutting on the river valley might be pronounced uncertain. The two Governments accordingly agreed to send commissioners to delimit the frontier of Afghanistan on the Pamirs, and the Amir, agreeing to place his interests in the hands of the British, withdrew from Roshan and Shignan. In

September, 1895, General Gerard and General Schweikovski brought to a successful and satisfactory conclusion their labours for the delimitation of the north-east frontier of Afghanistan. This gave the Amir Wood's Lake (Lake Victoria) and a long strip of territory, embracing the Little Pamir and overlapping the whole of the Russian region past the Chinese frontier at Sirikul.

The same year that witnessed the close of the Pamir negotiations was marked by the troubles that followed the death of the Mehtar of Chitral and the siege and heroic defence of the Residency. The relief of Chitral, effected by the main expedition ably commanded by Sir Robert Low, and also by the gallant dash of the small rescuing force led across ice-bound mountain paths and glaciers by Colonel Kelly from Gilgit, was a very satisfactory performance. The severe frontier war in 1897 with the Afridis of the Khyber, culminating in the dramatic assault of Dargai, was less satisfactory from every point of view. Never did the savage hillmen fight with greater tenacity or skill, never were our losses (433 killed, including 36 officers; 1,321 wounded, including 81 officers) heavier, and the operations carried with them warning lessons, not merely of grave frontier perils, but also of serious military deficiencies. The greater part of Lord Elgin's term of power was consequently taken up with frontier operations, costly, irritating, and inconclusive, which formed no happy commencement for our assumption of control over the tribes of the No Man's Land, known to the Afghans as Yaghistan, "the country of the unruly."

Lord Elgin was Viceroy for rather more than five years, and in December, 1898, his successor, Lord Curzon, arrived to take over the task of governing India. He came with a great reputation and a very full and comprehensive programme. Fate has not so far been kind to its realization, for a terrible famine and the ravages of plague have combined to absorb attention, hamper progress, and damp courage and enthusiasm. Two years have passed. It is possible that those to come may be more productive of events that can be considered as in the category of making history.

One event may be distributed between the last two viceroyalties. In 1897, suddenly, like a bolt from the blue, just as in 1857, two English officials were murdered in the city of Poona, the old capital of the Peishwa and the headquarters of many intriguers among the Brahmins. It was said to be a protest against the precautionary measures taken for fighting the plague, and as there was much excitement throughout Western India from the same cause which found expression in riots at Bombay, the statement may have been correct. Some of the assailants were captured through the evidence of two brothers named Dravid, and duly punished. This took place while Lord Elgin was still in the country, and nothing more was thought about the subject until in February, 1899, shortly after Lord Curzon's arrival, the brothers Dravid were suddenly and mysteriously assassinated. This was a very bad affair, pointing clearly to the existence of some secret political organization, of which the European officials had no suspicion and could find no trace. Our rule in India has been for so many years tranquil and pleasant in regard to our relations with her vast population, that it is easy to forget the perils that must always lurk beneath the surface.

Chapter XI

THE MATERIAL PROGRESS OF INDIA

IT is very difficult, if not impossible, to ascertain the exact amount of material progress which India made during the 19th century, but there is no difficulty in measuring the result if we confine the retrospect to the closing forty-two years of the century, or, in other words, to the India of the Queen. During the first and slightly longer half of the century, statistics were compiled in an uncertain and fragmentary fashion, partly due to the fact that the absorption of India was in a transitional phase, and partly to the circumstance that statistical inquiry everywhere was in an embryonic stage. Until the year 1813 the administration of the East India Company was conducted on strictly business principles, every office and station containing its ledgers and journals in which the commercial transactions of the Company were duly recorded and set forth. In that year the Charter was shorn of its commercial monopoly in India, and gradually the ledgers disappeared, giving place to the registers of land assessment and the lists of license holders, that rightly find places in the offices of regularly constituted governments. The commercial monopoly with China remained in force for another twenty years, and it was generally believed that the profit of the China trade in tea, silk and opium met the deficit of the Indian revenue, and supplied the shareholders of the East India Company with their dividend. There was more exaggeration than truth in this statement, and Lord William Bentinck showed that India could pay for its government, and also supply a surplus. The India of his day was only a part of that which passed under the sway of the Queen in 1858, and the succession of wars of conquest and consolidation during the quarter of a century after his departure added to the burden of the Government in both accumulated debt and annual expenditure. Then came the Mutiny, which added £40,000,000 to the debt, diminished for the time the revenue by £2,000,000 per annum, and increased the yearly expenditure by another £2,000,000. Even if the statistics for the earlier period were available, they would be useless at least for purposes of comparison, because the conditions of government during the second period were radically altered.

The simple statement that the East India Company never attempted to take a census will bring home to the reader's mind the shortcomings of its system, or at least the fact that it had very partially answered all the duties of an efficient administration. The first Indian census was taken in 1871. It was attended by all the difficulties of a first attempt, and was admittedly imperfect. It returned the population at 185,537,859. The second census in 1881 was naturally more complete and trustworthy; by it the total was given at 198,790,853. The third census in 1891 showed that the population had risen to 221,172,952, and to these totals must be added the population of the native states, viz., in 1881, 55,191,742, and in 1891, 66,050,479. Owing to the famine and the plague the population of India, according to the census of 1901, did not quite reach 295,000,000.

With regard to the sources of revenue, the Land Tax constituted the main contributary in the Company's time, providing latterly more than half the total annual receipts. A marked change has been effected in this matter, for whereas the receipts from the land have risen more than thirty per cent. since 1858, they now constitute no more than one-third of the total revenue. This improvement has not been due to the imposition of direct taxation, but to the development and expansion of India's general trade. In 1858 the land revenue was about £17,900,000; in 1888 it was over £23,000,000; and in 1898 £25,683,000. Salt and opium have not varied greatly in the last ten years, the former averaging £8,000,000 per annum, as against £4,000,000 in 1856, and the latter ranging from a maximum of £8,500,000 to a minimum of £6,500,000, as against less than £5,000,000 under the Company. The wheat cultivation is practically a new development of less than twenty years' existence, and that of cotton was introduced during the American Civil War, and has flourished with periods of depression ever since. Tea is another of the new and much increased products of India, although it has been somewhat overshadowed by the more remarkable output of Ceylon.

The lightness of the taxation on land may be inferred from the fact that the area under cultivation has doubled in forty years, while, owing to increased irrigation and improved means of transport, production per acre has become larger, and profits have at the same time grown. The main result is consequently that the Land Tax represents a smaller proportion of the receipts or profits from land than formerly.

At the same time that there has been this great progress in the money value of the output of every form of cultivation, there has been a gratifying and creditable improvement in the position and rights of the peasant proprietor. He has acquired practically fixity of tenure, even where the Permanent Settlement in Bengal and the recognition of the feudal system prevailing in Oude seemed to have left the zemindars of the one and the talukdars of the other province in a position of ascendancy. This progress has no doubt been facilitated by the enormous growth of wealth and prosperity of the Bengal landlords, who have regarded the development of tenant right with a more indulgent eye because their rents have multiplied four- or five-fold in the century, and more than doubled in thirty years.

Among material benefits conferred on the peoples of India, none surpasses the cheapening of salt in price, and the provision of that article in sufficient quantities to reach every household in India. It is computed that the rate of consumption to-day is fifty per cent higher than it was twenty years ago, while the abolition of the internal customs barriers has greatly simplified the distribution of this essential article.

Immediately after the Mutiny import duties were placed on a number of articles through the necessity of providing in some way or other a revenue. But in Lord Mayo's time the first step was taken towards their abolition, and in 1882 all customs duties were abolished except on salt, opium, wine, beer, spirits, petroleum and arms among imports, and opium and rice among exports. The excise has been increased in amount, and the revenue from it has risen five-fold since 1860, from £1,100,000 to about £5,000,000. The Income Tax introduced by Mr. Wilson, and resented by the Services, brings in about £1,500,000. All incomes under 500 rupees are exempt, as well as those derived from land or agriculture, which are considered to be sufficiently taxed in other ways. The Forest Department is another branch of the administration created since the fall of the Company, and not merely discharges a most beneficent work for the good of the country, but also brings in a considerable and increasing revenue.

Among material agencies introduced into the country since 1858, telegraphs and railways are of course the most important. They had indeed made their appearance before the Mutiny in the time of Lord Dalhousie, who had laid down the lines of the railway policy since pursued; but practically speaking they had not emerged from the stage of infancy. In 1857 there were 3,000 miles of telegraph of single wire; in 1887 the total was 30,000 miles of distance with over 86,000 miles of wire, and in 1898 50,000 of distance and 150,000 of wire. The Telegraph Department now shows a profit after paying a fair interest on the capital invested. In 1857 only 300 miles of railway were working or in course of construction. In 1889 this figure exceeded 15,000, and in 1898 it had risen to nearly 22,000. The rates for both passengers and goods are among the lowest in the world. The capital invested in these lines reaches nearly £200,000,000, and the net earnings exceeded five per cent. Notwithstanding the progress made, it is quite clear that railway construction in India is not yet on a par with either the necessities of the country or the possibilities of profitable investment. The railway policy of the Indian Government has been marked by timidity and a reluctance to press the subject on the attention of the investing public in Great Britain or America. But its very necessities must inspire boldness, and suggest departure from established rules of a narrow and cramping tendency. Railways provide the only weapon for coping with famines, and at the same time it is to them that India can alone look for outlets for her trade towards the East and the West. Checked in the latter direction by the fiscal policy of the Amir, she will sooner or later be compelled to turn with the more energy to the East, where interior China awaits the arrival of the iron horse from either the Bay of Bengal or the Gulf of Tonquin. The ordinary needs of India, including Burma, will not be supplied until she has a railway system of at least 100,000 miles.

In canal construction, including the improvement of pre-existing systems, the Government has done immense good work, and here its energy has been in no degree restrained by timidity or political apprehensions. Some of the canals, as for instance those of Scinde, are very remunerative, both as providing water routes and as means of irrigation; others, like the Sone, are non-remunerative and solely valuable as auxiliaries and agencies in coping with famine. Ten years ago it was computed that nearly 12,000,000 acres took water from irrigation works. About four-fifths of the irrigation from the great canals, and nearly all the navigation canals, are due to works carried out since the transfer to the Crown. High roads and feeder roads have been largely constructed in connection with canals and railways, but in this respect much remains to be done, and the question of light railways has not even been approached with any serious purpose or tangible result.

All these improvements, partial and incomplete as they may be, have in their way contributed to the expansion of India's trade. In 1857 India's external trade was given approximately by the Court of Directors at £25,500,000 of exports and £14,250,000 of imports. In 1888 these figures had risen respectively to £90,500,000 and £65,000,000 and the rate of imports had increased more rapidly than that of exports, from which we may infer that India was getting higher value for her produce. On the land frontier, unfortunately, the increase in trade has not been remarkable owing to the want of energy in the Indian Government, and to its having allowed its neighbours to close their frontiers in the face of Indian trade. While the external trade has developed in the manner described, it must also be remembered that a great cotton and weaving industry has been developed; Indian coal is being worked in large quantities, and with profitable results; new staples have been introduced in its agriculture, and that the benefits and profit of these industries and enterprise are far from being confined to external trade, but are felt in that internal trade and prosperity which defy or elude computation. The introduction of manufactures, still in a very early stage, has supplied with employment a very considerable class which formerly had nothing but agriculture to look to.

The increased cultivation of tea, coffee, and jute has led to the opening of fresh avenues of employment in India; and although an agitation is now on foot to increase what are alleged to be the starvation wages of the cultivator, forty years have been needed to reveal this hardship, and now no doubt the existing situation admits of some improvement in the scale of payment without injuring the trade. Nearly half a million persons are employed in the tea and coffee gardens of the country alone, and there seems no doubt that coffee cultivation at least might be largely increased. Cinchona cultivation, introduced from Brazil, which has been very successful, must be mainly regarded as a benefit to the health of the community, and not as a source of profit. To its introduction must be attributed the important fact that febrifuges are sold at one-fifth and one-sixth the price of former times.

To give the reader an idea of the general condition of the people of India, the following passages from a very interesting official report[1] should suffice:—

"The circumstances and condition of the people vary greatly in different parts of India. The plain of the Ganges, from Seharanpur to Dacca, bears a rural popu-

[1] *Some of the Results of Indian Administration during the past Thirty Years*, 1889.

lation of 80,000,000, at a rate of 400 to 800 to the square mile. The Central Provinces, Burma, Assam, Rajputana, and considerable areas in the Punjab and in Bombay, carry a rural population of less than 150 to the square mile. There are provinces where the rainfall is always abundant, ranging from 60 to 100 inches in the year, and there are vast plains where the rainfall is precarious, and is often less than 10 inches a year. There are tracts like Scinde, Tanjore, and parts of the North-West Provinces where one half or more than one half of the cultivated area is irrigated in one way or another. The tenures and the distribution of profits from land vary greatly. In the Punjab and parts of the North-West Provinces, in Bombay and Madras, in Burma and Assam, the profits of agriculture go wholly or in great part direct to a sturdy, and in ordinary years a prosperous, peasantry who till most of the land themselves; while in Behar, Oude, and Orissa most of the profits of agriculture go to landlords. In these latter provinces the pressure of population and the competition for land have forced up rents so as to leave in some cases only a bare margin for the support of tenants with small holdings. In any comparison between the condition of our people in India and in Europe it has to be remembered that in India every one marries and marries early; that the population increases yearly at a rate varying from half per cent. per annum in the Upper Ganges plain to four per cent. per annum in Burma; that there is no poor law or system of poor relief, but there is everywhere a widespread and open-handed charity, so that the infirm, the old, the sick, the cripples, priests, besides many who prefer a mendicant's life, are in ordinary years supported by the alms of their neighbours. Further, it must be borne in mind that in rural India, from the nature of the climate and by immemorial custom, the poorer classes have fewer wants and can satisfy them more cheaply than in Europe. Clothes, warmth, shelter, furniture cost very little for a rural family in India, and the bulk of the population is fully satisfied with two meals a day of millet cakes or porridge, some pulse or green vegetable, salt and oil. In coast districts, in Southern India and in Moslem families, a little salt fish or meat is added to the daily meal."

"So far as ordinary tests can be applied the average Indian landholder, trader, ryot or handicraftsman is better off than he was thirty years ago. He consumes more salt, more sugar, more tobacco and far more imported luxuries and conveniences than he did a generation back. Where house-to-house inquiries have been made it has been found that the average villager eats more food and has a better house than his father; that to a considerable extent brass or other metal vessels have taken the place of the coarse earthenware vessels of earlier times, and that his family possess more clothes than formerly. The greater part of India lies between two extremes of intense poverty and exceptional prosperity. On the whole the standard of comfort in an average Indian villager's household is reported to be better than it was thirty years ago. It is quite certain that the population of India absorb and hoard far more of the precious metals than they did formerly, for during the past thirty years India's net absorption of gold and silver from outside has amounted to £342,500,000 of 10 rupees, or an average of £11,500,000 a year, while during the twenty-two years ending with 1857 the net absorption of the precious metals by India averaged only £3,250,000 a year."

With regard to the material condition of the labouring classes the Government of India instituted a systematic inquiry after the famine of 1877, and eight years later Lord Dufferin's Government expressed the opinion on such of the reports as had been received that "the condition of the lower classes of the agricultural population is not one which need cause any great anxiety at present." There were exceptions, however, in this conclusion. In Behar, for instance, forty per cent. of a population exceeding 15,000,000 was in a state of agricultural degradation. In Bengal, Oude and the North-West Provinces, which contain between them half the population of India, things were better. The industrious classes found no difficulty in supplying their primary wants, and are as a rule well nourished, and the consensus of opinion was that the people generally are not underfed. In the Punjab the general level is higher, no doubt due to the opening for labour supplied by the cultivation of wheat, and it is only in years of scarcity that a pinch is felt. In Burma the natives are better off than in any part of India. The standard of wages is three or four times higher, and there are no poor in the province. These statements based on official returns do not give an unreasonably over-coloured picture of the situation. But at the same time it has to be noted that if material prosperity has increased in India the population has also advanced at such a rapid rate through the maintenance of peace and the improved health conditions introduced that the consequences of any interruption of prosperity or of any natural calamity are rendered more serious and appalling. In plain words the margin between the conditions of ordinary life, as represented by a living wage and the possibility of obtaining an adequate supply of food, and a state of absolute want, if not starvation, is so narrow that no absolute conviction as to the prosperity of India may be cherished in disregard to possibilities of famine and disease that may at any moment intervene to change the picture and destroy the prospect. While taking credit to itself for the progress and improvements achieved, the Government of India is bound by its duty to be ever prepared for the worst, and in years of smiling plenty to provide for the lean years that are never very long in recurrence.

The prevalence of famine in India since we became responsible for its government, and especially since the fall of the Company, is a mortifying fact which we can neither deny nor satisfactorily explain away. But we may at least lay this amount of satisfaction to our hearts, that the evidence of real prosperity in the country is too clear and of too varied a character to admit of any doubt as to the general merit of our system. The causes of famine must be sought elsewhere than in the detection of flaws in the policy and proceedings of the Government of India. They may lie in the visitation of natural calamities against which precautionary measures can be and are taken, but which in a never-ending war between man and nature must sometimes end in the victory of the latter. Or the cause may be concealed in some economic conditions that have not been properly taken into account. But whatever it be there can be no question that the evil has been much aggravated, and that its consequences have been extended by the increase in the population that has accompanied our rule and provided one of the most convincing proofs of its beneficence.

After the great famine in Mysore and Southern India in 1877 a long cessation of famines followed, giving rise to an optimistic feeling in official circles which was expressed in the following passages from the report cited :

"Against famine, the greatest of all troubles that

befall the population of India, the country is more fitted to contend than it was thirty years ago. Over many tracts of India the rainfall is occasionally short or unseasonable, and sometimes it fails altogether. Such a disaster causes loss of harvests and scarcity of food, deepening sometimes into famine. Happily drought or famine never afflicts the whole of India at once, and prosperous provinces always have surplus food to spare for their suffering neighbours. During the past thirty years (1888) there have occurred the Northern India drought of 1860, the Orissa famine of 1866, scarcity in the Upper Ganges Valley during 1869 and 1878, drought in Bengal in 1874, and the great famine in 1877. For the last ten years India has been exempt from serious drought or famine, though local failures of crops have occurred such as would have caused much misery if improved means of communication had not enabled supplies of food to flow from surplus districts to meet the local scarcity. It is quite certain that our Indian provinces and the Indian administration generally are now better prepared to meet a famine than they were thirty years ago. Every province has its plan of relief organization and of relief works thought out and sanctioned beforehand. Everywhere the urban and village organization is stronger than it was. The crop area protected from drought by irrigation has more than doubled since 1857. Means of communication and food transport from province to province have been established such as never existed before, while roads and carts for distributing food from railway stations have been multiplied. In the great South India famine of 1877, the most terrible Indian famine of which there is any authentic record, four railway lines were at one time carrying into the famine tracts 4,000 tons of food a day from the surplus of Bengal, Burma, Nagpore and North India. This represented a day's meal for nearly seven millions of people. Not one-tenth of this quantity could have reached the afflicted provinces or could have been distributed in time with the means of communication that existed in 1857."

These somewhat optimistic views have been refuted by the outbreak of the great famine of 1900, which affected parts of India that had been always considered to lie outside the famine area. This famine also covered a wider proportion of the country than any other, and the observation of local famines applied with less correctness to this visitation than to any of its predecessors. At the same time the official reporter seems to have discerned the weak spot in the situation, for he wrote by anticipation:

"In one respect only is an Indian province less prepared to resist famine than formerly. Before railways were made and trade had increased the surplus food of good harvests fetched very low prices, and used to be kept by the producers or by local dealers in underground or other granaries against a year of scarcity, or until the stores rotted. Nowadays the surplus is exported at once, and fetches the prices current in the markets of the outer world. And so when a year of scarcity comes the local reserve stocks of food are much smaller than they used to be."

There is no doubt that this furnishes the true explanation of the severity of the suffering caused by the famine of 1900. The absence of any reserve or stock must tell seriously in the early stages of a famine, especially when there is a not unnatural official reluctance to admit that scarcity signifies famine. It is only when the people are in the grip of want that the situation is appreciated, and then time is needed, even with improved means of communication, for the arrival of supplies. Relief works can be set on foot at twenty-four hours' notice; but the now universally adopted payment in money, while it has some advantages, does not altogether meet the situation in the early stages of a famine when food is exhausted. This is perhaps more noticeable in the Native States than in British India, for the well-filled granaries held in reserve for a famine by the chiefs under the pressure of popular opinion are now no longer to be seen. Their contents are turned into money after every harvest; and although money is valuable in providing improved means of communication and irrigation against famine, it is clear that a perfect famine policy for India must include reserves of food in public or state granaries. This can be carried out by Government purchases of bumper harvests, thus reducing the export of what is called the surplus produce of India, but which is only a surplus in an artificial sense, as it takes no account of lean years. The Government of India will sooner or later have to protect the food production of India, and in thus protecting the people it will protect itself, and at the same time lighten the heavy burden it has to bear in all years, and especially in those of famine.

The responsibilities and burdens of the Government of India, heavy at all times, have been much increased in the last few years by the invasion of the plague. Originally imported from Hong Kong, this scourge temporarily desolated a great part of Western India, including Bombay and Kurrachi. No doubt it found in those cities insanitary area favourable for its propagation, and the hostility shown by the people themselves to plague regulations was evidence in its way that the preservation of social customs and exclusiveness was deemed of greater importance than that of health. The difficulties of Indian legislation were never more clearly revealed than in the anti-plague measures adopted and in the popular hostility that they aroused. At the present time an elaborate and extensive scheme for the rebuilding of the greater part of Bombay is in progress, and no doubt this will be attended with beneficial results. But such sweeping measures are only possible in rich cities and centres of trade. The possibilities of plague invasion are a further cloud on the Indian horizon, and with the fell disease established in Mysore and other parts of India the prospect gives rise to misgiving and must not be treated lightly.

Still, with all deductions made and reasons for criticism admitted, there is an undoubted balance to the good in favour of what we have done to benefit India materially, quite apart from the advantages conferred politically and socially by the preservation of internal peace, and the dispensation of an even-handed justice. I think the reader may have no doubt or misgiving in accepting the main accuracy of the following official description of what the Government of India has done and is doing. "It may fairly be claimed that during the government under the Crown progress has been more rapid in India than during any previous period of the same length, and that the intentions and actions of the Government have been as much for the benefit of the Indian people as in the time of the Court of Directors. The polity, the progress and the requirements of India have been investigated by competent critics of many nations, and the general verdict has been that despite mistakes and shortcomings such as are inseparable from human effort, the administration of India by the Crown has been an earnest and fairly successful attempt to solve political, social, and material problems of much difficulty and complexity."

Chapter XII

A RETROSPECT AND FORECAST

IN glancing back to the beginning of the century that has now finally taken its place in the human records of time, the belief may be expressed that in no country, in no enterprise of man, has a more remarkable progress been effected than in the peninsula called after the Hindus. When the eighteenth century closed, all that could be positively affirmed was that the superiority of English courage, discipline, and military efficiency had been clearly established. But, apart from that incontestable fact, our rule was merely in an infantile stage as an imperial power. No one could tell whether it would develop or endure. The part of India left to be conquered or pacified was held by more formidable races than any that we had subdued. The possibility of outside intervention, and even of a rallying together of previously hostile elements, could not be eliminated, and with all our sense of self-confidence, no one could have foretold the issue of such a struggle. As the century progressed, one by one the doubts and dubious factors were removed, until, after the conquest of the Punjab, India might be said, without exaggeration and in real truth, to have become British. Then came the spasm of the Mutiny which threatened to undo all that had been accomplished, and to destroy our power by the agency which had created it.

The nineteenth century had, therefore, run more than half its course when the country, such as we know it, began to make its appearance. The event, which might well have wrecked native progress for a long period, introduced, through the wise policy defined by Queen Victoria, an era of peace, prosperity, and great private as well as national development. In the New India the races of that country felt that they enjoyed practical equality with the English as citizens together of the British Empire. The remaining badges of superiority among the white officials were either not very offensive, or where they related to the higher scale of pay required by European exigencies, felt to be not unreasonable. In the secondary and inferior grades of the administration the natives held and still hold by far the majority of offices; and this numerical preponderance was specially marked in the courts and departments of justice. The peoples of India could, therefore, say that if they did not altogether govern themselves, they at least judged themselves, with the happy reservation of a right of appeal to a High Court of mixed composition, and to the Privy Council in London.

If the opening out of new careers in the official and judicial worlds for the intelligent and educated classes in India was noteworthy, it is probable that in that of commerce the progress and development were still more remarkable, for here there were no official barriers to be levelled. The Bengali, or the Parsi, or the Madras merchant competed with the European on a footing of perfect equality. Such difference as existed was rather in their favour, because they were better acquainted with native prejudices, and knew how to coerce or to utilise labour. The cotton industry of Western India has become practically speaking a Parsi monopoly. Large fortunes have been amassed by such men as Sir Dinshaw Manockjee Petit in a way that would have been impossible under any native or national rule that was ever known. The gentleman named and others of the same class owe to British security, justice, and opposition to extortion, the fortunes derived from their own enterprise and success. They have shown their appreciation of the assistance rendered by the policy of the Government in the achievement of their own personal success by becoming philanthropists on a large scale. In this direction, too, evidence has been furnished of the accuracy of the statement hazarded as to the perfect equality existing in the commercial world, for the two merchant princes

SIR D. M. PETIT, BART., C.S.I.

[*To face page* 346.

and world philanthropists, Sir D. M. Petit and Sir J. J. Jeejeebhoy,[1] have been created baronets just as if they had been citizens and Lord Mayors of London.

This state of things based on practical equality and an increasing sense of good fellowship and identical interest was impossible before the Mutiny. It need only be suggested as a theme for investigation by native inquirers that there was something remarkable in an event, that might well have rendered the breach impassable, proving a means of reconciliation and reunion. The magnanimity with which the government of India has since been carried on is perhaps the most conspicuous of its merits, and it is in that sense that it has appealed most forcibly to the hearts of the peoples of India. Without asserting for a moment that there is perfect union, that dissatisfaction with the present and longing for the return of the past have disappeared as vital sentiments, and that all apprehension of a revival of internal strife and native animosity can be prudently dismissed, it may be affirmed that the opinion is largely and increasingly held in India that the British raj is in itself a good government, and that a better cannot be found for the country under present conditions. That sentiment is beyond dispute the main element of stability in India, and there is no doubt that it is increasing in strength and volume. The native of

[1] Reference is, of course, made to the first baronet, who has now been dead many years.

India is quite capable of judging for himself, and there are a certain number of facts which may be pronounced beyond question. He is not so ignorant of Russian methods in Central Asia as to fail to see by the standard of comparison that he lives under happier circumstances and superior conditions than would be his if the dispensers of the orders of Government were Russian instead of British officers.

It is probable that the appreciation of the merits of British rule is more just and more general among the masses of India than among some of the classes forming educated society. This is both natural and desirable, because our policy aims before all things at benefiting the millions of the country. We regard ourselves as having in charge a trusteeship for the helpless, ignorant, and long-suffering population of a country wherein good government has rarely condescended to look beyond the pleasure of princes and the pageantry of courts. But this policy has necessitated an accompanying attitude of censure towards the native rulers, not merely with regard to their past conduct towards their subjects, but also in reference to criticisms about their efforts to attain the British model of excellence in their own administration. These criticisms, this exhortation to live, as it were, a higher life, form the bulk of the correspondence passing between the Supreme Government and its feudatories; for it must be remembered that, whilst we very clearly guaranteed the princes their territory and while we have very faithfully kept that promise, there is a general underlying condition which is the maintenance of good government. It is only in accordance with human nature that these iterations of advice, this insistence on good conduct, should produce a sentiment of irritation, and even the most intelligent of princes may find a monitor ever at his elbow somewhat irksome. In discharging our high mission we should do well to temper zeal and rectitude of purpose with a spirit of forbearance and even of charity towards the shortcomings of princes, who cannot in a few generations get out of their convictions the old idea that the land is theirs, and the fatness thereof, and that the people are but the ministers of their princes' needs and pleasures.

It is probable that we have made least progress of all among the educated classes, and that among them we have to look for our most serious detractors and bitter enemies. The reasons for this are not far to seek. Our interposition in the affairs of India disturbed and destroyed the system on which Brahmin influence was based. We put an end to the race of hereditary functionaries and officials, who enjoyed their privileges and positions by caste and inheritance in precisely the same way as all the minor crafts and trades were inherited and possessed. Education has revived the Brahmin's pretensions to be a ruler in the land, but to nothing like the extent of his former monopoly. He is also a somewhat dissatisfied worker, disliking what he calls routine work, and pining to do something original, or at least out of the common. The burden of his complaint seems to be that in the British service he is merely a clerk, whereas he aspires to be an administrator, and even a statesman. A large proportion of this class of men takes service in the Native States, and as he finds the openings for originality confined by the prudent limitations of British control, his discontent is not appeased by his experience in whatever State he may serve. This class is probably the most deeply discontented and bitter towards us in India. They have a capacity for mischief like their comrades who go to the bar or write for the Press as political agitators, but it would be easy to exaggerate their importance. They may mislead a few princes, they may fan discontent into treason in some isolated cases, but their capacity for mischief can never be very great so long as the princes their employers are well enough satisfied in the main with their position, and convinced that they cannot better it.

One of the most striking changes of the century has occurred in the military position. When it dawned the English garrison did not exceed 12,000 men, a force which was engaged in unceasing warfare, and in coping with the ravages of fever and cholera that were more destructive than the bullets of the enemy. In 1817 this force had been doubled, and as one struggle succeeded another, the sepoy army had swelled, snowball fashion, by the absorption of the vanquished in anticipation of fresh struggles. There was no time for pause or reflection in that victorious progress. The goal was only reached with the outer portals of India, and when it was thought to apply the knife of reform to the inflated and overgrown military establishment of the Company, the sepoys took the matter in their own hands, and strove to show that they were the masters. After the struggle a wise reorganization was set on foot, and the balance of military power was wholly redistributed. The European garrison was raised to a fixed minimum of 55,000 men, which has since been increased, owing to the exigencies arising from the nearer approach of Russia, to 72,000 men, and the native was reduced to a regular force of 100,000 men, with irregular contingents of about 25,000 more. As the European force was increased it was found possible to increase the native army, which now contains about 135,000 regulars, 35,000 irregulars, and the Imperial Service Corps of 25,000 men *d'élite* from the Native States. With the exception of two or three batteries in the Punjab frontier force, the artillery is exclusively British, but quite recently it has been deemed safe to give the native infantry soldier the same magazine rifle as his British comrade.

There can be no doubt whatever of the military spirit of the Indian army. Largely composed of Sikhs, Goorkhas, Afghans and Rajputs, it represents a fighting caste to which there is no equal throughout the world. Now that they have been given an armament equal to modern exigencies, they are far superior to the majority of European conscript armies, and it is no secret that whatever else campaigning in China may have done it has given our sowars and sepoys a just idea of the sort of adversary that they will have to meet in Russian soldiers. At the same time, if there is no room for misgiving on the score of stomach for fighting about our native army, there is some reason to think that criticisms about the intelligence of the force may rest on a surer foundation. There is at least one obvious and glaring defect in the paucity of British officers attached to each native regiment. The existing system is an obvious anachronism and absurdity. A regiment of British infantry requires thirty officers at full strength to lead it into action, whereas a native regiment has only six combatant officers! So long as this glaring defect is maintained as part of the established system, there must be a weak point in our armour, and an opening for critics to attack the intelligence of our Indian army.

If we confine our scrutiny of the Anglo-Indian army to the question of internal security, there is no room for anxiety or disquietude. The proportions between the component items of the force are well observed, the native troops are open to no outside influence, and even when the imagination suggests that some influence might supervene it could only operate upon portions and not upon the whole of the force. The cause that would incite some troops against us would determine the loyalty of others in our favour, but in fact there is no ground for doubting the loyalty of any until at least we have had our first trial of strength with Russia. For that episode in our history the new sepoy army is waiting with considerable expectancy, some impatience and no doubt as to the result. Until it has occurred we need have no misgiving about the loyalty of the native army of India, and on the result of that struggle all things in India will naturally depend.

Having said this much in the way of retrospect, a few lines of the nature of forecast may be permitted. The growth of the British Empire in India has been traced to the present day. The question may reasonably be asked whether it will endure. Apart from the external danger from Russia, no hesitation need be felt in stating that it is absolutely secure against attack, and as much could never have been said in the days of the Company, whose power rested on a number of ifs and assumptions. Nor is there any reason to think that the flow of new vigorous blood from the United Kingdom to the civil and military garrisons of India, which has kept them at the highest point of efficiency and strength, will soon be stopped or weakened. Such a decline will only follow when the nation has lost something of its virile strength, its firmness of purpose, and the sense of its imperial duties. No sure evidence on these points can be furnished until we have been brought into collision with a great power, and that evidence will provide the clue not merely to the future of British rule in India, but of our whole Empire.

At the same time, it is clear that in the natural course of things the character of British rule in India must undergo a change. New Indian needs must arise, new Indian expectations will have to be satisfied. We cannot always keep Indian opinion in leading strings, and there are many matters of Indian interest that will neither wait upon the sluggish co-operation of English opinion nor admit of solution in deference and subjection to that opinion. There are rocks ahead, and these can only be removed by the prevalence of Indian views, because Indian interests and welfare will be at stake. As India's national necessities increase with the growth of population which is the concomitant of our rule, new avenues of prosperity and wealth will have to be opened out, and the latent resources of India will have to be developed by the introduction of hundreds and thousands of millions of capital. The Government of India will have to radically change the policy that it has hitherto followed, but the Government of India is so essentially official and bureaucratic that it may reasonably be doubted whether it can ever be moulded or modified so as to reflect popular wishes and attain popular requirements. In whatever direction it may have to be enlarged or strengthened, we must hope that it will not be in the direction of the National Congress, which is worked by wirepullers who represent the most hostile classes in India to our rule. To recognize that self-constituted body of tiresome windbags and vain theorists would be to pander to our foes and to slight our friends.

THE GAIKWAR OF BARODA.

[To face page 334.

The most hopeful practical solution seems to lie in the direction of an Imperial Council which would furnish a safe and sure mode of intercommunication between the Viceroy's Government and the responsible rulers, administrators and merchants of India. This body should be a deliberative rather than a debating society. Its object should be work and not talk. It would be the ally and complement of the Government, not its opponent and hindrance. The rank of Imperial Councillor should be the highest honour in the gift of the Viceroy, and it might be well to combine with it a seat on the Privy Council. This arrangement would be a first step towards satisfying the legitimate desire of the princes and peoples of India to share in the direct government of their country, and it would tend to bridge the gap that intervenes between the present Viceregal form of government and the inevitable moment when British power will have to be devolved to a separate British dynasty in India. The character of our present rule is too anomalous to endure for a very long time, but there is no sign at present of any native rule supplanting ours, or of one being found capable of performing our work. British rule will continue, but at the close of the present century the British public will perhaps be discussing the question of delegating the sovereignty of the country to a scion of our reigning house as Emperor of India.

There are two events of the immediate future that must tend in their several ways to consolidate Indian opinion behind us and to strengthen our position. The first is the introduction of the China question into the list of subjects in which India is interested, and the second is the growing and obvious peril from Russia. Neither of these matters will allow of any trifling on the part of the Indian public, any more than on that of the British Government. It is satisfactory to note that both subjects are being viewed by native thinkers and public men with the gravity they deserve, and with a complete absence of the old note of secret jubilation that our embarrassment might provide India's opportunity. We may confidently believe that under existing conditions India would present an united front to the assault of any adversary, and that an invader would meet with neither sympathy nor support. This improved sentiment is largely due to greater knowledge of Russian methods, but it is also the consequence of a more grateful appreciation of our own. But the determining influence of all has been the growth of a conviction that India's own interests demand a prolonged tutelage under the care of England, and the spread of this opinion provides the sure foundation on which rests the loyalty of India. India is becoming increasingly and sincerely loyal because her best men see that by loyalty they most promote the interests, welfare and happiness of their country.

In the sense, then, that it has provided a brake upon the excessive or uncontrolled indulgence of not unnatural anti-English sentiments among the natives of

India, to whom after all we are naturally foreigners, and to the extent of its having produced a sobering effect on Indian native opinion, the spectre of the Russian peril has not been without some compensating advantage. Far from us be the intention of contributing to spread unreasonable alarm in saying that that danger is much too grave and probably too near to be treated in either a light spirit or with indifference. In the days of Bentinck and Auckland Russia was over 1,500 miles distant from the British frontier. She had not conquered one of the Khanates, the Caucasus was unsubdued, there was not a Russian ship on the Caspian, or a mile of railway in existence. Yet there seemed nothing impossible to our best military authorities in the schemes of Napoleon and Russian generals for the invasion of India.

At the present moment the outposts of Russia on the Kushk are distant, by the high road traversed by so many conquerors in the past and by Ayoob Khan in 1880, from our outpost at Chaman less than 400 miles, whereas on the Pamirs the Russians are less than a hundred miles from Hunza or Gilgit. The Khanates are all annexed and the Caucasus is as much part of Russia as Finland. There are armed flotillas not only on the Caspian, but on the Jaxartes and the Oxus. There is a main line of railway connecting the Caspian with Turkistan and Siberia, and there is another connecting Turkistan *viâ* Siberia and Orenburg with the heart of the Empire. The conditions of the problem have all changed, and they have changed in favour of Russia. It would be manifestly absurd for any one to contend to-day that a Russian invasion of India is an impossibility. On the contrary it would be a perfectly feasible and comparatively easy operation, apart, of course, from the opposition it would encounter at our hands.

All that has to be noted is that an attack by Russia on India is no longer a visionary project, but one well within the compass of achievement. Nor can we seriously doubt when we watch the drift of Russia's policy that it may be sprung upon us at any moment, either by way of military experiment, or to neutralize our proceedings in Europe, or to assist the promotion of Russia's schemes in either Persia or China. If the present ruler of Russia were a different man from what he is, it is probable that the crisis in South Africa would have been taken advantage of by the military school to execute an experimental campaign against Herat. Moderate counsels, however, are never more than passing guests in the policy of Russia. No one has yet stayed her onward march. Her face is set towards India. Nothing but the blow that will send her reeling to the earth will turn her away.

It behoves us then to be up and doing in good time to meet a serious danger which will not be conjured away by fair words. Can any authority conscientiously say that we are ready in India to meet this peril if it occurred to-morrow? I know very well that no authority will put his name to that declaration. When

Lord Roberts left India in 1894 he had raised the garrison to a high point of efficiency and readiness to take the field. If Russia had come then, or if we had gone forth to meet her, it is probable that we should have given a very good account of any available Russian armies. But in the last seven years Russia has made relatively more progress than we have, and every year finds her power in Asia forging ahead. Another effort is needed to bring up the Indian garrison to a level with its present duties and responsibilities. There are some who would bid us regard the situation in Asia with a light heart and easy mind because of what we have done in South Africa. They will tell us that the country that sent a quarter of a million of men to fight the Boers could send double that number to meet Russia on the Indian frontier. Large as those totals may appear, they would not be half the strength that Russia before many more years will be able to direct against India. We must also remember that our experiences in South Africa are useless as a precedent for a war with Russia. The main characteristic of Boer warfare, and no aspersion of their courage is intended, has been to avoid fighting as regular armies fight. There will be no similar backwardness on the part of the Russians.

The Russian danger is the portentous fact which overshadows the present century, and when Russia absorbs Chinese Turkistan and brings her frontier down to the Himalayas—which is an event likely to happen before long—it will be impossible for the most wilfully blind not to see. The immediate responsibility rests on our Government to raise the Anglo-Indian garrison to the highest possible point of strength and efficiency. It will never again be safe to draw upon it for the means of meeting outside dangers as has been done in South Africa and China. There we took a liberty with Fortune which has had no untoward results, but which it would be folly to think of repeating. India's military resources are not greater than her constant requirements, and at any moment she may be called upon to use them in her own defence. The safety of India depends on her being in a state of military preparedness to resist invasion, and the belief that she is in that state is the best creative force of confidence and loyalty. We need not fear the result of any struggle with Russia if we are ready and prepared, but the desire to shirk the conclusion that such a struggle is inevitable is one of the chief reasons why Asiatics doubt our power and the issue of that contest when it comes. They do not understand our reluctance to face and admit the truth, and sometimes our forbearance is interpreted as cowardice. In the East we have not only to be brave and strong, but we have to be thought brave and strong.

THE END.